"Our mission is to im‚ stimulate research and inform debate within government and the wider community by providing a quality statistical service"

1992 Standard Industrial Classification of economic activities

London: The Stationery Office

Information services

For general enquiries about official statistics, please contact the Office for National Statistics Public Enquiry Service on the following telephone numbers:

Social and Economic Statistics	-	0171 533 6262/6363/6364
Business Statistics	-	01633 812973

Alternatively write to ONS Public Enquiry Service, Zone DG/19, 1 Drummond Gate, Pimlico, London, SW1V 2QQ. Fax 0171 533 5719.

For more information about ONS's publications, electronic data dissemination or other information services, contact the ONS Sales Office, Marketing and Customer Service Division, Zone B1/06, 1 Drummond Gate, Pimlico, London, SW1V 2QQ; tel 0171 533 5678 or fax 0171 533 5689.

Publications may also be obtained from the The Stationery Office Publications Centre, P.O. Box 276, London, SW8 5DT; tel 0171 873 9090 or fax 0171 873 8200.

Office for National Statistics

The Office for National Statistics (ONS) is the Government Agency responsible for compiling, analysing and disseminating many of the United Kingdom's economic, social and demographic statistics including the retail prices index, trade figures and labour market data as well as the periodic census of the population and health statistics. The head of ONS is also Registrar-General for England & Wales where the agency carries out all statutory registration of births, marriages and deaths.

ONS was formed in April 1996 from a merger of the Central Statistical Office and the Office of Population Censuses and Surveys. The Agency is independent of any other Government Department and is accountable to the Chancellor of the Exchequer.

 ## Government Statistical Service

ONS works in partnership with others in the Government Statistical Service (GSS) located throughout many different Government Departments. Together they provide a quality statistical service to a great many users, and this is reflected in the GSS Mission Statement:

"To provide Parliament, government and the wider community with the statistical information, analysis and advice needed to improve decision making, stimulate research and inform debate."

Each Department produces its own statistical publications, and the Office for National Statistics brings many of these statistics together in its compendia publications and databases. For further information on the source Departments, contact the ONS Public Enquiry Service on 0171 533 6262/6363.

Cover design by Michelle Franco, ONS design

CONTENTS

SUMMARY OF SECTIONS AND SUBSECTIONS

EXPLANATORY NOTES

INTRODUCTION TO STANDARD INDUSTRIAL CLASSIFICATION OF ECONOMIC ACTIVITIES - SIC(92)

Introduction

1.   A Standard Industrial Classification (SIC) was first introduced into the United Kingdom in 1948 for use in classifying business establishments and other statistical units by the type of economic activity in which they are engaged. The classification provides a framework for the collection, tabulation, presentation and analysis of data about economic activities. Its use promotes uniformity of data collected by various government departments and agencies. In addition it can be used for administrative purposes and by many non-government bodies as a convenient way of classifying industrial activities into a common structure.

Classification changes

2.   Since 1948 the classification has been revised in 1958, in 1968 and in 1980. The 1980 SIC has been used largely unchanged until the present 1992 revision. Revision is necessary because, over a period of time, new products and the new industries to produce them emerge and shifts of emphasis occur in existing industries, so that existing classifications are always having to be twisted and turned to accommodate them. This is not always possible so that after a period of time, updating the classification is the most sensible action.

3.   The need for change is equally true for all international classifications and they are revised from time to time to bring them up to date and reflect changes in industrial activity. Thus a new International Standard Industrial Classification of All Economic Activities (ISIC Rev 3) was agreed in the Statistical Commission of the United Nations in February 1989. (1) Whilst on 9 October 1990 the European Communities' Internal Market Council (of Ministers) passed a regulation to introduce a new statistical classification of economic activities in the European Communities (NACE Rev 1). (2)

International classifications

4.   From the outset, the UK SIC followed the same broad principles as the relevant international standards. UK statisticians played an important part in the formulation of the first ISIC issued by the United Nations in 1948 and revised in 1958, 1968 and 1989. Nevertheless, there were differences in detail between the two since ISIC reflected the structure of economic activity in the world as a whole rather than that in one particular country.

5.   In 1980 one of the principal objectives of the revision of the SIC was to examine and eliminate differences from the activity classification issued by Statistical Office of the European Communities (Eurostat) and entitled 'Nomenclature générale des activités économiques dans les Communautés européennes', usually abbreviated to NACE. The 1970 NACE could be rearranged to agree with ISIC at aggregated levels but departed from it at detailed levels. The 1980 revision of the SIC applied NACE as closely as was practicable to the structure of British industry.

6.   In 1990, however, the first revision of NACE was made by EC regulation and this presented a different set of circumstances.

EC Regulation

7.   A European Community regulation has general application and is directly applicable in all member states. It does not have to be confirmed by national parliaments in order to have binding effect. The NACE regulation, therefore, in effect makes it obligatory on the UK to introduce a new Standard Industrial Classification, SIC(92), based on NACE Rev 1 and to use NACE Rev 1 or SIC(92) in cases where the UK is required to transmit to the European Commission statistics broken down by economic activity.

8.   The NACE regulation gives effect to the wish of Eurostat to establish a common statistical classification of economic activities in order to guarantee comparability between national and Community classifications and therefore between national and Community statistics. The regulation only applies to the use of NACE Rev 1 for statistical purposes, although this does not stop a country using NACE for other administrative purposes. It does not "per se oblige Member States to collect, publish or supply data". NACE Rev 1 is only a language and all requests for data collection, transmission and publication must be specified elsewhere.

9.   As already indicated NACE was originally an acronym but for the future all countries will refer to "NACE" so that it is now intended to be English, German, Spanish etc. for the European Community Classification of Economic Activities.

SIC Structure

10.   SIC(92) is based exactly on NACE Rev 1 but where it was thought necessary or helpful a fifth digit has been added to form subclasses of the NACE Rev 1 four digit classes. Thus SIC(92) is a hierarchical five digit system. However, at the first or highest level of aggregation, unlike the SIC(80) which had 10 divisions, SIC(92) is divided into 17 sections, each denoted by a single letter from A to Q. Some sections are, in turn, divided into subsections (each denoted by the addition of a second letter). The letters of the sections or subsections do not need to be part of the SIC/NACE codes since they can be uniquely defined by the

next breakdown, the divisions (denoted by two digits). The divisions are then broken down into groups (3 digits), then into classes (4 digits) and, in several cases, again into subclasses (5 digits). So for example we have:

Section D	Manufacturing (comprising divisions 15 to 37)
Subsection DB	Manufacture of textiles and textile products (comprising divisions 17 and 18)
Division 17	Manufacture of textiles
Group 17.4	Manufacture of made-up textile articles, except apparel
Class 17.40	Manufacture of made-up textile articles, except apparel
Subclass 17.40/1	Manufacture of soft furnishings

There are 17 sections, 14 subsections, 60 divisions, 222 groups, 503 classes and 142 subclasses. The full structure of SIC(92) is shown on pages 5-30.

11.   As with SIC(80), the full number of possible subdivisions at each level is not necessarily used but is varied according to the diversity of activities included. For example, section A (agriculture, hunting and forestry), has no subsections and only two divisions, 01 and 02, whereas section D (manufacturing) is divided into 14 subsections and contains 23 divisions. The use of 0 as the final digit for a group or class normally indicates that it is the only subdivision at that level. Thus division 16 (manufacture of tobacco products) has only one group, 16.0 and only one class, 16.00.   On the other hand, division 17 (manufacture of textiles) has 7 groups and so is numbered 17.1 through to 17.7.

Links to international classifications

12.   To the four digit level, SIC(92) will follow NACE Rev 1 exactly. The difference will be in the addition of subclasses where a sequential fifth digit will be added. For example, in both NACE Rev 1 and SIC(92), class 55.11 represents "Hotels and motels, with restaurant". In SIC(92), however, two subclasses are used so that 55.11/1 is "Licensed hotels and motels" and 55.11/2 is "Unlicensed hotels and motels". The first two digits, the divisions, of SIC(92) and NACE Rev 1 are exactly the same as in ISIC Rev 3, i.e. in content and in coding.   Beyond this, and shown after a decimal point in the SIC and NACE codes, the three digit groups and the four digit classes can be directly converted to the ISIC headings but may have different code numbers (eg ISIC class 6519 = SIC/NACE class 65.12) or have to be combined to reach the ISIC heading (eg ISIC class 6022 = SIC/NACE classes 60.22 + 60.23 + 60.24).

Change from 1980 SIC

13.   In addition to the change in the numbering system, there are also some changes in the sequence in which different industries are listed. For example, SIC(80) division 1 (Energy and Water Supply Industries) has been split in SIC(92) into fuel extraction (section C, Mining and Quarrying); fuel processing and production (section D, Manufacturing) and energy production and distribution (section E, Electricity, Gas and Water Supply). Also of note is section D in SIC(92) which encompasses parts of SIC (80) divisions 1 and 2 and all of divisions 3 and 4, thereby being much larger as a section than it initially appears. Not surprisingly, therefore, section D is the most highly divided section into 14 subsections of manufacturing. The most marked change from a comparison with SIC(80) is the increase in headings in the services sector; which can be seen by looking at old division 9 "Other Services" which splits principally between eight of the new section headings.

14.   The table below gives a broad comparison between the sections of SIC(92) and the former divisions of SIC(80), although the correlation is not exact since relatively minor differences in coverage are ignored.

PRESENT SECTIONS	FORMER DIVISIONS (Brackets denote part of a division)
A AGRICULTURE, HUNTING AND FORESTRY	0 (Agriculture and Forestry)
B FISHING	0 (Fishing)
C MINING AND QUARRYING	1 (Extraction of fuels) 2 (Extraction of minerals and ores)
D MANUFACTURING	1 (Fuel processing and production) 2 (Manufacture of chemicals and man-made fibres) 3 Metal goods, engineering and vehicles industries 4 Other manufacturing industries
E ELECTRICITY, GAS AND WATER SUPPLY	1 (Production and distribution of electricity, gas; Water supply)
F CONSTRUCTION	5 Construction
G WHOLESALE AND RETAIL TRADE; REPAIR OF MOTOR VEHICLES, MOTORCYCLES AND PERSONAL AND HOUSEHOLD GOODS	6 (Wholesale and retail distribution; Commission agents; Repairs)
H HOTELS AND RESTAURANTS	6 (Hotels and catering)
I TRANSPORT, STORAGE AND COMMUNICATION	7 Transport and communication 9 (Tourist offices; Radio and tv transmission)

PRESENT SECTIONS	FORMER DIVISIONS (Brackets denote part of a division)
I FINANCIAL INTERMEDIATION	8 (Banking, finance and insurance)
K REAL ESTATE, RENTING AND BUSINESS ACTIVITIES	8 (Business services; Dealing in real estate) 9 (Research & development; Other services)
L PUBLIC ADMINISTRATION AND DEFENCE; COMPULSORY SOCIAL SECURITY	9 (Public administration, national defence and security)
M EDUCATION	9 (Education)
N HEALTH AND SOCIAL WORK	9 (Health and veterinary services; Other general services to the public)
O OTHER COMMUNITY, SOCIAL & PERSONAL SERVICE ACTIVITIES	9 (Sanitary, recreational and personal services)
P PRIVATE HOUSEHOLDS WITH EMPLOYED PERSONS	9 (Domestic services)
Q EXTRA - TERRITORIAL ORGANISATIONS AND BODIES	9 (Diplomatic representation, international organisations, allied armed forces)

15. The table cannot show within-section changes, such as that within section G where retail outlets are now rather more classified by type of outlet and not mainly by goods sold, as in SIC(80). A more detailed table of the main changes between the 1980 classification and the present revision will be available from the Central Statistical Office in 1993. It must be stressed, however, that it is not possible to automatically re-code from one classification where activities previously covered by one code are now covered by more than one code.

Related classifications

16.   There are several other classifications both national and international, which may be used in conjunction with the industrial classification. These include, for example, the classification of occupations, which relates to the jobs performed by individual workers rather than to the industry in which they work. The workers classified to a particular industry will fall into a number of different categories of an occupational classification and similarly the workers in some occupations may be found in many different industries. The UK use the Standard Occupational Classification. (3)

17. A second classification, used mainly in the national accounts, is that by institutional sector. In the UK this is the Sector Classification for the National Accounts. (4)

This groups units according to their organisation or ownership, ie it distinguishes between unincorporated businesses, companies, public corporations (nationalised industries), central or local government. The industrial classification does not make such distinctions but brings together units engaged in similar activities, irrespective of ownership.

18. A third classification is that of products - often a listing of individual products or groups of similar products according to the industries in which they are principally produced. The number of entries depends on how far it is desired to go in the separate identification of products usually produced in the same industry and for similar purposes but varying in the materials used, quality, size, shape etc. The amount of detail needed for statistical purposes is much less than that which would be required for, say, a manufacturer's catalogue. The classification can also be extended to cover not only the production of goods but distribution, transport and other service industries though the number of different types of service included will normally be much less than the number of different products of production industries. Each product (good or service) is in general classified only to one industry - that in which it is mainly produced. In practice many units produce not only the goods or services which are principal products of the industries to which the units are classified but also products mainly produced in other industries.

19. At the international level, the United Nations has the Provisional Central Product Classification (CPC). (5) The main intent of the CPC is to provide a general framework for international comparisons of product statistics. It applies to tradeable and non-tradeable goods and services. CPC was agreed at the UN Statistical Commission in February 1989 for review in four years time, after use. The UN documentation of the CPC provides direct links to the Harmonized System (HS) and the Standard International Trade Classification (SITC), which are described below. The European Community, however, preferred a product classification that was more akin to the industrial activity classification and devised the Classification of Products by Activity (CPA). The CPA will relate directly to the classification structure in NACE Rev 1 (ie the first four digits will be the same) and have links to CPC (via the fifth and sixth digits). So CPA provides detailed lists of products under each economic activity. CPA is currently under discussion in Europe but it is nearly complete and it will be introduced by regulation shortly.

20 One of the uses of the CPA is to code the PRODCOM list by extending the CPA code structure from six to eight digits. PRODCOM is from PRODucts of the European COMmunity, and is a list of some 4,400 products, developed by Eurostat, for which production data will be required from all Member States from 1993. (6) PRODCOM only covers sections C, D and E of the NACE Rev 1 classification.

21. The product lists associated with industrial activity classifications contrast with the classifications recording imports and exports. The United Nations Standard

International Trade Classification (SITC Revision 3) and the Harmonized Commodity Description and Coding System (HS) with which it is correlated have been widely adopted throughout the world as the basis for national classifications both for tariff and trade statistics purposes. The HS was devised by the Customs Cooperation Council to facilitate the interests of international trade and meet the requirements of Customs authorities, statisticians, carriers and producers. The SITC is the most commonly published format for foreign trade statistics. However, the Member States of the European Community use the more detailed Combined Nomenclature (CN) to collect trade data, through their Customs procedures, but from 1993 for intra-Community trade by means of a new statistical system linked to VAT returns. The CN is developed directly from the HS and is used for the collection of both intra-Community and external trade statistics.

Use of SIC(92)

22. For most purposes the SIC classification will be applied to statistical units according to the principal activity of the units, which in turn is often determined by the nature of the products produced. In general, the rules used with the 1980 SIC on how to apply the SIC, on what types of statistical units are appropriate and on how to assess the principal (and also secondary and ancillary) activities will continue to apply. However, the introduction to NACE Rev 1 will set these matters out in full and it is hoped to incorporate these rules in later editions of the SIC(92). The NACE Rev 1 introduction will also comment on conventions used in classifying installation, maintenance and repair activities in so far as they are not specifically mentioned in the classification.

SIC(92) Indexes

23. As with previous versions of the SIC, a separate book will be published containing detailed lists of products and activities contained in each SIC(92) class. However, to help the reader with this volume, a more limited index has been included which contains details of where to find each activity actually mentioned in the explanatory notes. Each of these indexes has been, or is being, generated at the Institute of Employment Research at the University of Warwick.

References

(1) ISIC Rev 3 was published by the Statistical Office of the United Nations as Statistical paper Series M No 4 Rev 3 (ISBN 92-1-161319-0).

(2) NACE Rev 1 regulation was published in the Official Journal of the European Communities L 293 Volume 33, 24 October 1990 (ISSN 0378-6978)

(3) The SOC was published in 1990 (Volume 1; HMSO ISBN 011 691284 7).

(4) The UK Sector Classification for the National Accounts is Business Monitor MA 23; available from HMSO Publications Office, PO Box 276, London SW8 5DT (Telephone orders: 071 873 9090).

(5) The CPC was published as United Nations Statistical papers Series M No. 77 ISBN 92-1-161329-9

(6) The PRODCOM Regulation (EEC)No 3924/91 was published in the Official Journal of the European Communities L 374/1, 31 December 1991

Central Statistical Office
Millbank Tower
LONDON SW1P 4QQ

1 September 1992

UK STANDARD INDUSTRIAL CLASSIFICATION OF ECONOMIC ACTIVITIES – SIC(92)

Division	Group	Class & sub class	Description
SECTION A			**AGRICULTURE, HUNTING AND FORESTRY**
01			AGRICULTURE, HUNTING AND RELATED SERVICE ACTIVITIES
	01.1		Growing of crops; market gardening; horticulture
		01.11	Growing of cereals and other crops not elsewhere classified
		01.12	Growing of vegetables, horticultural specialties and nursery products
		01.13	Growing of fruit, nuts, beverage and spice crops
	01.2		Farming of animals
		01.21	Farming of cattle, dairy farming
		01.22	Farming of sheep, goats, horses, asses, mules and hinnies
		01.23	Farming of swine
		01.24	Farming of poultry
		01.25	Other farming of animals
	01.3		Growing of crops combined with farming of animals (mixed farming)
		01.30	Growing of crops combined with farming of animals (mixed farming)
	01.4		Agricultural and animal husbandry service activities, except veterinary activities
		01.41	Agricultural service activities
		01.42	Animal husbandry service activities, except veterinary activities
	01.5		Hunting, trapping and game propagation including related service activities
		01.50	Hunting, trapping and game propagation including related service activities
02			FORESTRY, LOGGING AND RELATED SERVICE ACTIVITIES
	02.0		Forestry, logging and related service activities
		02.01	Forestry and logging
		02.02	Forestry and logging related service activities
SECTION B			**FISHING**
05			FISHING, OPERATION OF FISH HATCHERIES AND FISH FARMS; SERVICE ACTIVITIES INCIDENTAL TO FISHING
	05.0		Fishing, operation of fish hatcheries and fish farms; service activities incidental to fishing
		05.01	Fishing
		05.02	Operation of fish hatcheries and fish farms
SECTION C			**MINING AND QUARRYING**
Subsection CA			MINING AND QUARRYING OF ENERGY PRODUCING MATERIALS
10			MINING OF COAL AND LIGNITE; EXTRACTION OF PEAT

Division	Group	Class & sub class	Description
	10.1		Mining and agglomeration of hard coal
		10.10	Mining and agglomeration of hard coal
		10.10/1	Deep coal mines
		10.10/2	Opencast coal working
		10.10/3	Manufacture of solid fuel
	10.2		Mining and agglomeration of lignite
		10.20	Mining and agglomeration of lignite
	10.3		Extraction and agglomeration of peat
		10.30	Extraction and agglomeration of peat
11			EXTRACTION OF CRUDE PETROLEUM AND NATURAL GAS; SERVICE ACTIVITIES INCIDENTAL TO OIL AND GAS EXTRACTION EXCLUDING SURVEYING
	11.1		Extraction of crude petroleum and natural gas
		11.10	Extraction of crude petroleum and natural gas
	11.2		Service activities incidental to oil and gas extraction excluding surveying
		11.20	Service activities incidental to oil and gas extraction excluding surveying
12			MINING OF URANIUM AND THORIUM ORES
	12.0		Mining of uranium and thorium ores
		12.00	Mining of uranium and thorium ores

Subsection CB MINING AND QUARRYING EXCEPT ENERGY PRODUCING MATERIALS

Division	Group	Class & sub class	Description
13			MINING OF METAL ORES
	13.1		Mining of iron ores
		13.10	Mining of iron ores
	13.2		Mining of non-ferrous metal ores, except uranium and thorium ores
		13.20	Mining of non-ferrous metal ores, except uranium and thorium ores
14			OTHER MINING AND QUARRYING
	14.1		Quarrying of stone
		14.11	Quarrying of stone for construction
		14.12	Quarrying of limestone, gypsum and chalk
		14.13	Quarrying of slate
	14.2		Quarrying of sand and clay
		14.21	Operation of gravel and sand pits
		14.22	Mining of clays and kaolin
	14.3		Mining of chemical and fertilizer minerals
		14.30	Mining of chemical and fertilizer minerals

Division	Group	Class & sub class	Description
	14.4		Production of salt
		14.40	Production of salt
	14.5		Other mining and quarrying not elsewhere classified
		14.50	Other mining and quarrying not elsewhere classified

SECTION D　　　　　　　　**MANUFACTURING**

Subsection DA　　　　　　MANUFACTURE OF FOOD PRODUCTS; BEVERAGES AND TOBACCO

15　　　　　　　　　　　　MANUFACTURE OF FOOD PRODUCTS AND BEVERAGES

Division	Group	Class & sub class	Description
	15.1		Production, processing and preserving of meat and meat products
		15.11	Production and preserving of meat
		15.11/1	Slaughtering of animals other than poultry and rabbits
		15.11/2	Animal by-product processing
		15.11/3	Fellmongery
		15.12	Production and preserving of poultry meat
		15.13	Production of meat and poultry meat products
		15.13/1	Bacon and ham production
		15.13/2	Other meat and poultry meat processing
	15.2		Processing and preserving of fish and fish products
		15.20	Processing and preserving of fish and fish products
		15.20/1	Freezing of fish
		15.20/2	Other fish processing and preserving
	15.3		Processing and preserving of fruit and vegetables
		15.31	Processing and preserving of potatoes
		15.32	Manufacture of fruit and vegetable juice
		15.33	Processing and preserving of fruit and vegetables not elsewhere classified
	15.4		Manufacture of vegetable and animal oils and fats
		15.41	Manufacture of crude oils and fats
		15.42	Manufacture of refined oils and fats
		15.43	Manufacture of margarine and similar edible fats
	15.5		Manufacture of dairy products
		15.51	Operation of dairies and cheese making
		15.51/1	Liquid milk and cream production
		15.51/2	Butter and cheese production
		15.51/3	Manufacture of other milk products
		15.52	Manufacture of ice cream
	15.6		Manufacture of grain mill products, starches and starch products
		15.61	Manufacture of grain mill products
		15.61/1	Grain milling
		15.61/2	Manufacture of breakfast cereals and cereals-based foods
		15.62	Manufacture of starches and starch products

Division Group		Class & sub class	Description
	15.7		Manufacture of prepared animal feeds
		15.71	Manufacture of prepared feeds for farm animals
		15.72	Manufacture of prepared pet foods
	15.8		Manufacture of other food products
		15.81	Manufacture of bread; manufacture of fresh pastry goods and cakes
		15.82	Manufacture of rusks and biscuits; manufacture of preserved pastry goods and cakes
		15.83	Manufacture of sugar
		15.84	Manufacture of cocoa; chocolate and sugar confectionery
		15.84/1	Manufacture of cocoa and chocolate confectionery
		15.84/2	Manufacture of sugar confectionery
		15.85	Manufacture of macaroni, noodles, couscous and similar farinaceous products
		15.86	Processing of tea and coffee
		15.86/1	Tea processing
		15.86/2	Production of coffee and coffee substitutes
		15.87	Manufacture of condiments and seasonings
		15.88	Manufacture of homogenised food preparations and dietetic food
		15.89	Manufacture of other food products not elsewhere classified
		15.89/1	Manufacture of soups
		15.89/2	Manufacture of other food products not elsewhere classified
	15.9		Manufacture of beverages
		15.91	Manufacture of distilled potable alcoholic beverages
		15.92	Production of ethyl alcohol from fermented materials
		15.93	Manufacture of wines
		15.93/1	Manufacture of wine of fresh grapes and grape juice
		15.93/2	Manufacture of wine based on concentrated grape must
		15.94	Manufacture of cider and other fruit wines
		15.94/1	Manufacture of cider and perry
		15.94/2	Manufacture of other fermented fruit beverages
		15.95	Manufacture of other non-distilled fermented beverages
		15.96	Manufacture of beer
		15.97	Manufacture of malt
		15.98	Production of mineral waters and soft drinks
16			MANUFACTURE OF TOBACCO PRODUCTS
	16.0		Manufacture of tobacco products
		16.00	Manufacture of tobacco products
Subsection DB			MANUFACTURE OF TEXTILES AND TEXTILE PRODUCTS
17			MANUFACTURE OF TEXTILES
	17.1		Preparation and spinning of textile fibres
		17.11	Preparation and spinning of cotton-type fibres
		17.12	Preparation and spinning of woollen-type fibres
		17.13	Preparation and spinning of worsted-type fibres
		17.14	Preparation and spinning of flax-type fibres
		17.15	Throwing and preparation of silk including from noils and throwing and texturing of synthetic or artificial filament yarns

Division	Group	Class & sub class	Description
		17.16	Manufacture of sewing threads
		17.17	Preparation and spinning of other textile fibres
	17.2		Textile weaving
		17.21	Cotton-type weaving
		17.22	Woollen-type weaving
		17.23	Worsted-type weaving
		17.24	Silk-type weaving
		17.25	Other textile weaving
	17.3		Finishing of textiles
		17.30	Finishing of textiles
	17.4		Manufacture of made-up textile articles, except apparel
		17.40	Manufacture of made-up textile articles, except apparel
		17.40/1	Manufacture of soft furnishings
		17.40/2	Manufacture of canvas goods, sacks, etc
		17.40/3	Manufacture of household textiles
	17.5		Manufacture of other textiles
		17.51	Manufacture of carpets and rugs
		17.51/1	Manufacture of woven carpets and rugs
		17.51/2	Manufacture of tufted carpets and rugs
		17.51/3	Manufacture of other carpets and rugs
		17.52	Manufacture of cordage, rope, twine and netting
		17.53	Manufacture of nonwovens and articles made from nonwovens, except apparel
		17.54	Manufacture of other textiles not elsewhere classified
		17.54/1	Manufacture of lace
		17.54/2	Manufacture of narrow fabrics
		17.54/3	Manufacture of other textiles not elsewhere classified
	17.6		Manufacture of knitted and crocheted fabrics
		17.60	Manufacture of knitted and crocheted fabrics
	17.7		Manufacture of knitted and crocheted articles
		17.71	Manufacture of knitted and crocheted hosiery
		17.72	Manufacture of knitted and crocheted pullovers, cardigans and similar articles
18			MANUFACTURE OF WEARING APPAREL; DRESSING AND DYEING OF FUR
	18.1		Manufacture of leather clothes
		18.10	Manufacture of leather clothes
	18.2		Manufacture of other wearing apparel and accessories
		18.21	Manufacture of workwear
		18.22	Manufacture of other outerwear
		18.22/1	Manufacture of other men's outerwear
		18.22/2	Manufacture of other women's outerwear
		18.23	Manufacture of underwear
		18.23/1	Manufacture of men's underwear
		18.23/2	Manufacture of women's underwear
		18.24	Manufacture of other wearing apparel and accessories not elsewhere classified

Division	Group	Class & sub class	Description
		18.24/1	Manufacture of hats
		18.24/2	Manufacture of other wearing apparel and accessories
	18.3		Dressing and dyeing of fur; manufacture of articles of fur
		18.30	Dressing and dyeing of fur; manufacture of articles of fur

Subsection DC   MANUFACTURE OF LEATHER AND LEATHER PRODUCTS

Division	Group	Class & sub class	Description
19			TANNING AND DRESSING OF LEATHER; MANUFACTURE OF LUGGAGE, HANDBAGS, SADDLERY, HARNESS AND FOOTWEAR
	19.1		Tanning and dressing of leather
		19.10	Tanning and dressing of leather
	19.2		Manufacture of luggage, handbags and the like, saddlery and harness
		19.20	Manufacture of luggage, handbags and the like, saddlery and harness
	19.3		Manufacture of footwear
		19.30	Manufacture of footwear

Subsection DD   MANUFACTURE OF WOOD AND WOOD PRODUCTS

Division	Group	Class & sub class	Description
20			MANUFACTURE OF WOOD AND OF PRODUCTS OF WOOD AND CORK, EXCEPT FURNITURE; MANUFACTURE OF ARTICLES OF STRAW AND PLAITING MATERIALS
	20.1		Sawmilling and planing of wood, impregnation of wood
		20.10	Sawmilling and planing of wood, impregnation of wood
	20.2		Manufacture of veneer sheets; manufacture of plywood, laminboard, particle board, fibre board and other panels and boards
		20.20	Manufacture of veneer sheets; manufacture of plywood, laminboard, particle board, fibre board and other panels and boards
	20.3		Manufacture of builders' carpentry and joinery
		20.30	Manufacture of builders' carpentry and joinery
	20.4		Manufacture of wooden containers
		20.40	Manufacture of wooden containers
	20.5		Manufacture of other products of wood; manufacture of articles of cork, straw and plaiting materials
		20.51	Manufacture of other products of wood
		20.52	Manufacture of articles of cork, straw and plaiting materials

Subsection DE   MANUFACTURE OF PULP, PAPER AND PAPER PRODUCTS; PUBLISHING AND PRINTING

Division	Group	Class & sub class	Description
21			MANUFACTURE OF PULP, PAPER AND PAPER PRODUCTS
	21.1		Manufacture of pulp, paper and paperboard

Division	Group	Class & sub class	Description
		21.11	Manufacture of pulp
		21.12	Manufacture of paper and paperboard
	21.2		Manufacture of articles of paper and paperboard
		21.21	Manufacture of corrugated paper and paperboard and of containers of paper and paperboard
		21.21/1	Manufacture of corrugated paper and paperboard, sacks and bags
		21.21/2	Manufacture of cartons, boxes, cases and other containers
		21.22	Manufacture of household and sanitary goods and of toilet requisites
		21.23	Manufacture of paper stationery
		21.24	Manufacture of wallpaper
		21.25	Manufacture of other articles of paper and paperboard not elsewhere classified
22			PUBLISHING, PRINTING AND REPRODUCTION OF RECORDED MEDIA
	22.1		Publishing
		22.11	Publishing of books
		22.12	Publishing of newspapers
		22.13	Publishing of journals and periodicals
		22.14	Publishing of sound recordings
		22.15	Other publishing
	22.2		Printing and service activities related to printing
		22.21	Printing of newspapers
		22.22	Printing not elsewhere classified
		22.23	Bookbinding and finishing
		22.24	Composition and plate-making
		22.25	Other activities related to printing
	22.3		Reproduction of recorded media
		22.31	Reproduction of sound recording
		22.32	Reproduction of video recording
		22.33	Reproduction of computer media

Subsection DF   MANUFACTURE OF COKE, REFINED PETROLEUM PRODUCTS AND NUCLEAR FUEL

Division	Group	Class & sub class	Description
23			MANUFACTURE OF COKE, REFINED PETROLEUM PRODUCTS AND NUCLEAR FUEL
	23.1		Manufacture of coke oven products
		23.10	Manufacture of coke oven products
	23.2		Manufacture of refined petroleum products
		23.20	Manufacture of refined petroleum products
		23.20/1	Mineral oil refining
		23.20/2	Other treatment of petroleum products (excluding petrochemicals manufacture)
	23.3		Processing of nuclear fuel
		23.30	Processing of nuclear fuel

Division	Group	Class & sub class	Description
Subsection DG			MANUFACTURE OF CHEMICALS, CHEMICAL PRODUCTS AND MAN-MADE FIBRES
24			MANUFACTURE OF CHEMICALS AND CHEMICAL PRODUCTS
	24.1		Manufacture of basic chemicals
		24.11	Manufacture of industrial gases
		24.12	Manufacture of dyes and pigments
		24.13	Manufacture of other inorganic basic chemicals
		24.14	Manufacture of other organic basic chemicals
		24.15	Manufacture of fertilizers and nitrogen compounds
		24.16	Manufacture of plastics in primary forms
		24.17	Manufacture of synthetic rubber in primary forms
	24.2		Manufacture of pesticides and other agro-chemical products
		24.20	Manufacture of pesticides and other agro-chemical products
	24.3		Manufacture of paints, varnishes and similar coatings, printing ink and mastics
		24.30	Manufacture of paints, varnishes and similar coatings, printing ink and mastics
		24.30/1	Manufacture of paints, varnishes and similar coatings
		24.30/2	Manufacture of printing ink
		24.30/3	Manufacture of mastics and sealants
	24.4		Manufacture of pharmaceuticals, medicinal chemicals and botanical products
		24.41	Manufacture of basic pharmaceutical products
		24.42	Manufacture of pharmaceutical preparations
		24.42/1	Manufacture of medicaments
		24.42/2	Manufacture of non-medicaments
	24.5		Manufacture of soap and detergents, cleaning and polishing preparations, perfumes and toilet preparations
		24.51	Manufacture of soap and detergents, cleaning and polishing preparations
		24.51/1	Manufacture of soap and detergents
		24.51/2	Manufacture of cleaning and polishing preparations
		24.52	Manufacture of perfumes and toilet preparations
	24.6		Manufacture of other chemical products
		24.61	Manufacture of explosives
		24.62	Manufacture of glues and gelatine
		24.63	Manufacture of essential oils
		24.64	Manufacture of photographic chemical material
		24.65	Manufacture of prepared unrecorded media
		24.66	Manufacture of other chemical products not elsewhere classified
	24.7		Manufacture of man-made fibres
		24.70	Manufacture of man-made fibres
Subsection DH			MANUFACTURE OF RUBBER AND PLASTIC PRODUCTS
25			MANUFACTURE OF RUBBER AND PLASTIC PRODUCTS

Division	Group	Class & sub class	Description
	25.1		Manufacture of rubber products
		25.11	Manufacture of rubber tyres and tubes
		25.12	Retreading and rebuilding of rubber tyres
		25.13	Manufacture of other rubber products
	25.2		Manufacture of plastic products
		25.21	Manufacture of plastic plates, sheets, tubes and profiles
		25.22	Manufacture of plastic packing goods
		25.23	Manufacture of builders' ware of plastic
		25.23/1	Manufacture of plastic floor covering
		25.23/2	Manufacture of other builders' ware of plastic
		25.24	Manufacture of other plastic products

Subsection DI   MANUFACTURE OF OTHER NON-METALLIC MINERAL PRODUCTS

Division	Group	Class & sub class	Description
26			MANUFACTURE OF OTHER NON-METALLIC MINERAL PRODUCTS
	26.1		Manufacture of glass and glass products
		26.11	Manufacture of flat glass
		26.12	Shaping and processing of flat glass
		26.13	Manufacture of hollow glass
		26.14	Manufacture of glass fibres
		26.15	Manufacture and processing of other glass including technical glassware
	26.2		Manufacture of non-refractory ceramic goods other than for construction purposes; manufacture of refractory ceramic products
		26.21	Manufacture of ceramic household and ornamental articles
		26.22	Manufacture of ceramic sanitary fixtures
		26.23	Manufacture of ceramic insulators and insulating fittings
		26.24	Manufacture of other technical ceramic products
		26.25	Manufacture of other ceramic products
		26.26	Manufacture of refractory ceramic products
	26.3		Manufacture of ceramic tiles and flags
		26.30	Manufacture of ceramic tiles and flags
	26.4		Manufacture of bricks, tiles and construction products, in baked clay
		26.40	Manufacture of bricks, tiles and construction products, in baked clay
	26.5		Manufacture of cement, lime and plaster
		26.51	Manufacture of cement
		26.52	Manufacture of lime
		26.53	Manufacture of plaster
	26.6		Manufacture of articles of concrete, plaster and cement
		26.61	Manufacture of concrete products for construction purposes
		26.62	Manufacture of plaster products for construction purposes
		26.63	Manufacture of ready-mixed concrete
		26.64	Manufacture of mortars
		26.65	Manufacture of fibre cement
		26.66	Manufacture of other articles of concrete, plaster and cement

Division	Group	Class & sub class	Description
	26.7		Cutting, shaping and finishing of stone
		26.70	Cutting, shaping and finishing of stone
	26.8		Manufacture of other non-metallic mineral products
		26.81	Production of abrasive products
		26.82	Manufacture of other non-metallic mineral products not elsewhere classified
		26.82/1	Manufacture of asbestos
		26.82/2	Manufacture of other non-metallic mineral products not elsewhere classified

Subsection DJ   MANUFACTURE OF BASIC METALS AND FABRICATED METAL PRODUCTS

Division	Group	Class & sub class	Description
27			MANUFACTURE OF BASIC METALS
	27.1		Manufacture of basic iron and steel and of ferro-alloys (ECSC)
		27.10	Manufacture of basic iron and steel and of ferro-alloys (ECSC)
	27.2		Manufacture of tubes
		27.21	Manufacture of cast iron tubes
		27.22	Manufacture of steel tubes
	27.3		Other first processing of iron and steel and production of non-ECSC ferro-alloys
		27.31	Cold drawing
		27.32	Cold rolling of narrow strip
		27.33	Cold forming or folding
		27.34	Wire drawing
		27.35	Other first processing of iron and steel not elsewhere classified; production of non-ECSC ferro-alloys
	27.4		Manufacture of basic precious and non-ferrous metals
		27.41	Precious metals production
		27.42	Aluminium production
		27.43	Lead, zinc and tin production
		27.44	Copper production
		27.45	Other non-ferrous metal production
	27.5		Casting of metals
		27.51	Casting of iron
		27.52	Casting of steel
		27.53	Casting of light metals
		27.54	Casting of other non-ferrous metals
28			MANUFACTURE OF FABRICATED METAL PRODUCTS, EXCEPT MACHINERY AND EQUIPMENT
	28.1		Manufacture of structural metal products
		28.11	Manufacture of metal structures and parts of structures
		28.12	Manufacture of builders' carpentry and joinery of metal
	28.2		Manufacture of tanks, reservoirs and containers of metal; manufacture of central heating radiators and boilers
		28.21	Manufacture of tanks, reservoirs and containers of metal
		28.22	Manufacture of central heating radiators and boilers

Division	Group	Class & sub class	Description
	28.3		Manufacture of steam generators, except central heating hot water boilers
		28.30	Manufacture of steam generators, except central heating hot water boilers
	28.4		Forging, pressing, stamping and roll forming of metal; powder metallurgy
		28.40	Forging, pressing, stamping and roll forming of metal; powder metallurgy
	28.5		Treatment and coating of metals; general mechanical engineering
		28.51	Treatment and coating of metals
		28.52	General mechanical engineering
	28.6		Manufacture of cutlery, tools and general hardware
		28.61	Manufacture of cutlery
		28.62	Manufacture of tools
		28.63	Manufacture of locks and hinges
	28.7		Manufacture of other fabricated metal products
		28.71	Manufacture of steel drums and similar containers
		28.72	Manufacture of light metal packaging
		28.73	Manufacture of wire products
		28.74	Manufacture of fasteners, screw machine products, chain and springs
		28.75	Manufacture of other fabricated metal products not elsewhere classified

Subsection DK MANUFACTURE OF MACHINERY AND EQUIPMENT NOT ELSEWHERE CLASSIFIED

29 MANUFACTURE OF MACHINERY AND EQUIPMENT NOT ELSEWHERE CLASSIFIED

Division	Group	Class & sub class	Description
	29.1		Manufacture of machinery for the production and use of mechanical power, except aircraft, vehicle and cycle engines
		29.11	Manufacture of engines and turbines, except aircraft, vehicle and cycle engines
		29.12	Manufacture of pumps and compressors
		29.12/1	Manufacture of pumps
		29.12/2	Manufacture of compressors
		29.13	Manufacture of taps and valves
		29.14	Manufacture of bearings, gears, gearing and driving elements
	29.2		Manufacture of other general purpose machinery
		29.21	Manufacture of furnaces and furnace burners
		29.22	Manufacture of lifting and handling equipment
		29.23	Manufacture of non-domestic cooling and ventilation equipment
		29.24	Manufacture of other general purpose machinery not elsewhere classified
	29.3		Manufacture of agricultural and forestry machinery
		29.31	Manufacture of agricultural tractors
		29.32	Manufacture of other agricultural and forestry machinery
	29.4		Manufacture of machine tools
		29.40	Manufacture of machine tools
	29.5		Manufacture of other special purpose machinery
		29.51	Manufacture of machinery for metallurgy

Division	Group	Class & sub class	Description
		29.52	Manufacture of machinery for mining, quarrying and construction
		29.52/1	Manufacture of machinery for mining
		29.52/2	Manufacture of earth-moving equipment
		29.52/3	Manufacture of equipment for concrete crushing and screening and roadworks
		29.53	Manufacture of machinery for food, beverage and tobacco processing
		29.54	Manufacture of machinery for textile, apparel and leather production
		29.55	Manufacture of machinery for paper and paperboard production
		29.56	Manufacture of other special purpose machinery not elsewhere classified
	29.6		Manufacture of weapons and ammunition
		29.60	Manufacture of weapons and ammunition
	29.7		Manufacture of domestic appliances not elsewhere classified
		29.71	Manufacture of electric domestic appliances
		29.72	Manufacture of non-electric domestic appliances

Subsection DL MANUFACTURE OF ELECTRICAL AND OPTICAL EQUIPMENT

Division	Group	Class & sub class	Description
30			MANUFACTURE OF OFFICE MACHINERY AND COMPUTERS
	30.0		Manufacture of office machinery and computers
		30.01	Manufacture of office machinery
		30.02	Manufacture of computers and other information processing equipment
31			MANUFACTURE OF ELECTRICAL MACHINERY AND APPARATUS NOT ELSEWHERE CLASSIFIED
	31.1		Manufacture of electric motors, generators and transformers
		31.10	Manufacture of electric motors, generators and transformers
	31.2		Manufacture of electricity distribution and control apparatus
		31.20	Manufacture of electricity distribution and control apparatus
	31.3		Manufacture of insulated wire and cable
		31.30	Manufacture of insulated wire and cable
	31.4		Manufacture of accumulators, primary cells and primary batteries
		31.40	Manufacture of accumulators, primary cells and primary batteries
	31.5		Manufacture of lighting equipment and electric lamps
		31.50	Manufacture of lighting equipment and electric lamps
	31.6		Manufacture of electrical equipment not elsewhere classified
		31.61	Manufacture of electrical equipment for engines and vehicles not elsewhere classified
		31.62	Manufacture of other electrical equipment not elsewhere classified
32			MANUFACTURE OF RADIO, TELEVISION AND COMMUNICATION EQUIPMENT AND APPARATUS
	32.1		Manufacture of electronic valves and tubes and other electronic components
		32.10	Manufacture of electronic valves and tubes and other electronic components

Division	Group	Class & sub class	Description
	32.2		Manufacture of television and radio transmitters and apparatus for line telephony and line telegraphy
		32.20	Manufacture of television and radio transmitters and apparatus for line telephony and line telegraphy
		32.20/1	Manufacture of telegraph and telephone apparatus and equipment
		32.20/2	Manufacture of radio and electronic capital goods
	32.3		Manufacture of television and radio receivers, sound or video recording or reproducing apparatus and associated goods
		32.30	Manufacture of television and radio receivers, sound or video recording or reproducing apparatus and associated goods
33			MANUFACTURE OF MEDICAL, PRECISION AND OPTICAL INSTRUMENTS, WATCHES AND CLOCKS
	33.1		Manufacture of medical and surgical equipment and orthopaedic appliances
		33.10	Manufacture of medical and surgical equipment and orthopaedic appliances
	33.2		Manufacture of instruments and appliances for measuring, checking, testing, navigating and other purposes, except industrial process control equipment
		33.20	Manufacture of instruments and appliances for measuring, checking, testing, navigating and other purposes, except industrial process control equipment
		33.20/1	Manufacture of electronic instruments and appliances for measuring, checking, testing, navigating and other purposes, except industrial process control equipment
		33.20/2	Manufacture of non-electronic instruments and appliances for measuring, checking, testing, navigating and other purposes, except industrial process control equipment
	33.3		Manufacture of industrial process control equipment
		33.30	Manufacture of industrial process control equipment
		33.30/1	Manufacture of electronic industrial process control equipment
		33.30/2	Manufacture of non-electronic industrial process control equipment
	33.4		Manufacture of optical instruments and photographic equipment
		33.40	Manufacture of optical instruments and photographic equipment
		33.40/1	Manufacture of spectacles and unmounted lenses
		33.40/2	Manufacture of optical precision instruments
		33.40/3	Manufacture of photographic and cinematographic equipment
	33.5		Manufacture of watches and clocks
		33.50	Manufacture of watches and clocks

Subsection DM MANUFACTURE OF TRANSPORT EQUIPMENT

Division	Group	Class & sub class	Description
34			MANUFACTURE OF MOTOR VEHICLES, TRAILERS AND SEMI-TRAILERS
	34.1		Manufacture of motor vehicles
		34.10	Manufacture of motor vehicles
	34.2		Manufacture of bodies (coachwork) for motor vehicles; manufacture of trailers and semi-trailers

Division	Group	Class & sub class	Description
		34.20	Manufacture of bodies (coachwork) for motor vehicles; manufacture of trailers and semi-trailers
		34.20/1	Manufacture of bodies (coachwork) for motor vehicles (except caravans)
		34.20/2	Manufacture of trailers and semi-trailers
		34.20/3	Manufacture of caravans
	34.3		Manufacture of parts and accessories for motor vehicles and their engines
		34.30	Manufacture of parts and accessories for motor vehicles and their engines
35			MANUFACTURE OF OTHER TRANSPORT EQUIPMENT
	35.1		Building and repairing of ships and boats
		35.11	Building and repairing of ships
		35.12	Building and repairing of pleasure and sporting boats
	35.2		Manufacture of railway and tramway locomotives and rolling stock
		35.20	Manufacture of railway and tramway locomotives and rolling stock
	35.3		Manufacture of aircraft and spacecraft
		35.30	Manufacture of aircraft and spacecraft
	35.4		Manufacture of motorcycles and bicycles
		35.41	Manufacture of motorcycles
		35.42	Manufacture of bicycles
		35.43	Manufacture of invalid carriages
	35.5		Manufacture of other transport equipment not elsewhere classified
		35.50	Manufacture of other transport equipment not elsewhere classified
Subsection DN			MANUFACTURING NOT ELSEWHERE CLASSIFIED
36			MANUFACTURE OF FURNITURE; MANUFACTURING NOT ELSEWHERE CLASSIFIED
	36.1		Manufacture of furniture
		36.11	Manufacture of chairs and seats
		36.12	Manufacture of other office and shop furniture
		36.13	Manufacture of other kitchen furniture
		36.14	Manufacture of other furniture
		36.15	Manufacture of mattresses
	36.2		Manufacture of jewellery and related articles
		36.21	Striking of coins and medals
		36.22	Manufacture of jewellery and related articles not elsewhere classified
	36.3		Manufacture of musical instruments
		36.30	Manufacture of musical instruments
	36.4		Manufacture of sports goods
		36.40	Manufacture of sports goods
	36.5		Manufacture of games and toys

Division	Group	Class & sub class	Description
		36.50	Manufacture of games and toys
		36.50/1	Manufacture of professional and arcade games and toys
		36.50/2	Manufacture of other games and toys not elsewhere classified
	36.6		Miscellaneous manufacturing not elsewhere classified
		36.61	Manufacture of imitation jewellery
		36.62	Manufacture of brooms and brushes
		36.63	Other manufacturing not elsewhere classified
		36.63/1	Manufacture of miscellaneous stationers' goods
		36.63/2	Other manufacturing not elsewhere classified
37			RECYCLING
	37.1		Recycling of metal waste and scrap
		37.10	Recycling of metal waste and scrap
	37.2		Recycling of non-metal waste and scrap
		37.20	Recycling of non-metal waste and scrap

SECTION E ELECTRICITY, GAS AND WATER SUPPLY

Division	Group	Class & sub class	Description
40			ELECTRICITY, GAS, STEAM AND HOT WATER SUPPLY
	40.1		Production and distribution of electricity
		40.10	Production and distribution of electricity
		40.10/1	Electricity generation
		40.10/2	Electricity transmission, distribution and supply
	40.2		Manufacture of gas; distribution of gaseous fuels through mains
		40.20	Manufacture of gas; distribution of gaseous fuels through mains
	40.3		Steam and hot water supply
		40.30	Steam and hot water supply
41			COLLECTION, PURIFICATION AND DISTRIBUTION OF WATER
	41.0		Collection, purification and distribution of water
		41.00	Collection, purification and distribution of water

SECTION F CONSTRUCTION

Division	Group	Class & sub class	Description
45			CONSTRUCTION
	45.1		Site preparation
		45.11	Demolition and wrecking of buildings; earth moving
		45.12	Test drilling and boring
	45.2		Building of complete constructions or parts thereof; civil engineering
		45.21	General construction of buildings and civil engineering works
		45.22	Erection of roof covering and frames
		45.23	Construction of highways, roads, airfields and sport facilities
		45.24	Construction of water projects

Division	Group	Class & sub class	Description
		45.25	Other construction work involving special trades
	45.3		Building installation
		45.31	Installation of electrical wiring and fittings
		45.32	Insulation work activities
		45.33	Plumbing
		45.34	Other building installation
	45.4		Building completion
		45.41	Plastering
		45.42	Joinery installation
		45.43	Floor and wall covering
		45.44	Painting and glazing
		45.45	Other building completion
	45.5		Renting of construction or demolition equipment with operator
		45.50	Renting of construction or demolition equipment with operator

SECTION G — WHOLESALE AND RETAIL TRADE; REPAIR OF MOTOR VEHICLES, MOTORCYCLES AND PERSONAL AND HOUSEHOLD GOODS

Division	Group	Class & sub class	Description
50			SALE, MAINTENANCE AND REPAIR OF MOTOR VEHICLES AND MOTORCYCLES; RETAIL SALE OF AUTOMOTIVE FUEL
	50.1		Sale of motor vehicles
		50.10	Sale of motor vehicles
	50.2		Maintenance and repair of motor vehicles
		50.20	Maintenance and repair of motor vehicles
	50.3		Sale of motor vehicle parts and accessories
		50.30	Sale of motor vehicle parts and accessories
	50.4		Sale, maintenance and repair of motorcycles and related parts and accessories
		50.40	Sale, maintenance and repair of motorcycles and related parts and accessories
	50.5		Retail sale of automotive fuel
		50.50	Retail sale of automotive fuel
51			WHOLESALE TRADE AND COMMISSION TRADE, EXCEPT OF MOTOR VEHICLES AND MOTORCYCLES
	51.1		Wholesale on a fee or contract basis
		51.11	Agents involved in the sale of agricultural raw materials, live animals, textile raw materials and semi-finished goods
		51.12	Agents involved in the sale of fuels, ores, metals and industrial chemicals
		51.13	Agents involved in the sale of timber and building materials
		51.14	Agents involved in the sale of machinery, industrial equipment, ships and aircraft
		51.15	Agents involved in the sale of furniture, household goods, hardware and ironmongery
		51.16	Agents involved in the sale of textiles, clothing, footwear and leather goods

Division	Group	Class & sub class	Description
		51.17	Agents involved in the sale of food, beverages and tobacco
		51.18	Agents specialising in the sale of particular products or ranges of products not elsewhere classified
		51.19	Agents involved in the sale of a variety of goods
	51.2		Wholesale of agricultural raw materials and live animals
		51.21	Wholesale of grain, seeds and animal feeds
		51.22	Wholesale of flowers and plants
		51.23	Wholesale of live animals
		51.24	Wholesale of hides, skins and leather
		51.25	Wholesale of unmanufactured tobacco
	51.3		Wholesale of food, beverages and tobacco
		51.31	Wholesale of fruit and vegetables
		51.32	Wholesale of meat and meat products
		51.33	Wholesale of dairy produce, eggs and edible oils and fats
		51.34	Wholesale of alcoholic and other beverages
		51.35	Wholesale of tobacco products
		51.36	Wholesale of sugar and chocolate and sugar confectionery
		51.37	Wholesale of coffee, tea, cocoa and spices
		51.38	Wholesale of other food including fish, crustaceans and molluscs
		51.39	Non-specialised wholesale of food, beverages and tobacco
	51.4		Wholesale of household goods
		51.41	Wholesale of textiles
		51.42	Wholesale of clothing and footwear
		51.43	Wholesale of electrical household appliances and radio and television goods
		51.44	Wholesale of china and glassware, wallpaper and cleaning materials
		51.45	Wholesale of perfume and cosmetics
		51.46	Wholesale of pharmaceutical goods
		51.47	Wholesale of other household goods
		51.47/1	Wholesale of furniture
		51.47/2	Wholesale of other household goods not elsewhere classified
	51.5		Wholesale of non-agricultural intermediate products, waste and scrap
		51.51	Wholesale of solid, liquid and gaseous fuels and related products
		51.51/1	Wholesale of petroleum and petroleum products
		51.51/2	Wholesale of other fuels and related products
		51.52	Wholesale of metals and metal ores
		51.53	Wholesale of wood, construction materials and sanitary equipment
		51.54	Wholesale of hardware, plumbing and heating equipment and supplies
		51.55	Wholesale of chemical products
		51.56	Wholesale of other intermediate products
		51.57	Wholesale of waste and scrap
	51.6		Wholesale of machinery, equipment and supplies
		51.61	Wholesale of machine tools
		51.62	Wholesale of construction machinery
		51.63	Wholesale of machinery for the textile industry, and of sewing and knitting machines
		51.64	Wholesale of office machinery and equipment
		51.65	Wholesale of other machinery for use in industry, trade and navigation

Division	Group	Class & sub class	Description
		51.66	Wholesale of agricultural machinery and accessories and implements, including tractors
	51.7		Other wholesale
		51.70	Other wholesale
52			RETAIL TRADE, EXCEPT OF MOTOR VEHICLES AND MOTORCYCLES; REPAIR OF PERSONAL AND HOUSEHOLD GOODS
	52.1		Retail sale in non-specialised stores
		52.11	Retail sale in non-specialised stores with food, beverages or tobacco predominating
		52.12	Other retail sale in non-specialised stores
	52.2		Retail sale of food, beverages and tobacco in specialised stores
		52.21	Retail sale of fruit and vegetables
		52.22	Retail sale of meat and meat products
		52.23	Retail sale of fish, crustaceans and molluscs
		52.24	Retail sale of bread, cakes, flour confectionery and sugar confectionery
		52.25	Retail sale of alcoholic and other beverages
		52.26	Retail sale of tobacco products
		52.27	Other retail sale of food, beverages and tobacco in specialised stores
	52.3		Retail sale of pharmaceutical and medical goods, cosmetic and toilet articles
		52.31	Dispensing chemists
		52.32	Retail sale of medical and orthopaedic goods
		52.33	Retail sale of cosmetic and toilet articles
	52.4		Other retail sale of new goods in specialised stores
		52.41	Retail sale of textiles
		52.42	Retail sale of clothing
		52.43	Retail sale of footwear and leather goods
		52.44	Retail sale of furniture, lighting equipment and household articles not elsewhere classified
		52.45	Retail sale of electrical household appliances and radio and television goods
		52.46	Retail sale of hardware, paints and glass
		52.47	Retail sale of books, newspapers and stationery
		52.48	Other retail sale in specialised stores
		52.48/1	Retail sale of floor coverings
		52.48/2	Retail sale of photographic, optical and precision equipment, office supplies and equipment (including computers, etc)
		52.48/3	Other retail sale in specialised stores not elsewhere classified
	52.5		Retail sale of second-hand goods in stores
		52.50	Retail sale of second-hand goods in stores
	52.6		Retail sale not in stores
		52.61	Retail sale via mail order houses
		52.62	Retail sale via stalls and markets
		52.63	Other non-store retail sale

Division	Group	Class & sub class	Description
	52.7		Repair of personal and household goods
		52.71	Repair of boots, shoes and other articles of leather
		52.72	Repair of electrical household goods
		52.73	Repair of watches, clocks and jewellery
		52.74	Repair not elsewhere classified

SECTION H   HOTELS AND RESTAURANTS

55			HOTELS AND RESTAURANTS
	55.1		Hotels
		55.11	Hotels and motels, with restaurant
		55.11/1	Licensed hotels and motels
		55.11/2	Unlicensed hotels and motels
		55.12	Hotels and motels, without restaurant
	55.2		Camping sites and other provision of short-stay accommodation
		55.21	Youth hostels and mountain refuges
		55.22	Camping sites, including caravan sites
		55.23	Other provision of lodgings not elsewhere classified
		55.23/1	Holiday centres and holiday villages
		55.23/2	Other self-catering holiday accommodation
		55.23/3	Other tourist or short-stay accommodation
	55.3		Restaurants
		55.30	Restaurants
		55.30/1	Licensed restaurants
		55.30/2	Unlicensed restaurants and cafes
		55.30/3	Take-away food shops
	55.4		Bars
		55.40	Bars
		55.40/1	Licensed clubs with entertainment
		55.40/2	Public houses and bars
	55.5		Canteens and catering
		55.51	Canteens
		55.52	Catering

SECTION I   TRANSPORT, STORAGE AND COMMUNICATION

60			LAND TRANSPORT; TRANSPORT VIA PIPELINES
	60.1		Transport via railways
		60.10	Transport via railways
		60.10/1	Inter-city services
		60.10/2	Other transport via railways
	60.2		Other land transport
		60.21	Other scheduled passenger land transport

Division	Group	Class & sub class	Description
		60.21/1	Inter-city coach services
		60.21/2	Other scheduled passenger land transport not elsewhere classified
		60.22	Taxi operation
		60.23	Other passenger land transport
		60.24	Freight transport by road
	60.3		Transport via pipelines
		60.30	Transport via pipelines
61			WATER TRANSPORT
	61.1		Sea and coastal water transport
		61.10	Sea and coastal water transport
		61.10/1	Passenger sea and coastal water transport
		61.10/2	Freight sea and coastal water transport
	61.2		Inland water transport
		61.20	Inland water transport
		61.20/1	Passenger inland water transport
		61.20/2	Other inland water transport
62			AIR TRANSPORT
	62.1		Scheduled air transport
		62.10	Scheduled air transport
		62.10/1	Scheduled passenger air transport
		62.10/2	Other scheduled air transport
	62.2		Non-scheduled air transport
		62.20	Non-scheduled air transport
		62.20/1	Non-scheduled passenger air transport
		62.20/2	Other non-scheduled air transport
	62.3		Space transport
		62.30	Space transport
63			SUPPORTING AND AUXILIARY TRANSPORT ACTIVITIES; ACTIVITIES OF TRAVEL AGENCIES
	63.1		Cargo handling and storage
		63.11	Cargo handling
		63.12	Storage and warehousing
	63.2		Other supporting transport activities
		63.21	Other supporting land transport activities
		63.22	Other supporting water transport activities
		63.23	Other supporting air transport activities
	63.3		Activities of travel agencies and tour operators; tourist assistance activities not elsewhere classified
		63.30	Activities of travel agencies and tour operators; tourist assistance activities not elsewhere classified

Division	Group	Class & sub class	Description
		63.30/1	Activities of travel agencies
		63.30/2	Activities of travel organisers
		63.30/3	Activities of tour guides
		63.30/4	Other tourist assistance activities not elsewhere classified
	63.4		Activities of other transport agencies
		63 40	Activities of other transport agencies
64			POST AND TELECOMMUNICATIONS
	64.1		Post and courier activities
		64.11	National post activities
		64.12	Courier activities other than national post activities
	64.2		Telecommunications
		64.20	Telecommunications

SECTION J — FINANCIAL INTERMEDIATION

Division	Group	Class & sub class	Description
65			FINANCIAL INTERMEDIATION, EXCEPT INSURANCE AND PENSION FUNDING
	65.1		Monetary intermediation
		65.11	Central banking
		65.12	Other monetary intermediation
		65.12/1	Banks
		65.12/2	Building societies
	65.2		Other financial intermediation
		65.21	Financial leasing
		65.22	Other credit granting
		65.22/1	Credit granting by non-deposit taking finance houses and other specialist consumer credit grantors
		65.22/2	Factoring
		65.22/3	Activities of mortgage finance companies
		65.22/4	Other credit granting not elsewhere classified
		65.23	Other financial intermediation not elsewhere classified
		65.23/1	Activities of investment trusts
		65.23/2	Activities of unit trusts and property unit trusts
		65.23/3	Security dealing on own account
		65.23/4	Activities of bank holding companies
		65.23/5	Activities of venture and development capital companies
		65.23/6	Financial intermediation not elsewhere classified
66			INSURANCE AND PENSION FUNDING, EXCEPT COMPULSORY SOCIAL SECURITY
	66.0		Insurance and pension funding, except compulsory social security
		66.01	Life insurance
		66.02	Pension funding
		66.03	Non-life insurance

Division	Group	Class & sub class	Description
67			ACTIVITIES AUXILIARY TO FINANCIAL INTERMEDIATION
	67.1		Activities auxiliary to financial intermediation, except insurance and pension funding
		67.11	Administration of financial markets
		67.12	Security broking and fund management
		67.12/1	Fund management activities
		67.12/2	Security broking and related activities
		67.13	Activities auxiliary to financial intermediation not elsewhere classified
	67.2		Activities auxiliary to insurance and pension funding
		67.20	Activities auxiliary to insurance and pension funding
SECTION K			**REAL ESTATE, RENTING AND BUSINESS ACTIVITIES**
70			REAL ESTATE ACTIVITIES
	70.1		Real estate activities with own property
		70.11	Development and selling of real estate
		70.12	Buying and selling of own real estate
	70.2		Letting of own property
		70.20	Letting of own property
		70.20/1	Letting of conference and exhibition centres
		70.20/2	Other letting of own property
	70.3		Real estate activities on a fee or contract basis
		70.31	Real estate agencies
		70.32	Management of real estate on a fee or contract basis
71			RENTING OF MACHINERY AND EQUIPMENT WITHOUT OPERATOR AND OF PERSONAL AND HOUSEHOLD GOODS
	71.1		Renting of automobiles
		71.10	Renting of automobiles
	71.2		Renting of other transport equipment
		71.21	Renting of other land transport equipment
		71.21/1	Renting of passenger land transport equipment
		71.21/2	Renting of other land transport equipment
		71.22	Renting of water transport equipment
		71.22/1	Renting of passenger water transport equipment
		71 22/2	Renting of other water transport equipment
		71.23	Renting of air transport equipment
		71.23/1	Renting of passenger air transport equipment
		71.23/2	Renting of other air transport equipment
	71.3		Renting of other machinery and equipment
		71.31	Renting of agricultural machinery and equipment
		71.32	Renting of construction and civil engineering machinery and equipment
		71.33	Renting of office machinery and equipment including computers
		71.34	Renting of other machinery and equipment not elsewhere classified

Division	Group	Class & sub class	Description
	71.4		Renting of personal and household goods not elsewhere classified
		71.40	Renting of personal and household goods not elsewhere classified
		71.40/1	Renting of sporting and recreational equipment
		71.40/2	Renting of other personal and household goods not elsewhere classified
72			COMPUTER AND RELATED ACTIVITIES
	72.1		Hardware consultancy
		72.10	Hardware consultancy
	72.2		Software consultancy and supply
		72.20	Software consultancy and supply
	72.3		Data processing
		72.30	Data processing
	72.4		Data base activities
		72.40	Data base activities
	72.5		Maintenance and repair of office, accounting and computing machinery
		72.50	Maintenance and repair of office, accounting and computing machinery
	72.6		Other computer related activities
		72.60	Other computer related activities
73			RESEARCH AND DEVELOPMENT
	73.1		Research and experimental development on natural sciences and engineering
		73.10	Research and experimental development on natural sciences and engineering
	73.2		Research and experimental development on social sciences and humanities
		73.20	Research and experimental development on social sciences and humanities
74			OTHER BUSINESS ACTIVITIES
	74.1		Legal, accounting, book-keeping and auditing activities; tax consultancy; market research and public opinion polling; business and management consultancy; holdings
		74.11	Legal activities
		74.12	Accounting, book-keeping and auditing activities; tax consultancy
		74.13	Market research and public opinion polling
		74.14	Business and management consultancy activities
		74.15	Management activities of holding companies
	74.2		Architectural and engineering activities and related technical consultancy
		74.20	Architectural and engineering activities and related technical consultancy
	74.3		Technical testing and analysis
		74.30	Technical testing and analysis
	74.4		Advertising
		74.40	Advertising

Division	Group	Class & sub class	Description
	74.5		Labour recruitment and provision of personnel
		74.50	Labour recruitment and provision of personnel
	74.6		Investigation and security activities
		74.60	Investigation and security activities
	74.7		Industrial cleaning
		74.70	Industrial cleaning
	74.8		Miscellaneous business activities not elsewhere classified
		74.81	Photographic activities
		74.82	Packaging activities
		74.83	Secretarial and translation activities
		74.84	Other business activities not elsewhere classified

SECTION L   **PUBLIC ADMINISTRATION AND DEFENCE; COMPULSORY SOCIAL SECURITY**

Division	Group	Class & sub class	Description
75			PUBLIC ADMINISTRATION AND DEFENCE; COMPULSORY SOCIAL SECURITY
	75.1		Administration of the State and the economic and social policy of the community
		75.11	General (overall) public service activities
		75.12	Regulation of the activities of agencies that provide health care, education, cultural services and other social services excluding social security
		75.13	Regulation of and contribution to more efficient operation of business
		75.14	Supporting service activities for the government as a whole
	75.2		Provision of services to the community as a whole
		75.21	Foreign affairs
		75.22	Defence activities
		75.23	Justice and judicial activities
		75.24	Public security, law and order activities
		75.25	Fire service activities
	75.3		Compulsory social security activities
		75.30	Compulsory social security activities

SECTION M   **EDUCATION**

Division	Group	Class & sub class	Description
80			EDUCATION
	80.1		Primary education
		80.10	Primary education
	80.2		Secondary education
		80.21	General secondary education
		80.22	Technical and vocational secondary education
	80.3		Higher education
		80.30	Higher education
		80.30/1	Sub-degree level higher education

Division	Group	Class & sub class	Description
		80.30/2	First-degree level higher education
		80.30/3	Post-graduate level higher education
	80.4		Adult and other education
		80.41	Driving school activities
		80.42	Adult and other education not elsewhere classified
		80.42/1	Activities of private training providers
		80.42/2	Other adult and other education not elsewhere classified

SECTION N — HEALTH AND SOCIAL WORK

Division	Group	Class & sub class	Description
85			HEALTH AND SOCIAL WORK
	85.1		Human health activities
		85.11	Hospital activities
		85.12	Medical practice activities
		85.13	Dental practice activities
		85.14	Other human health activities
	85.2		Veterinary activities
		85.20	Veterinary activities
	85.3		Social work activities
		85.31	Social work activities with accommodation
		85.32	Social work activities without accommodation

SECTION O — OTHER COMMUNITY, SOCIAL AND PERSONAL SERVICE ACTIVITIES

Division	Group	Class & sub class	Description
90			SEWAGE AND REFUSE DISPOSAL, SANITATION AND SIMILAR ACTIVITIES
	90.0		Sewage and refuse disposal, sanitation and similar activities
		90.00	Sewage and refuse disposal, sanitation and similar activities
91			ACTIVITIES OF MEMBERSHIP ORGANISATIONS NOT ELSEWHERE CLASSIFIED
	91.1		Activities of business, employers and professional organisations
		91.11	Activities of business and employers organisations
		91.12	Activities of professional organisations
	91.2		Activities of trade unions
		91.20	Activities of trade unions
	91.3		Activities of other membership organisations
		91.31	Activities of religious organisations
		91.32	Activities of political organisations
		91.33	Activities of other membership organisations not elsewhere classified
92			RECREATIONAL, CULTURAL AND SPORTING ACTIVITIES
	92.1		Motion picture and video activities

Division	Group	Class & sub class	Description
		92.11	Motion picture and video production
		92.12	Motion picture and video distribution
		92.13	Motion picture projection
	92.2		Radio and television activities
		92.20	Radio and television activities
	92.3		Other entertainment activities
		92.31	Artistic and literary creation and interpretation
		92.31/1	Live theatrical presentations
		92.31/2	Other artistic and literary creation and interpretation
		92.32	Operation of arts facilities
		92.33	Fair and amusement park activities
		92.34	Other entertainment activities not elsewhere classified
	92.4		News agency activities
		92.40	News agency activities
	92.5		Library, archives, museums and other cultural activities
		92.51	Library and archives activities
		92.52	Museum activities and preservation of historical sites and buildings
		92.53	Botanical and zoological gardens and nature reserves activities
	92.6		Sporting activities
		92.61	Operation of sports arenas and stadiums
		92.62	Other sporting activities
	92.7		Other recreational activities
		92.71	Gambling and betting activities
		92.72	Other recreational activities not elsewhere classified
93			OTHER SERVICE ACTIVITIES
	93.0		Other service activities
		93.01	Washing and dry cleaning of textile and fur products
		93.02	Hairdressing and other beauty treatment
		93.03	Funeral and related activities
		93.04	Physical well-being activities
		93.05	Other service activities not elsewhere classified

SECTION P — PRIVATE HOUSEHOLDS WITH EMPLOYED PERSONS

Division	Group	Class & sub class	Description
95			PRIVATE HOUSEHOLDS WITH EMPLOYED PERSONS
	95.0		Private households with employed persons
		95.00	Private households with employed persons

SECTION Q — EXTRA-TERRITORIAL ORGANISATIONS AND BODIES

Division	Group	Class & sub class	Description
99			EXTRA-TERRITORIAL ORGANISATIONS AND BODIES
	99.0		Extra-territorial organisations and bodies
		99.00	Extra-territorial organisations and bodies

EXPLANATORY NOTES

SECTION A   AGRICULTURE, HUNTING AND FORESTRY

01   AGRICULTURE, HUNTING AND RELATED SERVICE ACTIVITIES

01.1   Growing of crops; market gardening; horticulture

01.11   Growing of cereals and other crops not elsewhere classified

This class includes:
- growing of cereal grains: hard and soft wheat, rye, barley, oats, maize, etc.
- growing of potatoes
- growing of sugar beet
- growing of oil seeds: soya, colza, etc.
- production of sugar beet seeds and forage plant seeds (including grasses)
- growing of hop cones, roots and tubers with a high starch or inulin content
- growing of diverse textile plants; retting of plants bearing vegetable fibres
- growing of dried leguminous vegetables such as field peas and beans
- growing of plants used chiefly in pharmacy or for insecticidal, fungicidal or similar purposes
- growing of crops not elsewhere classified

This class excludes:
- *production of flower and vegetable seeds cf. 01.12*
- *growing of sweet corn cf. 01.12*
- *growing of other vegetables cf. 01.12*
- *growing of melons cf. 01.12*
- *growing of horticultural specialities cf. 01.12*
- *growing of flowers cf. 01.12*
- *growing of nuts cf. 01.13*
- *growing of spice crops cf. 01.13*
- *gathering of forest products and other wild growing material cf. 02.01*
- *growing of vegetable materials used for plaiting cf. 02.01*

01.12   Growing of vegetables, horticultural specialties and nursery products

This class includes:
- growing of vegetables: tomatoes, melons, onions, cabbages, lettuce, cucumbers, carrots, beans, cress, sweet corn, courgettes, egg-plants, leeks
- growing of seasoning herbs and vegetables: capers, "peppers", fennel, parsley, chervil, tarragon, sweet marjoram
- growing of mushrooms and gathering of forest mushrooms
- growing of flowers
- production of seeds for flowers, fruit or vegetables
- growing of plants for planting or ornamental purposes, including turf for transplanting

This class excludes:
- *growing of oil seeds cf. 01.11*
- *growing of vegetable textile materials cf. 01.11*
- *growing of potatoes cf. 01.11*
- *growing of roots and tubers with a high starch or inulin content cf. 01.11*
- *growing of sugar beets cf. 01.11*
- *growing of spice crops cf. 01.13*
- *growing of Christmas trees cf. 02.01*
- *operation of forest tree nurseries cf. 02.01*

01.13 Growing of fruit, nuts, beverage and spice crops

This class includes:
- production of fruit: apples, pears, apricots, strawberries, berries, cherries, peaches, etc.
- production of wine grapes and table grapes
- production of wine from self-produced grapes
- production of edible nuts
- growing of spice crops: bay, basil, coriander, etc.

This class excludes:
- *growing of hop cones cf. 01.11*
- *growing of fruit bearing vegetables e.g. cucumbers, tomatoes, melons, etc. cf. 01.12*
- *growing of fresh "peppers", parsley and tarragon cf. 01.12*
- *manufacture of olive oil cf. 15.42*
- *manufacture of cocoa cf. 15.84/1*
- *processing of tea leaves and coffee cf. 15.86*
- *manufacture of wines other than from self-produced grapes cf. 15.93*

01.2 Farming of animals

01.21 Farming of cattle, dairy farming

This class includes:
- farming of cattle
- production of raw cow milk

This class excludes:
- *animal boarding and care cf. 01.42*
- *processing of milk cf. 15.51*

01.22 Farming of sheep, goats, horses, asses, mules and hinnies

This class includes:
- farming and breeding of horses, asses, mules or hinnies
- farming of sheep and goats
- production of raw wool
- production of raw sheep or goat milk

This class excludes:
- *sheep shearing on a fee or contract basis cf. 01.42*
- *production of pulled wool cf. 15.11/3*
- *operation of racing stables and riding academies cf. 92.62*

01.23 Farming of swine

01.24 Farming of poultry

This class includes:
- raising of poultry
- production of eggs

This class excludes:
- *farming of other birds cf. 01.25*
- *production of feathers or down cf. 15.12*

01.25   Other farming of animals

This class includes:
- bee keeping and production of honey and beeswax
- raising of rabbits
- breeding of pet animals
- raising of fur animals, production of raw furskins
- raising of silk worms, production of silk worm cocoons
- raising of diverse animals

This class excludes:
- *animal boarding and care cf. 01.42*
- *production of hides and skins originating from hunting and trapping cf. 01.50*
- *training of dogs for security reasons cf. 74.60*
- *training of pet animals cf. 92.72*

01.3   Growing of crops combined with farming of animals (mixed farming)

01.30   Growing of crops combined with farming of animals (mixed farming)

This class includes:
- crop growing in combination with farming of livestock at mixed activity units with a specialisation ratio in either one of less than 66% of standard gross margins

This class excludes:
- *mixed cropping or mixed livestock units cf. their main activity*

01.4   Agricultural and animal husbandry service activities, except veterinary activities

01.41   Agricultural service activities

This class includes:
- agricultural activities on a fee or contract basis:
  . preparation of fields
  . establishing a crop
  . treatment of crops
  . crop spraying including by air
  . trimming of fruit trees and vines
  . thinning of beets
  . harvesting and preparation of crops for primary markets ie cleaning, trimming, grading, decorticating, retting,
    cooling or bulk packaging
  . pest control (including rabbits) in connection with agriculture
- operation of irrigation systems
- laying out, planting and maintenance of gardens, parks and green areas for sport installations and the like

This class also includes:
- tree pruning and hedge trimming
- renting of agricultural machinery and equipment with operator

This class excludes:
- *preparation of vegetable fibres cf. 17.1*
- *marketing activities of commission merchants and co-operative associations cf. 51*
- *activities of agronomists and agricultural economists cf. 74.14*
- *planning and design of gardens and sport installations cf. 74.20*
- *organisation of agricultural shows and fairs cf. 74.84*

01.42 Animal husbandry service activities, except veterinary activities

This class includes:
- agricultural activities on a fee or contract basis:
  . activities related to artificial insemination
  . herd testing services, droving services, agistment services, poultry caponising, coop cleaning, etc.
  . activities to promote propagation, growth and output of animals
  . animal boarding and care

This class excludes:
- *provision of feed lot services cf. 01.2*
- *service activities to promote commercial hunting and trapping cf. 01.50*
- *marketing activities of commission merchants and co-operative associations cf. 51*
- *activities of agronomists and agricultural economists cf. 74.14*
- *veterinary activities cf. 85.20*

01.5 Hunting, trapping and game propagation including related service activities

01.50 Hunting, trapping and game propagation including related service activities

This class includes:
- hunting and trapping of animals for food, fur, skin, or for use in research, in zoos or as pets
- production of furskins or bird skins from hunting or trapping activities
- game propagation
- service activities to promote commercial hunting and trapping

This class also includes:
- catching of sea mammals such as walrus and seal

This class excludes:
- *production of furskins or bird skins from ranching operations cf. 01.25*
- *raising of animals on ranching operations cf. 01.25*
- *catching of whales cf. 05.01*
- *production of hides and skins originating from slaughterhouses cf. 15.1111*
- *hunting for sport or recreation cf. 92.62*

02 FORESTRY, LOGGING AND RELATED SERVICE ACTIVITIES

02.0 Forestry, logging and related service activities

02.01 Forestry and logging

This class includes:
- growing of standing timber: planting, replanting, transplanting, thinning and conserving of forests and timber tracts
- growing of coppice and pulpwood
- operation of forest tree nurseries
- growing of Christmas trees
- logging: felling of timber and production of wood in the rough such as pit-props, split poles, pickets or fuel wood
- growing of vegetable materials used for plaiting

This class also includes:
- gathering of wild growing forest materials: lac, resins, balsams, vegetable hair, eel grass, acorns, horse-chestnuts, mosses, lichens

This class excludes:
- growing and gathering of mushrooms cf. 01.12
- gathering of berries or nuts cf. 01.13
- production of wood chips cf. 20.10

02.02   Forestry and logging related service activities

This class includes:
- forestry service activities: forestry inventories, timber evaluation, fire protection
- logging service activities: transport of logs within the forest

SECTION B FISHING

05   FISHING, OPERATION OF FISH HATCHERIES AND FISH FARMS; SERVICE ACTIVITIES
INCIDENTAL TO FISHING

05.0   Fishing, operation of fish hatcheries and fish farms; service activities incidental to fishing

05.01   Fishing

This class includes:
- fishing in ocean, coastal or inland waters
- taking of marine and freshwater crustaceans and molluscs
- hunting of aquatic animals: sea-squirts, tunicates, sea urchins, etc.

This class also includes:
- gathering of marine materials: sponges, algae
- service activities incidental to fishing

This class excludes:
- *capturing of sea mammals, except whales, e.g. walruses, seals cf. 01.50*
- *processing of fish, crustaceans and molluscs not connected to fishing, i.e. on vessels only engaged in processing and preserving fish, or in factories ashore cf. 15.20*
- *fishing practised for sport or recreation and related services cf. 92.72*

05.02   Operation of fish hatcheries and fish farms

This class includes:
- production of oyster spat, mussels, lobsterlings, shrimp post-larvae, fish fry and fingerlings
- growing of laver and other edible seaweeds
- fish farming in sea and fresh water
- cultivation of oysters

This class also includes:
- service activities incidental to the operation of fish hatcheries and fish farms

This class excludes:
- *operation of sport fishing preserves cf. 92.72*

SECTION C   MINING AND QUARRYING

Mining and quarrying include extraction of minerals occurring naturally as solids (coal and ores), liquids (petroleum), or gases (natural gas). Extraction can be by underground or surface mining or well operation. This section includes supplementary operations aimed at preparing the crude materials rendering them marketable: milling, dressing, desalting and beneficiation

Mining activities are classified into divisions, groups and classes on the basis of the principal mineral produced

This section also includes:
- agglomeration of coals and ores

This section excludes:
- *bottling of natural spring and mineral waters at springs and wells cf. 15.98*
- *crushing, grinding or otherwise treating certain earths, rocks and minerals not carried on in conjunction with mining and quarrying cf. 26.81, 26.82*
- *collection, purification and distribution of water cf. 41.00*
- *mineral prospecting cf. 74.20*

SUBSECTION CA   MINING AND QUARRYING OF ENERGY PRODUCING MATERIALS

10   MINING OF COAL AND LIGNITE; EXTRACTION OF PEAT

10.1   Mining and agglomeration of hard coal

10.10   Mining and agglomeration of hard coal

10.10/1   Deep coal mines

This subclass includes:
- mining of hard coal: underground mining
- cleaning, sizing, grading, pulverising, etc. of deep-mined coal

10.10/2   Opencast coal working

This subclass includes:
- mining of hard coal: surface mining
- cleaning, sizing, grading, pulverising, etc. of opencast coal

This subclass also includes:
- recovery of hard coal from tips

10.10/3   Manufacture of solid fuel

This subclass includes:
- manufacture of solid fuels whether carbonised or not, in the form of briquettes, ovoids or other coal agglomerates

This subclass excludes:
- *coke ovens and low temperature carbonisation plants producing solid fuels cf. 23.10*

10.2   Mining and agglomeration of lignite

10.20   Mining and agglomeration of lignite

This class includes:
- mining of lignite (brown coal): underground or surface mining
- washing, dehydrating, pulverising of lignite
- agglomeration of lignite

10.3 Extraction and agglomeration of peat

10.30 Extraction and agglomeration of peat

This class includes:
- peat digging
- peat agglomeration

This class excludes:
- *manufacture of articles of peat cf. 26.82/2*

11 EXTRACTION OF CRUDE PETROLEUM AND NATURAL GAS; SERVICE ACTIVITIES INCIDENTAL TO OIL AND GAS EXTRACTION EXCLUDING SURVEYING

11.1 Extraction of crude petroleum and natural gas

11.10 Extraction of crude petroleum and natural gas

This class includes:
- extraction of crude petroleum
- production of crude gaseous hydrocarbon (natural gas)
- extraction of condensates
- draining and separation of liquid hydrocarbon fractions
- liquefaction and regasification of natural gas for transportation
- gas desulphurisation

This class also includes:
- extraction of bituminous shale and sand
- production of crude petroleum from bituminous shale and sand

This class excludes:
- *service activities incidental to oil and gas extraction cf. 11.20*
- *manufacture of refined petroleum products cf. 23.20*
- *recovery of liquefied petroleum gases in the refining of petroleum cf. 23.20/1*
- *operation of pipelines cf. 60.30*
- *oil and gas exploration cf. 74.20*

11.2 Service activities incidental to oil and gas extraction excluding surveying

11.20 Service activities incidental to oil and gas extraction excluding surveying

This class includes:
- oil and gas extraction service activities provided on a fee or contract basis: test drilling and testhole boring; directional drilling and redrilling; "spudding in"; derrick erection in situ, repairing and dismantling; cementing oil and gas well casings; pumping of wells; plugging and abandoning wells, etc.

This class excludes:
- *geophysical, geological and seismographic surveys cf. 74.20*

12 MINING OF URANIUM AND THORIUM ORES

12.0 Mining of uranium and thorium ores

12.00 Mining of uranium and thorium ores

This class includes:
- mining of uranium and thorium ores
- concentration of such ores
- manufacture of yellowcake

This class excludes:
- *enrichment of uranium and thorium ores cf. 23.30*
- *production of fissile or fertile material cf. 23.30*
- *production of uranium metal cf. 23.30*

SUBSECTION CB   MINING AND QUARRYING EXCEPT ENERGY PRODUCING MATERIALS

13 MINING OF METAL ORES

This division includes:
- underground and opencast extraction of metal ores and native metals
- preparation of ores:
  . crushing and grinding of ores, washing of ores
  . concentrating of ores by magnetic or gravimetric separation
  . flotation, screening, grading, drying, calcination and roasting of ores

This division excludes:
- *mining of uranium and thorium ores cf. 12.00*
- *roasting of iron pyrites cf. 24.13*
- *production of aluminium oxide cf. 27.42*

13.1 Mining of iron ores

13.10 Mining of iron ores

This class includes:
- mining of ores valued chiefly for iron content
- beneficiation and agglomeration of iron ores

This class excludes:
- *pyrites and pyrrhotite mining and preparation cf. 14.30*

13.2 Mining of non-ferrous metal ores, except uranium and thorium ores

13.20 Mining of non-ferrous metal ores, except uranium and thorium ores

This class includes:
- mining and preparation of ores valued chiefly for non-ferrous metal content:
  . mining and preparation of ores of aluminium (bauxite), copper, lead, zinc, tin, manganese, chrome, nickel, cobalt, molybdenum, tantalum, vanadium, etc.
  . mining and preparation of ores of precious metals:
  preparation of ores of gold, silver, platinum

This class excludes:
- *mining and preparation of uranium and thorium ores cf. 12.00*
- *production of aluminium oxide and mattes of nickel or of copper cf. 27.4*

14 OTHER MINING AND QUARRYING

14.1 Quarrying of stone

14.11 Quarrying of stone for construction

This class includes:
- quarrying, rough trimming and sawing of monumental and building stone such as marble, granite, sandstone, etc.

This class excludes:
- *cutting, shaping and finishing of stone outside quarries cf. 26.70*

14.12 Quarrying of limestone, gypsum and chalk

This class includes:
- quarrying, crushing and breaking of limestone for industrial and constructional uses
- mining of gypsum and anhydrite
- mining of chalk

14.13 Quarrying of slate

14.2 Quarrying of sand and clay

14.21 Operation of gravel and sand pits

This class includes:
- extraction and dredging of industrial sand, sand for construction and gravel
- breaking and crushing of shingle, gravel and sand

This class excludes:
- *mining of bituminous sand cf. 11.10*

14.22 Mining of clays and kaolin

This class includes:
- extraction of clays for brick, pipe and tile making
- extraction of special clays including ball clay, china clay, fire-clay, fuller's earth, etc.

14.3 Mining of chemical and fertilizer minerals

14.30 Mining of chemical and fertilizer minerals

This class includes:
- mining of natural phosphates and natural potassium salts
- mining of native sulphur
- extraction and preparation of pyrites and pyrrhotite
- mining of natural barium sulphate and carbonate (barytes and witherite), natural borates, natural magnesium sulphates (kieserite)
- mining of earth colours and fluorspar

This class also includes:
- guano mining

This class excludes:
- *production of salt cf. 14.40*
- *roasting of iron pyrites cf. 24.13*
- *manufacture of synthetic fertilizers and nitrogen compounds cf. 24.15*

14.4   Production of salt

14.40   Production of salt

This class includes:
- extraction of salt from underground including by dissolving and pumping
- salt production by evaporation of sea water or other saline waters
- production of brine and other saline solutions
- crushing, purification and refining of salt

This class excludes:
- *potable water production by evaporation of saline water cf. 41.00*

14.5   Other mining and quarrying not elsewhere classified

14.50   Other mining and quarrying not elsewhere classified

This class includes:
- mining and quarrying of various minerals and materials:
  . abrasive materials, asbestos, siliceous fossil meals, natural graphite, steatite (talc), feldspar, etc.
  . gem stones, quartz, mica, etc.
  . natural asphalt and bitumen

SECTION D MANUFACTURING

SUBSECTION DA   MANUFACTURE OF FOOD PRODUCTS; BEVERAGES AND TOBACCO

15   MANUFACTURE OF FOOD PRODUCTS AND BEVERAGES

15.1   Production, processing and preserving of meat and meat products

15.11   Production and preserving of meat

15.11/1   Slaughtering of animals other than poultry and rabbits

This subclass includes:
- production of fresh, chilled or frozen meat, in carcasses
- production of fresh, chilled or frozen meat, in cuts

This subclass also includes:
- production of hides and skins originating from slaughterhouses

This subclass excludes:
- *packaging of meat for own account by the wholesale trade cf. 51.32*
- *packaging of meat on a fee or contract basis cf. 74.82*

15.11/2   Animal by-product processing

This subclass includes:
- rendering of edible fats of animal origin
- processing of animal offal; production of flours and meals of meat

15.11/3   Fellmongery

This subclass includes:
- production of pulled wool

15.12   Production and preserving of poultry meat

This class includes:
- slaughtering of poultry
- preparation of poultry meat
- production of fresh or frozen poultry meat in individual portions

This class also includes:
- slaughtering of rabbits and the like
- preparation of rabbit meat and the like
- production of feathers and down

This class excludes:
- *packaging of poultry meat for own account by the wholesale trade cf. 51.32*
- *packaging of poultry meat on a fee or contract basis cf. 74.82*

15.13   Production of meat and poultry meat products

15.13/1   Bacon and ham production

This subclass includes:
- production of bacon and ham, including boiled ham

This subclass excludes:
- *packaging of bacon and ham for own account by the wholesale trade cf. 51.32*
- *packaging of bacon and ham on a fee or contract basis cf. 74.82*

15.13/2   Other meat and poultry meat processing

This subclass includes:
- production of other dried, salted or smoked meat
- production of meat products: sausages, salami, puddings, "andouillettes", saveloys, bolognas, pates, galantines, rillettes; meat extracts and juices
- production of prepared meat dishes

This subclass excludes:
- *packaging of meat and poultry meat for own account by the wholesale trade cf. 51.32*
- *packaging of meat and poultry meat on a fee or contract basis cf. 74.82*

15.2   Processing and preserving of fish and fish products

15.20   Processing and preserving of fish and fish products

15.20/1   Freezing of fish

This subclass includes:
- preservation of fish, crustaceans and molluscs: freezing and deep freezing

This subclass also includes:
- activities of vessels only engaged in processing and preserving fish by freezing

This subclass excludes:
- *activities of vessels engaged both in fishing and in processing and freezing of fish cf. 05.01*

15.20/2   Other fish processing and preserving

This subclass includes:
- preservation of fish, crustaceans and molluscs: drying, smoking, salting, immersing in brine, canning, etc.
- production of fish, crustaceans and molluscs products:
  cooked fish, fish fillets, roes, caviar, caviar substitutes, etc.
- production of prepared fish dishes

This subclass also includes:
- activities of vessels only engaged in processing and preserving fish other than by freezing

This subclass excludes:
- *activities of vessels engaged both in fishing and in processing and preserving of fish cf. 05.01*
- *production of oils and fats from marine material cf. 15.41*
- *manufacture of fish soups cf. 15.89/1*

15.3   Processing and preserving of fruit and vegetables

15.31   Processing and preserving of potatoes

This class includes:
- production of prepared frozen potatoes
- production of dehydrated mashed potatoes

- production of potato snacks
- production of potato crisps
- manufacture of potato flour and meal

This class also includes:
- industrial peeling of potatoes

15.32   Manufacture of fruit and vegetable juice

This class also includes:
- production of concentrates and nectars

This class excludes:
- *production of fruit syrup cf. 15.98*

15.33   Processing and preserving of fruit and vegetables not elsewhere classified

This class includes:
- preserving of fruit, nuts or vegetables: freezing, drying, immersing in oil or in vinegar, canning, etc.
- manufacture of fruit or vegetable food products
- manufacture of jams, marmalades and table jellies

This class excludes:
- *manufacture of flour or meal of dried leguminous vegetables cf.15.61/2*
- *preservation of fruit and nuts in sugar cf. 15.84/2*

15.4   Manufacture of vegetable and animal oils and fats

15.41   Manufacture of crude oils and fats

This class includes:
- production of crude vegetable oils: olive oil, soya-bean oil, palm oil, sunflower-seed oil, cotton seed oil, rape, colza or mustard oil, linseed oil, etc.
- production of non-defatted flour or meal of oil-seeds, oil nuts or oil kernels

This class also includes:
- production of non-edible animal oils and fats
- extraction of fish and marine mammal oils

Note:
- cotton linters, oil cakes and other residual products of oil production are by-products of this class

This class excludes:
- *rendering and refining of lard and other edible animal fats cf. 15.11/2*
- *wet corn milling cf. 15.62*
- *production of essential oils cf. 24.63*

15.42   Manufacture of refined oils and fats

This class includes:
- production of refined vegetable oils: olive oil, soya-bean oil, etc.
- processing of vegetable oils: blowing, boiling, oxidation, polymerisation, dehydration, hydrogenation, etc.

This class excludes:
- *production of non-edible animal oils and fats cf. 15.41*
- *extraction of fish and marine mammal oils cf. 15.41*

15.43 Manufacture of margarine and similar edible fats

This class includes:
- manufacture of margarine
- manufacture of melanges and similar spreads
- manufacture of compound cooking fats

15.5 Manufacture of dairy products

15.51 Operation of dairies and cheese making

15.51/1 Liquid milk and cream production

This subclass includes:
- production of fresh liquid milk, pasteurised, sterilised, homogenised and/or ultra heat treated
- production of cream from fresh liquid milk, pasteurised, sterilised, homogenised

This subclass excludes:
- *production of fresh whole raw cow milk cf. 01.21*

15.51/2 Butter and cheese production

This subclass includes:
- production of butter
- production of cheese and curd

15.51/3 Manufacture of other milk products

This subclass includes:
- manufacture of dried or concentrated milk whether or not sweetened
- production of yogurt
- production of whey
- production of casein or lactose

15.52 Manufacture of ice cream

This class includes:
- production of ice cream and other edible ice such as sorbet

This class excludes:
- *activities of ice cream parlours cf. 55.30/3*

15.6 Manufacture of grain mill products, starches and starch products

15.61 Manufacture of grain mill products

15.61/1 Grain milling

This subclass includes:
- grain milling: production of flour, groats, meal or pellets of wheat, rye, oats, maize (corn) or other cereal grains
- manufacture of prepared blended flour for bread, cake, biscuits or pancakes

This subclass excludes:
- *wet corn milling cf. 15.62*

15.61/2   Manufacture of breakfast cereals and cereals-based foods

This subclass includes:
- manufacture of cereal breakfast foods
- rice milling: production of milled, polished, glazed, parboiled or converted rice; production of rice flour
- vegetable milling: production of flour or meal of dried leguminous vegetables, of roots or tubers, or of edible nuts

This subclass excludes:
- *manufacture of potato flour and meal cf. 15.31*

15.62   Manufacture of starches and starch products

This class includes:
- manufacture of starches from rice, potatoes, maize, etc.
- wet corn milling
- manufacture of glucose, glucose syrup, maltose, etc.
- manufacture of gluten
- manufacture of tapioca
- manufacture of corn oil

This class excludes:
- *manufacture of lactose cf. 15.51/3*
- *production of cane or beet sugar cf. 15.83*

15.7   Manufacture of prepared animal feeds

15.71   Manufacture of prepared feeds for farm animals

This class includes:
- manufacture of prepared feeds for farm animals including animal feed supplements
- preparation of unmixed (single) feeds for farm animals

This class excludes:
- *production of fishmeal for animal feed cf. 15.20/2*
- *production of oil seed cake cf. 15.41*

15.72   Manufacture of prepared pet foods

15.8   Manufacture of other food products

15.81   Manufacture of bread; manufacture of fresh pastry goods and cakes

This class includes:
- manufacture of bread and rolls
- manufacture of fresh pastry, cakes, pies, tarts, etc.

This class excludes:
- *manufacture of farinaceous products (pastas) cf. 15.85*

15.82   Manufacture of rusks and biscuits; manufacture of preserved pastry goods and cakes

This class includes:
- manufacture of rusks and biscuits and "dry" bakery products
- manufacture of preserved pastry goods and cakes
- manufacture of snack products whether sweet or salted

15.83   Manufacture of sugar

This class includes:
- manufacture or refining of sugar (sucrose) and sugar substitutes from the juice of cane, beet, maple and palm

This class excludes:
- *manufacture of glucose, glucose syrup, maltose cf. 15.62*

15.84   Manufacture of cocoa; chocolate and sugar confectionery

15.84/1   Manufacture of cocoa and chocolate confectionery

This subclass includes:
- manufacture of cocoa, cocoa butter, cocoa fat, cocoa oil
- manufacture of chocolate and chocolate confectionery

15.84/2   Manufacture of sugar confectionery

This subclass includes:
- manufacture of sugar confectionery
- manufacture of chewing gum
- preserving in sugar of fruit, nuts, fruit-peels and other parts of plants
- manufacture of medicated confectionery

This subclass excludes:
- *production of sucrose sugar cf. 15.83*

15.85   Manufacture of macaroni, noodles, couscous and similar farinaceous products

This class includes:
- manufacture of pastas such as macaroni and noodles: cooked or not cooked, whether or not stuffed
- manufacture of couscous

15.86   Processing of tea and coffee

15.86/1   Tea processing

This subclass includes:
- blending of tea and mate
- packing of tea including packing in tea-bags

15.86/2   Production of coffee and coffee substitutes

This subclass includes:
- decaffeination and roasting of coffee
- production of coffee products:
  . ground coffee
  . soluble coffee
  . extracts and concentrates of coffee
- manufacture of coffee substitutes

15.87   Manufacture of condiments and seasonings

This class includes:
- manufacture of spices, sauces and condiments:

. mayonnaise
. mustard flour and meal
. prepared mustard, etc.
- manufacture of vinegar

This class excludes:
- *growing of spice crops cf. 01.13*
- *manufacture of table salt cf. 14.40*

15.88   Manufacture of homogenised food preparations and dietetic food

This class includes:
- manufacture of foods for particular nutritional uses (Council directive, Official Journal of the European Communities No L186 dated 30 June 1989):
  . infant formulae
  . follow-up milk and other follow-up foods
  . baby foods
  . low-energy and energy-reduced foods intended for weight control
  . dietary foods for special medical purposes
  . low-sodium foods, including low-sodium or sodium-free dietary salts
  . gluten-free foods
  . foods intended to meet the expenditure of intense muscular effort, especially for sportsmen
  . foods for persons suffering from carbohydrate-metabolism disorders (diabetes)

15.89   Manufacture of other food products not elsewhere classified

15.89/1   Manufacture of soups

This subclass includes:
- manufacture of soups and broths

15.89/2   Manufacture of other food products not elsewhere classified

This subclass includes:
- manufacture of yeast, powdered or reconstituted eggs

15.9   Manufacture of beverages

15.91   Manufacture of distilled potable alcoholic beverages

This class includes:
- manufacture of distilled, potable, alcoholic beverages:
  manufacture of whisky, brandy, gin, liqueurs, etc.

This class excludes:
- *manufacture of non-distilled alcoholic beverages cf. 15.92, 15.93, 15.94*

15.92   Production of ethyl alcohol from fermented materials

This class includes:
- production of ethyl alcohol from fermented materials
- production of neutral spirits

15.93   Manufacture of wines

15.93/1   Manufacture of wine of fresh grapes and grape juice

This subclass includes:
- manufacture of wine:
  . table wine
  . QWPSR wine (Quality wine produced in specified regions)
- manufacture of sparkling wine

This subclass excludes:
- *manufacture of wine from self-produced grapes cf. 01.13*
- *bottling and packaging without transformation of the wine cf. 51.34, 74.82*

15.93/2   Manufacture of wine based on concentrated grape must

This subclass includes:
- manufacture of wine from concentrated grape must

This subclass excludes:
- *bottling and packaging without transformation of the wine cf. 51.34, 74.82*

15.94   Manufacture of cider and other fruit wines

15.94/1   Manufacture of cider and perry

15.94/2   Manufacture of other fermented fruit beverages

15.95   Manufacture of other non-distilled fermented beverages

This class includes:
- manufacture of vermouth and the like

15.96   Manufacture of beer

15.97   Manufacture of malt

15.98   Production of mineral waters and soft drinks

This class includes:
- bottling of waters including production of natural mineral waters
- production of soft drinks:
  . non-alcoholic flavoured and/or sweetened waters:
    lemonade, orangeade, cola, fruit drinks, tonic waters, etc.

This class excludes:
- *production of fruit and vegetable juice cf. 15.32*

16   MANUFACTURE OF TOBACCO PRODUCTS

16.0   Manufacture of tobacco products

16.00   Manufacture of tobacco products

This class includes:
- manufacture of tobacco products: cigarettes, cigarette tobacco, cigars, pipe tobacco, chewing tobacco, snuff
- manufacture of "homogenised" or "reconstituted" tobacco

SUBSECTION DB   MANUFACTURE OF TEXTILES AND TEXTILE PRODUCTS

17   MANUFACTURE OF TEXTILES

17.1   Preparation and spinning of textile fibres

17.11   Preparation and spinning of cotton-type fibres

This class includes:
- preparatory operations on cotton-type fibres, carding and combing
- manufacture of cotton-type yarn, either with cotton or artificial or synthetic fibres, for weaving, knitting, etc.

This class excludes:
- *manufacture of sewing thread cf. 17.16*

17.12   Preparation and spinning of woollen-type fibres

This class includes:
- preparatory operations on woollen-type fibres: degreasing and carbonising of wool, carding
- manufacture of woollen-type yarns, either with wool or artificial or synthetic fibres, for weaving, knitting, etc.

17.13   Preparation and spinning of worsted-type fibres

This class includes:
- combing of worsted-type fibres
- manufacture of worsted-type yarns, either with wool or artificial or synthetic fibres, for weaving, knitting, etc.
- preparation and spinning of semi-worsted-type (carded but not fully combed) fibres

17.14   Preparation and spinning of flax-type fibres

This class includes:
- scutching of flax
- manufacture of flax-type yarns, either with flax or artificial or synthetic fibres, for weaving, knitting, etc.

17.15   Throwing and preparation of silk including from noils and throwing and texturing of synthetic or artificial filament yarns

This class includes:
- reeling, washing and throwing of silk
- carding and combing of silk waste
- manufacture of silk-type yarns, either with silk or artificial or synthetic fibres, for weaving, knitting, etc.
- texturising, twisting, folding, cabling and dipping of synthetic or artificial filament yarns

17.16   Manufacture of sewing threads

This class includes:
- manufacture of sewing thread of any textile material including mixtures

This class excludes:
- *manufacture of knitting and crocheting yarn cf. 17.11-17.15, 17.17*

17.17   Preparation and spinning of other textile fibres

This class includes:
- preparatory operations and spinning of other textile fibres, such as jute or bast fibres

This class also includes:
- manufacture of paper yarn

This class excludes:
- *manufacture of synthetic or artificial fibres and tows, manufacture of single yarns (including high tenacity yarn and yarn for carpets) of synthetic or artificial fibres cf. 24.70*
- *manufacture of glass fibres cf. 26.14*
- *spinning of asbestos yarn cf. 26.82/1*

17.2 Textile weaving

17.21 Cotton-type weaving

This class includes:
- manufacture of broad woven cotton-type fabrics, either with cotton or artificial or synthetic yarns

This class also includes:
- manufacture of woven pile or chenille fabrics, terry towelling, gauze, etc.

This class excludes:
- *manufacture of textile floor coverings cf. 17.51*
- *manufacture of nonwovens cf. 17.53*
- *manufacture of narrow fabrics cf. 17.54/2*
- *manufacture of knitted and crocheted fabrics cf. 17.60*

17.22 Woollen-type weaving

This class includes:
- manufacture of broad woven woollen-type fabrics, either with wool or artificial or synthetic yarns

This class excludes:
- *manufacture of textile floor coverings cf. 17.51*
- *manufacture of nonwovens cf. 17.53*
- *manufacture of knitted and crocheted fabrics cf. 17.60*

17.23 Worsted-type weaving

This class includes:
- manufacture of broad woven worsted-type fabrics, either with wool or artificial or synthetic yarns

This class excludes:
- *manufacture of textile floor coverings cf. 17.51*
- *manufacture of nonwovens cf. 17.53*
- *manufacture of knitted and crocheted fabrics cf. 17.60*

17.24 Silk-type weaving

This class includes:
- manufacture of broad woven silk-type fabrics either with silk or artificial or synthetic yarns

This class excludes:
- *manufacture of nonwovens cf. 17.53*

17.25 Other textile weaving

This class includes:
- manufacture of other broad woven fabrics, using flax, ramie, hemp, jute, bast fibres and special yarns
- manufacture of polypropylene fabrics

This class also includes:
- manufacture of woven fabrics of glass fibres

This class excludes:
- *manufacture of textile floor coverings cf. 17.51*
- *manufacture of nonwovens cf. 17.53*
- *weaving of asbestos yarn cf. 26.82/1*

17.3   Finishing of textiles

17.30   Finishing of textiles

This class includes:
- bleaching, dyeing and printing (including thermo-printing) of not self-produced textiles and textile articles
- dressing, drying, steaming, shrinking, sanforizing, mercerising of not self-produced textiles and textile articles

This class excludes:
- *finishing of textile articles made from self-produced materials cf. 17.1, 17.2 and 17.5*
- *impregnation, coating, covering and lamination of textiles with plastics cf. 17.54/3*

17.4   Manufacture of made-up textile articles, except apparel

17.40   Manufacture of made-up textile articles, except apparel

17.40/1   Manufacture of soft furnishings

This subclass includes:
- manufacture of made-up soft furnishing articles of any textile material including of knitted or crocheted fabrics:
  . cushions, pouffes, pillows, curtains, furniture covers, blinds such as Festoon, Austrian, Roman, etc.

17.40/2   Manufacture of canvas goods, sacks, etc.

This subclass includes:
- manufacture of made-up canvas goods, sacks, etc.:
. tarpaulins, tents, camping goods, sails, sacks, blinds, sun blinds, machine covers, loose covers for cars
. flags, banners, pennants, etc.
. life jackets, parachutes, etc.

17.40/3   Manufacture of household textiles

This subclass includes:
- manufacture of made-up household textile articles of any textile material including of knitted and crocheted fabrics:
  . blankets including travelling rugs
  . bed, table, toilet or kitchen linen
  . quilts, eiderdowns, sleeping bags, etc.
  . valances, bedspreads, etc.
  . dust-cloths, dish-cloths and similar articles

This subclass also includes:
- manufacture of the textile part of electric blankets

This subclass excludes:
- *manufacture of textile articles for technical use cf. 17.54/3*

17.5   Manufacture of other textiles

17.51   Manufacture of carpets and rugs

17.51/1   Manufacture of woven carpets and rugs

This subclass includes:
- manufacture of pile carpets and rugs from wool, cotton and man-made fibres by weaving processes

17.51/2   Manufacture of tufted carpets and rugs

This subclass includes:
- manufacture of pile carpets, rugs and tiles from wool, cotton and man-made fibres by tufting processes

17.51/3   Manufacture of other carpets and rugs

This subclass includes:
- manufacture of needleloom and bonded fibre carpets, rugs and tiles and needlefelt underlay
- manufacture of jute carpets and mats
- manufacture of knotted carpets
- manufacture of mats and matting of coir, sisal and other hard fibres

This subclass excludes:
- *manufacture of mats and matting of plaiting materials cf. 20.52*
- *manufacture of floor coverings of cork, rubber or plastic materials, even when textile backed cf. 20.52, 25.13, 25.23/1*
- *manufacture of linoleum and hard non-plastic surface floor coverings cf. 36.63/2*

17.52   Manufacture of cordage, rope, twine and netting

This class includes:
- manufacture of twine, cordage, rope and cables of textile fibres or strip or the like, whether or not impregnated, coated, covered or sheathed with rubber or plastics
- manufacture of knotted netting of twine, cordage or rope
- manufacture of products of rope or netting: fishing nets, ships' fenders, unloading cushions, loading slings, rope or cable fitted with metal rings, etc.

This class excludes:
- *manufacture of hair nets cf. 18.24/2*

17.53   Manufacture of nonwovens and articles made from nonwovens, except apparel

This class includes:
- manufacture of nonwovens and articles made from nonwovens, except apparel

17.54   Manufacture of other textiles not elsewhere classified

17.54/1   Manufacture of lace

This subclass includes:
- manufacture of tulles and other net fabrics; of lace in the piece, in strips or in motifs; of embroidery
- manufacture of net and window furnishing type fabrics of lace knitted on Raschel or similar machines

17.54/2 Manufacture of narrow fabrics

This subclass includes:
- manufacture of narrow woven fabrics, including fabrics consisting of warp without weft assembled by means of an adhesive
- manufacture of labels, badges, etc.
- manufacture of ornamental trimmings:
  . braids, tassels, pompons, etc.
- manufacture of rubber thread and cord covered with textile material
- manufacture of diverse textile articles: textile wicks, hosepiping, transmission or conveyor belts or belting

17.54/3 Manufacture of other textiles not elsewhere classified

This subclass includes:
- manufacture of felt
- manufacture of fabrics impregnated, coated, covered or laminated with plastics
- manufacture of textile yarn or strip covered, impregnated, coated or sheathed with rubber or plastics
- manufacture of textile wadding and articles of wadding:
  . sanitary towels or tampons
- manufacture of metallised yarn or gimped yarn
- manufacture of diverse fabrics: tyre cord fabric of high-tenacity man-made yarn, tracing cloth, canvas prepared for use by painters, buckram and similar stiffened textile fabrics, fabrics coated with gum or amylaceous substances
- manufacture of diverse textile articles: incandescent gas mantles and tubular gas mantle fabric, bolting cloth, straining cloth

This subclass excludes:
- manufacture of needleloom felt floor coverings cf. 17.51/3
- manufacture of cloth of woven metal wire cf. 28.73

17.6 Manufacture of knitted and crocheted fabrics

17.60 Manufacture of knitted and crocheted fabrics

This class includes:
- manufacture of knitted or crocheted fabrics:
  . pile and terry fabrics
  . net and window furnishing type fabrics knitted on Raschel or similar machines
  . other knitted or crocheted fabrics

This class excludes:
- manufacture of net and window furnishing type fabrics of lace knitted on Raschel or similar machines cf. 17.54/1

17.7 Manufacture of knitted and crocheted articles

17.71 Manufacture of knitted and crocheted hosiery

This class includes:
- manufacture of hosiery, including socks, tights and panti-hose

17.72 Manufacture of knitted and crocheted pullovers, cardigans and similar articles

This class includes:
- manufacture of knitted or crocheted pullovers, cardigans, jerseys, waistcoats and similar articles

18 MANUFACTURE OF WEARING APPAREL; DRESSING AND DYEING OF FUR

18.1 Manufacture of leather clothes

18.10 Manufacture of leather clothes

This class includes:
- manufacture of wearing apparel made of leather or imitation leather

This class excludes:
- *manufacture of leather gloves and belts cf. 18.24/2*
- *manufacture of leather sports gloves and sports headgear cf. 36.40*

18.2 Manufacture of other wearing apparel and accessories

18.21 Manufacture of workwear

This class includes:
- manufacture of workwear

This class excludes:
- *manufacture of footwear cf. 19.30*
- *manufacture of wearing apparel of rubber or plastics which is not assembled by stitching but is merely sealed together cf. 25.13, 25.24*
- *manufacture of safety headgear cf. 25.24, 28.75*
- *repair of wearing apparel cf. 52.74*

18.22 Manufacture of other outerwear

18.22/1 Manufacture of other men's outerwear

This subclass includes:
- manufacture of other outerwear made of woven, knitted or crocheted fabric, nonwovens, etc. for men and boys:
  . coats, suits, jackets, trousers, etc.

This subclass also includes:
- custom tailoring

This subclass excludes:
- *manufacture of wearing apparel of furskins cf. 18.30*
- *manufacture of wearing apparel of rubber or plastics which is not assembled by stitching but is merely sealed together cf. 25.13, 25.24*
- *repair of wearing apparel cf. 52.74*

18.22/2 Manufacture of other women's outerwear

This subclass includes:
- manufacture of other outerwear made of woven, knitted or crocheted fabric, nonwovens, etc. for women and girls:
  . coats, suits, ensembles, jackets, dresses, slacks, skirts, etc.

This subclass also includes:
- custom tailoring

This subclass excludes:
- *manufacture of wearing apparel of furskins cf. 18.30*
- *manufacture of wearing apparel of rubber or plastics which is not assembled by stitching but is merely sealed together cf. 25.13, 25.24*
- *repair of wearing apparel cf. 52.74*

18.23 Manufacture of underwear

18.23/1 Manufacture of men's underwear

This subclass includes:
- manufacture of underwear made of woven, knitted or crocheted fabric, etc. for men and boys:
  . shirts, t-shirts, underpants, briefs, pyjamas, dressing gowns, etc.

18.23/2 Manufacture of women's underwear

This subclass includes:
- manufacture of underwear made of woven, knitted or crocheted fabric, lace, etc. for women and girls:
  . blouses, lingerie, slips, brassieres, corsets, nightdresses, dressing gowns, etc.

18.24 Manufacture of other wearing apparel and accessories not elsewhere classified

18.24/1 Manufacture of hats

This subclass includes:
- manufacture of hats and caps

This subclass also includes:
- manufacture of headgear of furskins

This subclass excludes:
- *manufacture of safety headgear cf. 25.24, 28.75*
- *manufacture of sports headgear cf. 36.40*

18.24/2 Manufacture of other wearing apparel and accessories

This subclass includes:
- manufacture of babies garments, tracksuits, skisuits, swimwear, etc.
- manufacture of other clothing accessories: gloves, belts, shawls, ties, cravats, hair nets, etc.

This subclass also includes:
- manufacture of footwear of textile material without applied soles

This subclass excludes:
- *manufacture of leather sports gloves cf. 36.40*
- *repair of wearing apparel cf. 52.74*

18.3 Dressing and dyeing of fur; manufacture of articles of fur

18.30 Dressing and dyeing of fur; manufacture of articles of fur

This class includes:
- dressing and dyeing of furskins and hides with the hair on: scraping, currying, tanning, bleaching, shearing and plucking and dyeing of furskins

- manufacture of articles made of furskins:
  . fur wearing apparel and clothing accessories
  . assemblies of furskins such as "dropped" furskins, plates, mats, strips, etc.
  . diverse articles of furskins: rugs, unstuffed pouffes, industrial polishing cloths

This class also includes:
- manufacture of artificial fur and articles thereof

This class excludes:
- *production of raw furskins cf. 01.25, 01.50*
- *production of raw hides and skins cf. 15.11/1*
- *manufacture of imitation furs (long hair cloth obtained by weaving or knitting) cf. 17.2, 17.60*
- *manufacture of fur hats cf. 18.24/1*
- *manufacture of apparel trimmed with fur cf. 18.24/2*
- *manufacture of boots or shoes containing fur parts cf. 19.30*

SUBSECTION DC   MANUFACTURE OF LEATHER AND LEATHER PRODUCTS

19   TANNING AND DRESSING OF LEATHER; MANUFACTURE OF LUGGAGE, HANDBAGS, SADDLERY, HARNESS AND FOOTWEAR

19.1   Tanning and dressing of leather

19.10   Tanning and dressing of leather

This class includes:
- production of tanned leather
- manufacture of chamois dressed, parchment dressed, patent or metallised leathers
- manufacture of composition leather

This class excludes:
- *production of raw hides and skins cf. 15.11/1*
- *manufacture of leather apparel cf. 18.10*
- *tanning or dressing of furskins or hides with the hair on cf. 18.30*
- *manufacture of imitation leather not based on natural leather cf. 17.2, 25.13, 25.24*

19.2   Manufacture of luggage, handbags and the like, saddlery and harness

19.20   Manufacture of luggage, handbags and the like, saddlery and harness

This class includes:
- manufacture of luggage, handbags and the like, of leather, composition leather and of any other materials, such as plastic sheeting, textile materials, vulcanised fibre or paperboard, where the same technology is used as for leather
- manufacture of non-metallic watch straps
- manufacture of diverse articles of leather or composition leather: driving belts, packings, etc.
- manufacture of saddlery and harness

This class excludes:
- *manufacture of leather wearing apparel cf. 18.10*
- *manufacture of leather gloves and hats cf. 18.24*
- *manufacture of footwear cf. 19.30*
- *manufacture of metallic watch straps cf. 33.50*

19.3   Manufacture of footwear

19.30   Manufacture of footwear

This class includes:
- manufacture of footwear for all purposes, of any material, by any process including moulding
- manufacture of gaiters, leggings and similar articles
- manufacture of parts of footwear: manufacture of uppers and parts of uppers, outer and inner soles, heels, etc.

This class excludes:
- *manufacture of footwear of textile material without applied soles cf. 18.24/2*
- *manufacture of footwear of asbestos cf. 26.82/1*
- *manufacture of orthopaedic shoes cf. 33.10*

SUBSECTION DD   MANUFACTURE OF WOOD AND WOOD PRODUCTS

20   MANUFACTURE OF WOOD AND OF PRODUCTS OF WOOD AND CORK, EXCEPT FURNITURE; MANUFACTURE OF ARTICLES OF STRAW AND PLAITING MATERIALS

20.1   Sawmilling and planing of wood, impregnation of wood

20.10   Sawmilling and planing of wood, impregnation of wood

This class includes:
- sawing, planing and machining of wood
- manufacture of wooden railway sleepers
- manufacture of unassembled wooden flooring
- manufacture of wood wool, wood flour, chips, particles

This class also includes:
- drying of wood
- impregnation or chemical treatment of wood with preservatives or other materials

This class excludes:
- *logging and production of wood in the rough cf. 02.01*
- *manufacture of shingles and shakes, beadings and mouldings cf. 20.30*

20.2   Manufacture of veneer sheets; manufacture of plywood, laminboard, particle board, fibre board and other panels and boards

20.20   Manufacture of veneer sheets; manufacture of plywood, laminboard, particle board, fibre board and other panels and boards

This class also includes:
- manufacture of blockboard

20.3   Manufacture of builders' carpentry and joinery

20.30   Manufacture of builders' carpentry and joinery

This class includes:
- manufacture of wooden goods intended to be used primarily in the construction industry:
  . beams, rafters, roof struts

. doors, windows, shutters and their frames
. stairs, railings
. wooden beadings and mouldings, shingles and shakes
. parquet floor blocks, strips, etc., assembled into panels
- manufacture of prefabricated buildings or elements thereof, of wood

This class excludes:
- *manufacture of unassembled wooden flooring cf. 20.10*

20.4   Manufacture of wooden containers

20.40   Manufacture of wooden containers

This class includes:
- manufacture of packing cases, boxes, crates, drums and similar packings of wood
- manufacture of pallets, box pallets and other load boards of wood
- manufacture of barrels, vats, tubs and other coopers' products, of wood
- manufacture of wooden cable-drums

This class excludes:
- *manufacture of luggage cf. 19.20*
- *manufacture of cases of plaiting material cf. 20.52*

20.5   Manufacture of other products of wood; manufacture of articles of cork, straw and plaiting materials

20.51   Manufacture of other products of wood

This class includes:
- manufacture of various wood products:
  . wooden handles and bodies for tools, brooms, brushes
  . wooden boot or shoe lasts and trees, clothes hangers
  . household utensils and kitchen-ware of wood; coat and hat racks
  . wooden statuettes and ornaments, wood marquetry, inlaid wood
  . wooden caskets and cases for jewellery, cutlery and similar articles
  . wooden spools, cops, bobbins, sewing thread reels and similar articles of turned wood
  . other articles of wood

This class excludes:
- *manufacture of luggage cf. 19.20*
- *manufacture of wooden footwear cf. 19.30*
- *manufacture of lamps and lighting fittings cf. 31.50*
- *manufacture of clock cases cf. 33.50*
- *manufacture of furniture cf. 36.1*
- *manufacture of wooden toys cf. 36.50*
- *manufacture of imitation jewellery cf. 36.61*
- *manufacture of brushes and brooms cf. 36.62*
- *manufacture of walking sticks and umbrella handles cf. 36.63/2*
- *manufacture of matches cf. 36.63/2*

20.52   Manufacture of articles of cork, straw and plaiting materials

This class includes:
- natural cork processing
- manufacture of articles of natural or agglomerated cork

- manufacture of plaits and products of plaiting materials: mats, mattings, screens, etc.
- manufacture of basket ware and wickerwork

This class excludes:
- *manufacture of mats or matting of textile materials cf. 17.51*
- *manufacture of furniture cf. 36.1*

SUBSECTION DE   MANUFACTURE OF PULP, PAPER AND PAPER PRODUCTS; PUBLISHING AND PRINTING

21   MANUFACTURE OF PULP, PAPER AND PAPER PRODUCTS

21.1   Manufacture of pulp, paper and paperboard

21.11   Manufacture of pulp

This class includes:
- manufacture of bleached, semi-bleached or unbleached paper pulp:
  . manufacture by mechanical, chemical (dissolving or non-dissolving) or semi-chemical processes of paper pulp
- removal of ink and manufacture of pulp from waste paper

21.12   Manufacture of paper and paperboard

This class includes:
- manufacture of paper and paperboard intended for further industrial processing

This class also includes:
- coating, covering and impregnation of paper and paperboard
- manufacture of creped or crinkled paper
- manufacture of cellulose wadding and webs of cellulose fibres

This class excludes:
- *manufacture of corrugated paperboard cf. 21.21/1*
- *manufacture of further processed articles of paper cf. 21.21, 21.22, 21.23, 21.24, 21.25*

21.2   Manufacture of articles of paper and paperboard

21.21   Manufacture of corrugated paper and paperboard and of containers of paper and paperboard

21.21/1   Manufacture of corrugated paper and paperboard, sacks and bags

This subclass includes:
- manufacture of corrugated paper and paperboard
- manufacture of sacks and bags of paper

21.21/2   Manufacture of cartons, boxes, cases and other containers

This subclass includes:
- manufacture of containers of corrugated paper or paperboard
- manufacture of folding paperboard containers
- manufacture of other containers of paper and paperboard
- manufacture of containers of solid board
- manufacture of office box files and similar articles

This subclass excludes:
- manufacture of envelopes cf. 21.23

21.22 Manufacture of household and sanitary goods and of toilet requisites

This class includes:
- manufacture of household and personal hygiene paper and cellulose wadding products:
  . manufacture of cleansing tissues
  . manufacture of handkerchiefs, towels, serviettes
  . manufacture of toilet-paper
  . manufacture of sanitary towels and tampons, napkins and napkin liners for babies
  . manufacture of cups, dishes and trays

21.23 Manufacture of paper stationery

This class includes:
- manufacture of printing and writing paper ready for use
- manufacture of computer print-out paper
- manufacture of self-copy paper ready for use
- manufacture of duplicator stencils and carbon paper ready for use
- manufacture of gummed or adhesive paper ready for use
- manufacture of envelopes and letter-cards
- manufacture of boxes, pouches, wallets and writing compendiums containing an assortment of paper
  stationery

21.24 Manufacture of wallpaper

This class includes:
- manufacture of wallpaper and similar wallcoverings including vinyl coated wall paper
- manufacture of textile wall coverings

21.25 Manufacture of other articles of paper and paperboard not elsewhere classified

This class includes:
- manufacture of labels
- manufacture of filter paper and paperboard
- manufacture of paper and paperboard bobbins, spools, cops, cards for use on Jacquard machines, etc.
- manufacture of egg trays and other moulded pulp packaging products

This class excludes:
- manufacture of paper or paperboard in bulk cf. 21.12
- manufacture of games and toys of paper or paperboard cf. 36.50
- manufacture of playing cards cf. 36.50/2

22 PUBLISHING, PRINTING AND REPRODUCTION OF RECORDED MEDIA

22.1 Publishing

22.11 Publishing of books

This class includes:
- publishing of books, brochures, leaflets and similar publications including publishing of dictionaries and
  encyclopaedias
- publishing of maps and charts
- publishing of printed music

22.12   Publishing of newspapers

This class includes:
- publishing of newspapers, including advertising newspapers

22.13   Publishing of journals and periodicals

22.14   Publishing of sound recordings

This class includes:
- publishing of gramophone records, compact discs and tapes with music or other sound recordings

22.15   Other publishing

This class includes:
- publishing of:
  . photos, engravings and postcards
  . timetables
  . forms
  . posters, reproduction of works of art
  . other printed matter such as postcards reproduced by mechanical or photo-mechanical means

22.2   Printing and service activities related to printing

22.21   Printing of newspapers

22.22   Printing not elsewhere classified

This class includes:
- printing of magazines and other periodicals, books and brochures, music and music manuscripts, maps, atlases, posters, advertising catalogues, prospectuses and other printed advertising, postage stamps, taxation stamps, documents of title, cheques and other security papers, registers, albums, diaries, calendars, business forms and other commercial printed matter, personal stationery and other printed matter by letterpress, offset, photogravure, flexographic, screen printing and other printing presses, duplicating machines, computer printers, embossers, photocopiers and thermocopiers

This class excludes:
- *printing of labels cf. 21.25*
- *publishing cf. 22.1*

22.23   Bookbinding and finishing

This class includes:
- finishing of printed sheets, e.g. into books, brochures, magazines, catalogues, etc. by folding, assembling, stitching, gluing, collating, basting, adhesive binding, trimming, gold stamping
- finishing of printed paper or board, e.g. for business forms, displays, sample cards, labels, calendars, advertising literature for mailing, prospectuses by folding, stamping, drilling, punching, perforating, embossing, sticking, gluing, laminating

22.24   Composition and plate-making

This class includes:
- composing, e.g. text and image on film, photographic paper and normal paper
- reproduction: production of letterpress printing formes (e.g. flexographic or rubber plates, plastic plates, nylon printing plates, zinc or photopolymer plates, stereos and electros, embossing matrixes), offset reproduction and printing plates (e.g. offset lithos, offset plates such as mono- or multi-metal plates, screen printing stencils, film assemblers), gravure reproductions and gravure cylinders (e.g. half-tone copies and scanner films for cylinder engraving)

22.25   Other activities related to printing

This class includes:
- production of other reprographic products: overhead projection foils, sketches, lay-outs, dummies, etc.
- preparation of digital data, e.g. enhancement, selection, linkage of digital data stored on EDP data carriers
- other graphic activities

22.3   Reproduction of recorded media

22.31   Reproduction of sound recording

This class includes:
- reproduction from master copies of gramophone records, compact discs and tapes with music or other sound recordings

22.32   Reproduction of video recording

This class includes:
- reproduction from master copies of records, compact discs and tapes with motion pictures and other video recordings

22.33   Reproduction of computer media

This class includes:
- reproduction from master copies of software and data on discs and tapes

SUBSECTION DF   MANUFACTURE OF COKE, REFINED PETROLEUM PRODUCTS AND NUCLEAR FUEL

23   MANUFACTURE OF COKE, REFINED PETROLEUM PRODUCTS AND NUCLEAR FUEL

23.1   Manufacture of coke oven products

23.10   Manufacture of coke oven products

This class includes:
- production of coke
- production at low temperature carbonisation plants
- production of coke oven gas
- production of crude coal and lignite tars

This class excludes:
- *agglomeration of hard coal cf. 10.10/3*
- *agglomeration of lignite cf. 10.20*
- *production of pitch and pitch coke cf. 24.14*

23.2   Manufacture of refined petroleum products

23.20   Manufacture of refined petroleum products

23.20/1   Mineral oil refining

This subclass includes:
- refining crude and process oils or shale oil for the derivation of refined or partly refined petroleum products, cracking or other processes

- production of process oils: refinery feedstocks used in the manufacture of petroleum products
- production of motor fuel: petrol, automotive diesel, etc.
- production of other transport fuels: aviation turbine fuel, marine diesel, etc.
- production of fuel: other middle distillates such as gas oil, burning oil; heavy distillates - light, medium and heavy fuel oil; refinery gases such as ethane, propane, butane, etc.
- manufacture of products for the petrochemical industry and for the manufacture of road coverings
- manufacture of other products: such as solvents, e.g. white spirit, or petroleum jelly used as an ointment

23.20/2   Other treatment of petroleum products (excluding petrochemicals manufacture)

This subclass includes:
- processing, blending and compounding of mineral, animal and vegetable oils and greases other than at petroleum refineries
- manufacture of oil based lubricating oils or greases including from waste oil

23.3   Processing of nuclear fuel

23.30   Processing of nuclear fuel

This class includes:
- conversion of yellowcake to uranium tetrafluoride and uranium hexafluoride
- production of enriched uranium
- production of fuel elements for nuclear reactors
- production of radioactive elements for industrial or medical use
- reprocessing of spent nuclear fuel
- treatment of nuclear waste

This class excludes:
- *mining and concentration of uranium and thorium ores cf. 12.00*
- *manufacture of yellowcake cf. 12.00*

SUBSECTION DG   MANUFACTURE OF CHEMICALS, CHEMICAL PRODUCTS AND MAN-MADE FIBRES

24   MANUFACTURE OF CHEMICALS AND CHEMICAL PRODUCTS

24.1   Manufacture of basic chemicals

24.11   Manufacture of industrial gases

This class includes:
- manufacture of liquefied or compressed industrial or medical gases:
  . elemental gases
  . liquid or compressed air
  . refrigerant gases
  . mixed industrial gases
  . inert gases such as carbon dioxide
  . isolating gases

This class excludes:
- *extraction of methane, ethane, butane or propane cf. 11.10*
- *manufacture of fuel gases such as ethane, butane or propane in a petroleum refinery cf. 23.20/1*

24.12   Manufacture of dyes and pigments

This class includes:
- manufacture of dyes and pigments from any source in basic form or as concentrate

This class also includes:
- manufacture of products of a kind used as fluorescent brightening agents or as luminophores

This class excludes:
- *manufacture of prepared dyes and pigments cf. 24.30/1*

24.13   Manufacture of other inorganic basic chemicals

This class includes:
- manufacture of chemical elements except metals, industrial elemental gases and radioactive elements produced by the nuclear fuels industry
- manufacture of inorganic acids except nitric acid
- manufacture of alkalis, lyes and other inorganic bases except ammonia
- manufacture of other inorganic compounds

This class excludes:
- *manufacture of nitric and sulphonitric acids cf. 24.15*
- *manufacture of ammonia cf. 24.15*
- *manufacture of ammonium chloride cf. 24.15*
- *manufacture of phosphates of triammonium, ammonium carbonates cf. 24.15*
- *manufacture of nitrites and nitrates of potassium cf. 24.15*
- *manufacture of chemical substances used in the manufacture of pharmaceuticals cf. 24.41*
- *manufacture of artificial corundum cf. 26.81 and other aluminium oxide cf. 27.42*

24.14   Manufacture of other organic basic chemicals

This class includes:
- manufacture of other organic basic chemicals:
  . acyclic hydrocarbons, saturated and unsaturated
  . cyclic hydrocarbons, saturated and unsaturated
  . acyclic and cyclic alcohols, including synthetic ethyl alcohol
  . mono- and polycarboxyclic acids including acetic acid
  . other oxygen-function compounds including aldehydes, ketones, quinones and dual or poly oxygen-function compounds
  . nitrogen-function organic compounds including amines
  . other organic compounds including wood distillation products, etc.
- manufacture of charcoal
- production of pitch and pitch coke
- manufacture of synthetic aromatic products
- distillation of coal tar

This class excludes:
- *manufacture of ethyl alcohol from fermented materials cf. 15.92*
- *manufacture of plastics in primary forms cf. 24.16*
- *manufacture of synthetic rubber in primary forms cf. 24.17*
- *manufacture of salicylic and o-acetylsalicylic acids cf. 24.41*
- *manufacture of chemical substances used in the manufacture of pharmaceuticals cf. 24.41*
- *manufacture of crude glycerol cf. 24.51/1*
- *manufacture of essential oils cf. 24.63*

24.15   Manufacture of fertilizers and nitrogen compounds

This class includes:
- manufacture of fertilizers:
  . straight or complex nitrogenous, phosphatic or potassic fertilizers
  . urea, crude natural phosphates and crude natural potassium salts
- manufacture of associated nitrogen products:
  . nitric and sulphonitric acids, ammonia, ammonium chloride, nitrites and nitrates of potassium, phosphates of triammonium and ammonium carbonates

This class excludes:
- *mining of guano cf. 14.30*
- *manufacture of agro-chemical products cf. 24.20*

24.16   Manufacture of plastics in primary forms

This class includes:
- manufacture of plastics in primary forms:
  . polymers including those of ethylene, propylene, styrene, vinyl chloride, vinyl acetate and acrylics
  . polyamides
  . phenolic and epoxide resins and polyurethanes
  . alkyd and polyester resins and polyethers
  . silicones
  . ion-exchangers based on polymers

This class also includes:
- manufacture of cellulose

This class excludes:
- *recycling of plastics cf. 37.20*

24.17   Manufacture of synthetic rubber in primary forms

This class includes:
- manufacture of synthetic rubber in primary forms:
  . synthetic rubber
  . factice
- manufacture of mixtures of synthetic rubber and natural rubber or rubber-like gums (e.g. balata)

24.2   Manufacture of pesticides and other agro-chemical products

24.20   Manufacture of pesticides and other agro-chemical products

This class includes:
- manufacture of insecticides, rodenticides, fungicides, herbicides, anti-sprouting products, plant growth regulators, disinfectants and other agro-chemical products not elsewhere classified

This class excludes:
- *manufacture of fertilizers and nitrogen compounds cf. 24.15*

24.3   Manufacture of paints, varnishes and similar coatings, printing ink and mastics

24.30   Manufacture of paints, varnishes and similar coatings, printing ink and mastics

24.30/1   Manufacture of paints, varnishes and similar coatings

This subclass includes:
- manufacture of paints and varnishes, enamels or lacquers
- manufacture of prepared pigments, opacifiers and colours; manufacture of vitrifiable enamels and glazes and engobes and similar preparations
- manufacture of organic composite solvents and thinners
- manufacture of prepared paint or varnish removers

This subclass excludes:
- *manufacture of dyestuffs and pigments cf. 24.12*

24.30/2   Manufacture of printing ink

This subclass includes:
- manufacture of printing ink

This subclass excludes:
- *manufacture of writing and drawing ink cf. 24.66*

24.30/3   Manufacture of mastics and sealants

This subclass includes:
- manufacture of mastics
- manufacture of caulking compounds and similar non-refractory filling or surfacing preparations

24.4   Manufacture of pharmaceuticals, medicinal chemicals and botanical products

24.41   Manufacture of basic pharmaceutical products

This class includes:
- investigation, perfecting and production of medicinal active substances to be used for their pharmacological properties in the manufacture of medicaments
- processing of blood

This class also includes:
- manufacture of chemically pure sugars
- processing of glands and manufacture of extracts of glands, etc.

24.42   Manufacture of pharmaceutical preparations

24.42/1   Manufacture of medicaments

This subclass includes:
- manufacture of medicaments defined as such in Community law:
  . anti-sera and other blood fractions
  . vaccines
  . diverse medicaments, including homoeopathic preparations
- manufacture of chemical contraceptive products for external use and hormonal contraceptive medicaments

24.42/2   Manufacture of non-medicaments

This subclass includes:
- manufacture of dental fillings and bone reconstruction cements
- manufacture of medical impregnated wadding, gauze, bandages, dressings, surgical gut string, etc.

24.5   Manufacture of soap and detergents, cleaning and polishing preparations, perfumes and toilet preparations

24.51 Manufacture of soap and detergents, cleaning and polishing preparations

24.51/1 Manufacture of soap and detergents

This subclass includes:
- manufacture of organic surface-active agents
- manufacture of soap
- manufacture of crude glycerol
- manufacture of surface-active preparations:
  . washing powders in solid or liquid form and detergents
  . dish-washing preparations
  . textile softeners

24.51/2 Manufacture of cleaning and polishing preparations

This subclass includes:
- manufacture of cleaning and polishing products:
  . preparations for perfuming or deodorising rooms
  . artificial waxes and prepared waxes
  . polishes and creams for leather
  . polishes and creams for wood
  . polishes for coachwork, glass and metal
  . scouring pastes and powders

24.52 Manufacture of perfumes and toilet preparations

This class includes:
- manufacture of perfumes and toilet preparations:
  . perfumes and toilet water
  . beauty and make-up preparations
  . sunburn prevention and sun tan preparations
  . manicure and pedicure preparations
  . shampoos, hair lacquers, waving and straightening preparations
  . dentifrices and preparations for oral hygiene, including denture fixative preparations
  . shaving preparations
  . deodorants and bath salts
  . depilatories

This class excludes:
- *extraction and refining of essential oils cf. 24.63*

24.6 Manufacture of other chemical products

24.61 Manufacture of explosives

This class includes:
- manufacture of propellant powders
- manufacture of explosives
- manufacture of pyrotechnic products

24.62 Manufacture of glues and gelatine

This class includes:
- manufacture of gelatine and its derivatives, glues and prepared adhesives, including rubber based glues and adhesives

24.63 Manufacture of essential oils

This class includes:
- manufacture of extracts of natural aromatic products
- manufacture of resinoids
- manufacture of aromatic distilled waters
- manufacture of mixtures of odoriferous products for the manufacture of perfumes or food

This class excludes:
- *manufacture of synthetic aromatic products cf. 24.14*
- *manufacture of perfumes and toilet preparations cf. 24.52*

24.64 Manufacture of photographic chemical material

This class includes:
- manufacture of photographic plates, films, sensitised paper and other sensitised unexposed materials
- manufacture of chemical preparations for photographic uses

24.65 Manufacture of prepared unrecorded media

This class includes:
- manufacture of unrecorded media for sound or video recording
- manufacture of unrecorded computer discs and tapes

24.66 Manufacture of other chemical products not elsewhere classified

This class includes:
- manufacture of various chemical products:
  . peptones, peptone derivatives, other protein substances and their derivatives not elsewhere classified
  . chemically modified oils and fats
  . materials used in the finishing of textiles and leather
  . powders and pastes used in soldering, brazing or welding
  . substances used to pickle metal
  . prepared additives for cements
  . activated carbon, lubricating oil additives, prepared rubber accelerators, catalysts and other chemical products for industrial use
  . anti-knock preparations, anti-freeze preparations, liquids for hydraulic transmission
  . composite diagnostic or laboratory reagents

This class also includes:
- manufacture of writing and drawing ink

This class excludes:
- *manufacture of printing ink cf. 24.30/2*

24.7 Manufacture of man-made fibres

24.70 Manufacture of man-made fibres

This class includes:
- manufacture of artificial or synthetic filament tow
- manufacture of synthetic or artificial staple fibres, not carded, combed or otherwise processed for spinning
- manufacture of synthetic or artificial single yarn including high tenacity yarn
- manufacture of synthetic or artificial monofilament or strip

This class excludes:
- *spinning of synthetic or artificial fibres cf. 17.1*
- *manufacture of sewing thread of man-made filaments cf. 17.16*

SUBSECTION DH   MANUFACTURE OF RUBBER AND PLASTIC PRODUCTS

25   MANUFACTURE OF RUBBER AND PLASTIC PRODUCTS

25.1   Manufacture of rubber products

25.11   Manufacture of rubber tyres and tubes

This class includes:
- manufacture of rubber tyres for vehicles, equipment, mobile machinery and other uses:
  . pneumatic tyres
  . solid or cushion tyres
- manufacture of inner tubes for tyres
- manufacture of interchangeable tyre treads, tyre flaps, "camel-back" strips for retreading tyres, etc.

This class excludes:
- *manufacture of rubber repair materials cf. 25.13*
- *tyre and tube repair, fitting or replacement cf. 50.20*

25.12   Retreading and rebuilding of rubber tyres

This class includes:
- tyre rebuilding and retreading

This class excludes:
- *manufacture of rubber repair materials cf. 25.13*
- *repair of punctured tyres cf. 50.20*

25.13   Manufacture of other rubber products

This class includes:
- manufacture of other products of natural or synthetic rubber, unvulcanised, vulcanised or hardened:
  . manufacture of semi-finished rubber products:
    . rubber plates, sheets, strip, rods, profile shapes
  . manufacture of finished rubber products:
    . tubes, pipes and hoses
    . rubber conveyor or transmission belts or belting
    . rubber hygienic articles:
      sheath contraceptives, teats, hot water bottles, etc.
    . rubber articles of apparel
    . rubber floor coverings
    . rubberised textiles
    . rubber thread and rope
    . rubberised yarn and fabrics
    . rubber rings, fittings and seals
    . rubber roller coverings
    . inflatable rubber mattresses

This class also includes:
- manufacture of rubber repair materials

This class excludes:
- *manufacture of tyre cord fabrics cf. 17.54/3*
- *manufacture of apparel of elastic fabrics cf. 18.2*
- *manufacture of rubber footwear cf. 19.30*
- *manufacture of glues and adhesives based on rubber cf. 24.62*
- *manufacture of "camel-back" strips cf. 25.11*
- *manufacture of inflatable rafts and boats cf. 35.12*
- *manufacture of mattresses of uncovered cellular rubber cf. 36.15*
- *manufacture of rubber sports requisites cf. 36.40*
- *manufacture of rubber games and toys cf. 36.50*
- *reclaiming of rubber cf. 37.20*

25.2 Manufacture of plastic products

25.21 Manufacture of plastic plates, sheets, tubes and profiles

This class includes:
- manufacture of semi-manufactures of plastic products:
  . plastic plates, sheets, blocks, film, foil, strip, etc.
- manufacture of finished plastic products:
  . plastic tubes, pipes and hoses; hose and pipe fittings

This class excludes:
- *manufacture of plastics in primary forms cf. 24.16*
- *manufacture of plastic optical elements cf. 33.40/1*
- *manufacture of mattresses of uncovered cellular plastic cf. 36.15*

25.22 Manufacture of plastic packing goods

This class includes:
- manufacture of plastic articles for the packing of goods:
  . plastic bags, sacks, containers, boxes, cases, carboys, bottles, etc.

This class excludes:
- *manufacture of plastic travel goods cf. 19.20*
- *manufacture of articles of synthetic or natural rubber cf. 25.1*
- *packaging cf. 74.82*

25.23 Manufacture of builders' ware of plastic

25.23/1 Manufacture of plastic floor covering

This subclass includes:
- plastic floor coverings in rolls or in the form of tiles

This subclass excludes:
- *manufacture of linoleum and hard non-plastic surface floor coverings cf. 36.63/2*

25.23/2 Manufacture of other builders' ware of plastic

This subclass includes:
- manufacture of plastic builders' ware:
  . plastic doors, windows, frames, shutters, blinds, skirting boards
  . tanks, reservoirs
  . plastic wall or ceiling coverings in rolls or in the form of tiles, etc.

. plastic sanitary ware: manufacture of plastic baths, shower-baths, wash basins, lavatory pans, flushing cisterns, etc.

This subclass excludes:
- *manufacture of articles of synthetic or natural rubber cf. 25.1*

25.24   Manufacture of other plastic products

This class includes:
- manufacture of plastic tableware, kitchenware and toilet articles
- manufacture of diverse plastic products:
   . plastic headgear, insulating fittings, parts of lighting fittings, office or school supplies, articles of apparel, fittings for furniture, statuettes, transmission and conveyor belts, etc.

This class excludes:
- *manufacture of plastic travel goods cf. 19.20*
- *manufacture of plastic footwear cf. 19.30*
- *manufacture of plastic medical and dental appliances cf. 33.10*
- *manufacture of plastic optical elements cf. 33.40/1*
- *manufacture of plastic furniture cf. 36.1*
- *manufacture of mattresses of uncovered cellular plastic cf. 36.15*
- *manufacture of plastic sports requisites cf. 36.40*
- *manufacture of plastic games and toys cf. 36.50*
- *manufacture of linoleum and hard non-plastic surface floor coverings cf. 36.63/2*

SUBSECTION DI   MANUFACTURE OF OTHER NON-METALLIC MINERAL PRODUCTS

26   MANUFACTURE OF OTHER NON-METALLIC MINERAL PRODUCTS

26.1   Manufacture of glass and glass products

26.11   Manufacture of flat glass

This class includes:
- manufacture of flat glass including wired, coloured or tinted flat glass

26.12   Shaping and processing of flat glass

This class includes:
- manufacture of toughened or laminated flat glass
- manufacture of glass mirrors
- manufacture of multiple-walled insulating units of glass

26.13   Manufacture of hollow glass

This class includes:
- manufacture of bottles and other containers of glass or crystal
- manufacture of drinking glasses and other domestic glass or crystal articles
- manufacture of glass inners for vacuum flasks and other vacuum vessels

This class excludes:
- *manufacture of glass toys cf. 36.50*
- *manufacture of vacuum flasks and other vacuum vessels cf. 36.63/2*

26.14 Manufacture of glass fibres

This class includes:
- manufacture of glass fibres including glass wool and nonwoven products thereof

This class excludes:
- *manufacture of woven fabric of glass yarn cf. 17.25*
- *manufacture of optical fibre cables for coded data transmission cf. 31.30*
- *manufacture of optical fibres and optical fibre cables for live transmission of images cf. 33.40/1*

26.15 Manufacture and processing of other glass including technical glassware

This class includes:
- manufacture of laboratory, hygienic or pharmaceutical glassware
- manufacture of glass envelopes
- manufacture of clock or watch glasses, optical glass and optical elements not optically worked
- manufacture of glassware used in imitation jewellery
- manufacture of glass insulators and glass insulating fittings
- manufacture of glass paving blocks
- manufacture of glass in rods or tubes

This class excludes:
- *manufacture of syringes cf. 33.10*
- *manufacture of optical elements optically worked cf. 33.40/1*

26.2 Manufacture of non-refractory ceramic goods other than for construction purposes; manufacture of refractory ceramic products

26.21 Manufacture of ceramic household and ornamental articles

This class includes:
- manufacture of ceramic tableware and other domestic or toilet articles
- manufacture of statuettes and other ornamental ceramic articles

This class excludes:
- *manufacture of ceramic toys cf. 36.50*
- *manufacture of imitation jewellery cf. 36.61*

26.22 Manufacture of ceramic sanitary fixtures

This class excludes:
- *manufacture of refractory ceramic goods cf. 26.26*
- *manufacture of ceramic building materials cf. 26.30, 26.40*

26.23 Manufacture of ceramic insulators and insulating fittings

This class includes:
- manufacture of electrical insulators and insulating fittings of ceramics

This class excludes:
- *manufacture of refractory ceramic goods cf. 26.26*

26.24 Manufacture of other technical ceramic products

This class includes:
- manufacture of ceramic laboratory, chemical and industrial products

26.25 Manufacture of other ceramic products

This class includes:
- manufacture of ceramic pots, jars and similar containers of a kind used for the conveyance or packing of goods
- manufacture of ceramic products not elsewhere classified

This class excludes:
- *manufacture of refractory ceramic goods cf. 26.26*
- *manufacture of ceramic building materials cf. 26.30, 26.40*

26.26 Manufacture of refractory ceramic products

This class includes:
- manufacture of refractory mortars, concretes, etc.
- manufacture of refractory ceramic goods:
  . manufacture of heat-insulating ceramic goods of siliceous fossil meals
  . manufacture of refractory bricks and blocks
  . manufacture of refractory ceramic retorts, crucibles, muffles, nozzles, tubes, pipes, etc.

This class also includes:
- manufacture of articles containing magnesite, dolomite or cromite

26.3 Manufacture of ceramic tiles and flags

26.30 Manufacture of ceramic tiles and flags

This class includes:
- manufacture of non-refractory ceramic hearth or wall tiles, mosaic cubes, etc.
- manufacture of non-refractory ceramic flags and paving

This class excludes:
- *manufacture of refractory ceramic products cf. 26.26*

26.4 Manufacture of bricks, tiles and construction products, in baked clay

26.40 Manufacture of bricks, tiles and construction products, in baked clay

This class includes:
- manufacture of non-refractory structural clay building materials:
  . manufacture of ceramic bricks, roofing tiles, chimney-pots, pipes, conduits, etc.

This class also includes:
- manufacture of flooring blocks in baked clay

This class excludes:
- *manufacture of structural refractory ceramic products cf. 26.26*
- *manufacture of ceramic flags and paving cf. 26.30*

26.5 Manufacture of cement, lime and plaster

26.51 Manufacture of cement

This class includes:
- manufacture of clinkers and hydraulic cements including portland, aluminous cement, slag cement and superphosphate cements

This class excludes:
- *manufacture of cements used in dentistry cf. 24.42/2*
- *manufacture of refractory mortars, concrete, etc. cf. 26.26*
- *manufacture of articles of cement cf. 26.6*
- *manufacture of ready-mixed concrete and mortars cf. 26.63, 26.64*

26.52 Manufacture of lime

This class includes:
- manufacture of lime:
  . manufacture of quicklime, slaked lime and hydraulic lime

26.53 Manufacture of plaster

This class excludes:
- *manufacture of articles of plaster cf. 26.6*

26.6 Manufacture of articles of concrete, plaster and cement

26.61 Manufacture of concrete products for construction purposes

This class includes:
- manufacture of precast concrete, cement or artificial stone articles for use in construction:
  . manufacture of tiles, flagstones, bricks, boards, sheets, panels, pipes, posts, etc.
- manufacture of prefabricated structural components for building or civil engineering of cement, concrete or artificial stone

26.62 Manufacture of plaster products for construction purposes

This class includes:
- manufacture of plaster articles for use in construction:
  . manufacture of boards, sheets, panels, etc.

26.63 Manufacture of ready-mixed concrete

This class excludes:
- *manufacture of refractory cements cf. 26.26*

26.64 Manufacture of mortars

This class includes:
- manufacture of powdered mortars

This class excludes:
- *manufacture of refractory mortars cf. 26.26*

26.65 Manufacture of fibre cement

This class includes:
- manufacture of building materials of vegetable substances (wood wool, straw, reeds, rushes) agglomerated with cement, plaster or other mineral binder
- manufacture of articles of cellulose fibre-cement or the like:
  . corrugated sheets, other sheets, panels, tiles, tubes, pipes, reservoirs, troughs, basins, sinks, jars, furniture, window frames, etc.

26.66 Manufacture of other articles of concrete, plaster and cement

This class includes:
- manufacture of other articles of concrete, plaster, cement or artificial stone:
  . manufacture of statuary, furniture, bas- and haut-reliefs, vases, flowerpots, etc.

26.7 Cutting, shaping and finishing of stone

26.70 Cutting, shaping and finishing of stone

This class includes:
- cutting, shaping and finishing stone for use in construction, in cemeteries, etc.
- operations carried out on rough stone delivered by quarries

This class excludes:
- activities carried out by operators of quarries, e.g., production of rough cut stone cf. 14.11
- production of millstones, abrasive stones and similar products cf. 26.81

26.8 Manufacture of other non-metallic mineral products

26.81 Production of abrasive products

This class includes:
- manufacture of millstones, sharpening or polishing stones and natural or artificial abrasive products including abrasive products on a soft base
- manufacture of artificial corundum

26.82 Manufacture of other non-metallic mineral products not elsewhere classified

26.82/1 Manufacture of asbestos

This subclass includes:
- manufacture of asbestos yarn and fabric, clothing, headgear, footwear, cord, string, paper, felt, etc.

This subclass excludes:
- articles of asbestos cement cf. 26.65

26.82/2 Manufacture of other non-metallic mineral products not elsewhere classified

This subclass includes:
- manufacture of friction material and unmounted articles thereof with a basis of mineral substances (other than asbestos) or of cellulose
- manufacture of mineral insulating materials, other than of asbestos: manufacture of slag wool, rockwool and

similar mineral wools; exfoliated vermiculite, expanded clays and similar heat-insulating, sound-insulating or sound absorbing materials
- manufacture of articles of diverse mineral substances: manufacture of worked mica and articles of mica, of peat, of graphite (other than electrical articles), etc.

This subclass excludes:
- *manufacture of glass wool and glass wool products cf. 26.14*

SUBSECTION DJ   MANUFACTURE OF BASIC METALS AND FABRICATED METAL PRODUCTS

27   MANUFACTURE OF BASIC METALS

27.1   Manufacture of basic iron and steel and of ferro-alloys (ECSC)[1]

27.10   Manufacture of basic iron and steel and of ferro-alloys (ECSC)

This class includes activities of the iron and steel industry as defined in the ECSC treaty:
- production of pig iron and steel resulting from ore or scrap reduction:
  . production of foundry pig iron and steelmaking pig iron
  . production of ferrous products obtained by direct reduction of iron ore, and other spongy ferrous products in lumps, pellets or similar forms
  . production of steel in a converter, electric furnace or by other methods
- production of high-carbon ferro-manganese and spiegeleisen
- production of hot rolled or cold rolled steel products (including those obtained by continuous casting):
  . production of ingots, other primary forms and semi-finished products
  . production and/or continuous coating of hot rolled wide strip, narrow strip, plates and sheets and wide flats
  . production and/or continuous coating of cold rolled wide strip, plates and sheets
  . production of tinplate, electrolytically chromium coated sheet, blackplate
  . production of hot rolled steel bars and rod
  . production of hot rolled heavy and light sections and sheet piling
  . production of rails and other hot rolled railway materials

This class also includes:
- production of hot rolled products and cold rolled wide strip and sheet, coated or uncoated, further worked than simply surface-treated, but not thereby classified to another heading

This class excludes:
- *production of cold rolled narrow strip, coated or uncoated, of a width up to 500 mm (non-ECSC) by cold reduction of hot rolled flat products or by slitting cold rolled flat products (ECSC), coated or uncoated cf. 27.32*
- *production of granules and powders of pig iron, iron or steel cf. 27.35*
- *production of ferro-alloys other than high-carbon ferro-manganese cf. 27.35*
- *production of forged semi-finished products, blanks and bars cf. 27.35*
- *production of iron and steel castings cf. 27.5*

27.2   Manufacture of tubes

27.21   Manufacture of cast iron tubes

This class includes:
- manufacture of cast iron tubes and cast iron or steel centrifugally cast tubes
- manufacture of cast iron fittings: manufacture of non-malleable and malleable cast iron fittings and cast steel fittings for which connection is obtained by screwing for threaded fittings, by contact for socket fittings or by bolting for flange fittings

---

[1] European Coal and Steel Community

27.22   Manufacture of steel tubes

This class includes:
- manufacture of seamless tubes, by hot rolling, hot extrusion or hot drawing, or by cold drawing or cold rolling
- manufacture of welded tubes by cold or hot forming and welding, by forming and cold drawing, or by hot forming and reducing
- manufacture of steel tube fittings:
  . flat flanges and flanges with forged collars of steel
  . butt welding fittings of steel
  . threaded fittings and other fittings of steel

This class excludes:
- *manufacture of seamless tubes of centrifugally cast steel cf. 27.21*

27.3   Other first processing of iron and steel and production of non-ECSC ferro-alloys

27.31   Cold drawing

This class includes:
- manufacture of steel bars or sections by cold drawing, grinding or peeling

This class excludes:
- *wire drawing or stretching cf. 27.34*

27.32   Cold rolling of narrow strip

This class includes:
- manufacture of coated or uncoated flat rolled steel products in coils or in straight lengths of a width less than 500 mm (non-ECSC) by cold re-rolling of hot rolled flat products

27.33   Cold forming or folding

This class includes:
- manufacture of open sections by progressive forming on a roll mill or folding on a press of flat rolled products of steel

27.34   Wire drawing

This class includes:
- manufacture of steel wire by cold drawing or stretching

27.35   Other first processing of iron and steel not elsewhere classified; production of non-ECSC ferro-alloys

This class includes:
- production of ferro-alloys except high-carbon ferro-manganese and of ferro-phosphor
- production of granular iron and iron powder; production of iron of exceptional purity by electrolysis or other chemical processes
- production of permanent way material except rails
- production of metal sand for sandblasting

27.4   Manufacture of basic precious and non-ferrous metals

27.41 Precious metals production

This class includes:
- production of basic precious metals:
  . production and refining of unwrought precious metals: gold, silver, platinum, etc.
- production of precious metal alloys
- production of precious metal semi-products
- production of silver rolled onto base metals
- production of gold rolled onto base metals or silver
- production of platinum and platinum group metals rolled onto gold, silver or base metals

This class excludes:
- *manufacture of precious metal watch cases cf. 33.50*
- *manufacture of precious metal jewellery cf. 36.22*

27.42 Aluminium production

This class includes:
- production of aluminium from alumina
- production of aluminium from electrolytic refining of aluminium waste and scrap
- production of aluminium alloys
- semi-manufacturing of aluminium

This class also includes:
- production of aluminium oxide (alumina)

27.43 Lead, zinc and tin production

This class includes:
- production of lead, zinc and tin from ores
- production of lead, zinc and tin from electrolytic refining of lead, zinc and tin waste and scrap
- production of lead, zinc and tin alloys
- semi-manufacturing of lead, zinc and tin

27.44 Copper production

This class includes:
- production of copper from ores
- production of copper from electrolytic refining of copper waste and scrap
- production of copper alloys
- manufacture of fuse wire or strip
- semi-manufacturing of copper

27.45 Other non-ferrous metal production

This class includes:
- production of chrome, manganese, nickel, etc., from ores or oxides
- production of chrome, manganese, nickel, etc., from electrolytic and aluminothermic refining of chrome, manganese, nickel, etc., waste and scrap
- production of chrome, manganese, nickel, etc., alloys
- semi-manufacturing of chrome, manganese, nickel, etc.

This class also includes:
- production of mattes of nickel

27.5   Casting of metals

This group includes:
- manufacture of semi-finished products and various castings produced for third parties according to their specifications

This group excludes:
- manufacture of finished cast products such as pipes and related items cf. 27.21, boilers and radiators cf. 28.2 and 28.3, cast household items cf. 28.75, etc.

27.51   Casting of iron

This class includes:
- casting of finished or semi-finished iron products
- casting of grey iron castings
- casting of spheroidal graphite iron castings
- casting of malleable cast iron products

This class excludes:
- casting carried out in connection with the manufacture of metal products cf. divisions 27-36

27.52   Casting of steel

This class includes:
- casting of finished or semi-finished steel products
- casting of steel castings

This class excludes:
- casting carried out in connection with the manufacture of metal products cf. divisions 27-36

27.53   Casting of light metals

This class includes:
- casting of finished or semi-finished products of aluminium, magnesium, titanium, beryllium, scandium and yttrium
- casting of light metal castings

This class excludes:
- casting carried out in connection with the manufacture of metal products cf. divisions 27-36

27.54   Casting of other non-ferrous metals

This class includes:
- casting of finished or semi-finished heavy and precious metal products
- casting of heavy metal castings
- casting of precious metal castings

This class excludes:
- casting carried out in connection with the manufacture of metal products cf. divisions 27-36

28   MANUFACTURE OF FABRICATED METAL PRODUCTS, EXCEPT MACHINERY AND EQUIPMENT

28.1   Manufacture of structural metal products

28.11 Manufacture of metal structures and parts of structures

This class includes:
- manufacture of ossature in metal for construction
- manufacture of industrial ossature in metal (ossature for blast furnaces, lifting and handling equipment, etc.)
- manufacture of prefabricated buildings mainly of metal: construction site huts, modular exhibition elements, etc.

This class excludes:
- *manufacture of sections of ships cf. 35.11*

28.12 Manufacture of builders' carpentry and joinery of metal

This class includes:
- manufacture of metal doors, windows and their frames, shutters and gates

28.2 Manufacture of tanks, reservoirs and containers of metal; manufacture of central heating radiators and boilers

28.21 Manufacture of tanks, reservoirs and containers of metal

This class includes:
- manufacture of reservoirs, tanks and similar containers of metal, of a capacity exceeding 300 litres
- manufacture of metal containers for compressed or liquefied gas

This class excludes:
- *manufacture of metal casks, drums, cans, pails, boxes, etc. of a capacity less than 300 litres cf. 28.7*
- *manufacture of transport containers cf. 34.20/2*

28.22 Manufacture of central heating radiators and boilers

28.3 Manufacture of steam generators, except central heating hot water boilers

28.30 Manufacture of steam generators except central heating hot water boilers

This class includes:
- manufacture of steam or other vapour generators
- manufacture of auxiliary plant for use with steam generators: condensers, economizers, super-heaters, steam collectors and accumulators
- manufacture of nuclear reactors

This class also includes:
- pipe system construction comprising further processing of tubes generally to make pressure pipes or pipe systems together with the associated design and construction work

This class excludes:
- *manufacture of isotope separators cf. 29.56*

28.4 Forging, pressing, stamping and roll forming of metal; powder metallurgy

28.40 Forging, pressing, stamping and roll forming of metal; powder metallurgy

This class includes:
- forging, pressing, stamping and roll-forming of metal

- powder metallurgy: production of metal objects directly from metal powders by heat treatment (sintering) or under pressure

This class excludes:
- production of finely ground metal powder cf. 27

28.5   Treatment and coating of metals; general mechanical engineering

28.51   Treatment and coating of metals

This class includes:
- plating, anodizing, etc. of metal
- heat treatment of metal
- deburring, sand blasting, tumbling, cleaning of metals
- colouring, engraving, printing of metal
- non-metallic coating of metal: plastifying, enamelling, lacquering, etc.
- hardening, buffing of metal

28.52   General mechanical engineering

This class includes:
- boring, turning, milling, eroding, planing, lapping, broaching, levelling, sawing, grinding, sharpening, welding, splicing, etc. of metal work pieces

28.6   Manufacture of cutlery, tools and general hardware

28.61   Manufacture of cutlery

This class includes:
- manufacture of domestic cutlery such as knives, forks, spoons, etc.
- manufacture of various cutting articles:
  . razors and razor blades
  . scissors and hair clippers

This class excludes:
- manufacture of cutting blades for machines cf. 28.62
- manufacture of hollowware, dinnerware or flatware cf. 28.75
- manufacture of cutlery of precious metal cf. 36.22

28.62   Manufacture of tools

This class includes:
- manufacture of knives and cutting blades for machines or for mechanical appliances
- manufacture of hand tools such as pliers, screwdrivers, etc.
- manufacture of saws and sawblades, including circular sawblades and chainsaw blades
- manufacture of interchangeable tools for hand tools, whether or not power operated, or for machine tools:
  . drills, punches, dies, milling cutters
- manufacture of blacksmiths' tools: forges, anvils, etc.
- manufacture of vices, clamps

This class excludes:
- manufacture of power driven hand tools cf. 29.40

28.63   Manufacture of locks and hinges

This class includes:
- manufacture of padlocks, locks, keys, hinges and similar hardware for buildings, furniture, vehicles, etc.

28.7 Manufacture of other fabricated metal products

28.71 Manufacture of steel drums and similar containers

This class includes:
- manufacture of iron or steel boxes of a capacity less than 300 litres
- manufacture of pails, cans, drums, buckets

This class excludes:
- *manufacture of tanks and reservoirs cf. 28.21*

28.72 Manufacture of light metal packaging

This class includes:
- manufacture of tins and cans for food products, collapsible tubes and boxes
- manufacture of metallic closures

28.73 Manufacture of wire products

This class includes:
- manufacture of metal cable, plaited bands and similar articles
- manufacture of articles made of wire: barbed wire, wire fencing, grill, netting, cloth, etc.
- manufacture of nails and pins

28.74 Manufacture of fasteners, screw machine products, chain and springs

This class includes:
- manufacture of rivets, washers and similar non-threaded products
- manufacture of screw machine products: bolts, screws, nuts
- manufacture of springs:
  . leaf springs, helical springs, torsion bar springs
  . leaves for springs
- manufacture of chain, except power transmission chain

This class excludes:
- *manufacture of power transmission chain cf. 29.14*
- *manufacture of clock or watch springs cf. 33.50*

28.75 Manufacture of other fabricated metal products not elsewhere classified

This class includes:
- manufacture of metal household articles:
  . sauce-pans, frying pans and other non-electrical utensils for use at the table or in the kitchen
  . base metal flat ware
  . small kitchen appliances and accessories
  . metal scouring pads
- manufacture of soldering equipment
- manufacture of baths, sinks, wash basins and similar articles of base metal
- manufacture of small metal goods for office use
- manufacture of safes, strong-boxes, armoured doors, etc.
- manufacture of cutlasses, swords, bayonets, etc.
- manufacture of ships' propellers
- manufacture of various articles in base metal:
  . metal safety headgear
  . clasps, buckles, hooks
  . sign plates

SUBSECTION DK   MANUFACTURE OF MACHINERY AND EQUIPMENT NOT ELSEWHERE CLASSIFIED

29   MANUFACTURE OF MACHINERY AND EQUIPMENT NOT ELSEWHERE CLASSIFIED

29.1   Manufacture of machinery for the production and use of mechanical power, except aircraft, vehicle and cycle engines

29.11   Manufacture of engines and turbines except aircraft, vehicle and cycle engines

This class includes:
- manufacture of internal combustion piston engines and parts thereof except aircraft, motor vehicle and cycle engines:
  . marine engines and parts thereof
  . railway engines and parts thereof
- manufacture of turbines and parts thereof:
  . steam turbines and other vapour turbines
  . hydraulic turbines, water-wheels and regulators thereof
  . gas turbines

This class also includes:
- manufacture of inlet and exhaust valves of internal combustion engines

This class excludes:
- *manufacture of wind turbines cf. 29.12/2*
- *manufacture of electric generating sets cf. 31.10*
- *manufacture of electrical equipment and components of internal combustion engines cf. 31.61*
- *manufacture of motor vehicle, aircraft or cycle propulsion engines cf. 34.10, 35.30, 35.41*
- *manufacture of turbo-jets and turbo-propellers cf. 35.30*

29.12   Manufacture of pumps and compressors

29.12/1   Manufacture of pumps

This subclass includes:
- manufacture of air or vacuum pumps
- manufacture of pumps for liquids whether or not fitted with a measuring device

29.12/2   Manufacture of compressors

This subclass includes:
- manufacture of air or other gas compressors
- manufacture of fluid power equipment and pneumatic and wind power engines and motors

This subclass excludes:
- *manufacture of hydraulic transmission equipment cf. 29.14*

29.13   Manufacture of taps and valves

This class includes:
- manufacture of industrial taps and valves including regulating valves and intake taps
- manufacture of sanitary taps and valves
- manufacture of heating taps and valves

This class excludes:
- *manufacture of valves of unhardened vulcanised rubber, glass or of ceramic materials cf. 25.13, 26.15 or 26.24*
- *manufacture of inlet and exhaust valves of internal combustion engines cf. 29.11, 34.10, 35.30*

29.14   Manufacture of bearings, gears, gearing and driving elements

This class includes:
- manufacture of ball and roller bearings and parts thereof
- manufacture of mechanical power transmission equipment:
  . transmission shafts and cranks: cam shafts, crank shafts, cranks, etc.
  . bearing housings and plain shaft bearings
- manufacture of gears, gearing and gear boxes and other speed changers
- manufacture of clutches and shaft couplings
- manufacture of flywheels and pulleys
- manufacture of articulated link chain
- manufacture of hydraulic transmission equipment

This class excludes:
- *manufacture of other chain cf. 28.74*
- *manufacture of electromagnetic clutches cf. 31.62*

29.2   Manufacture of other general purpose machinery

29.21   Manufacture of furnaces and furnace burners

This class includes:
- manufacture of electrical and other industrial and laboratory furnaces and ovens including incinerators
- manufacture of burners

This class also includes:
- manufacture of mechanical stokers, grates, ash dischargers, etc.

This class excludes:
- *manufacture of non-electric bakery ovens cf. 29.53*
- *manufacture of agricultural dryers cf. 29.53*
- *manufacture of dryers for wood, paper pulp, paper or paperboard cf. 29.56*
- *manufacture of household ovens cf. 29.7*
- *manufacture of medical, surgical or laboratory sterilisers cf. 33.10*

29.22   Manufacture of lifting and handling equipment

This class includes:
- manufacture of hand operated or power driven lifting, handling, loading or unloading machinery:
  . pulley tackle and hoists, winches, capstans and jacks
  . derricks, cranes, mobile lifting frames, straddle carriers, etc.
  . works trucks, whether or not fitted with lifting or handling equipment whether or not self-propelled, of the
    type used in factories
  . mechanical manipulators and industrial robots specifically designed for lifting, handling, loading or unloading
- manufacture of conveyors, teleferics, liquid elevators, etc.
- manufacture of lifts, escalators and moving walkways

This class also includes:
- maintenance of lifts and escalators

This class excludes:
- *manufacture of mechanical shovels, excavators and shovel loaders cf. 29.52*

- *manufacture of continuous-action elevators and conveyors for underground use cf. 29.52/1*
- *manufacture of industrial robots for multiple uses cf. 29.56*
- *manufacture of crane-lorries, floating cranes, railway cranes, cf. 34.10, 35.11, 35.20*

29.23   Manufacture of non-domestic cooling and ventilation equipment

This class includes:
- manufacture of refrigerating or freezing industrial equipment
- manufacture of air-conditioning machines
- manufacture of heat exchangers
- manufacture of non-domestic fans

This class excludes:
- *manufacture of agricultural dryers cf. 29.53*
- *manufacture of domestic refrigerating or freezing equipment cf. 29.71*
- *manufacture of domestic fans cf. 29.71*

29.24   Manufacture of other general purpose machinery not elsewhere classified

This class includes:
- manufacture of weighing machinery (other than sensitive laboratory balances):
  . household and shop scales, platform scales, scales for continuous weighing, weigh-bridges, weights, etc.
- manufacture of filtering or purifying machinery and apparatus for liquids
- manufacture of equipment for projecting, dispersing or spraying liquids or powders: manufacture of spray guns, fire extinguishers, sand blasting machines, steam cleaning machines, etc.
- manufacture of packing and wrapping machinery: manufacture of filling, closing, sealing, capsuling or labelling machines, etc.
- manufacture of machinery for cleaning or drying bottles and for aerating beverages
- manufacture of distilling or rectifying plant for petroleum refineries, chemical industries, beverage industries, etc.
- manufacture of gas generators
- manufacture of calendering or other rolling machines and cylinders thereof
- manufacture of centrifuges
- manufacture of gaskets and similar joints made of a combination of materials or layers of the same material
- manufacture of automatic goods vending machines

This class excludes:
- *manufacture of agricultural spraying machinery cf. 29.32*
- *manufacture of metal or glass rolling machinery and cylinders thereof cf. 29.51, 29.56*
- *manufacture of cream separators cf. 29.53*
- *manufacture of domestic fans cf. 29.71*
- *manufacture of sensitive balances cf. 33.20*

29.3   Manufacture of agricultural and forestry machinery

29.31   Manufacture of agricultural tractors

This class includes:
- manufacture of tractors used in agriculture and forestry
- manufacture of walking (pedestrian controlled) tractors

This class excludes:
- *manufacture of road tractors for semi-trailers cf. 34.10*
- *manufacture of road trailers or semi-trailers cf. 34.20/2*

29.32   Manufacture of other agricultural and forestry machinery

This class includes:
- manufacture of mowers including lawn mowers
- manufacture of agricultural self-loading or self-unloading trailers or semi-trailers
- manufacture of agricultural machinery for soil preparation, planting or fertilizing:
  . ploughs, manure spreaders, seeders, harrows, etc.
- manufacture of harvesting or threshing machinery:
  . harvesters, threshers, sorters, etc.
- manufacture of milking machines
- manufacture of spraying machinery for agricultural use
- manufacture of diverse agricultural machinery:
  . poultry keeping machinery, bee-keeping machinery, equipment for preparing fodder, etc.
  . machines for cleaning, sorting or grading eggs, fruit, seed, grain, etc.

This class excludes:
- *manufacture of agricultural hand tools cf. 28.62*
- *manufacture of works trucks cf. 29.22*
- *manufacture of cream separators cf. 29.53*
- *manufacture of road trailers or semi-trailers cf. 34.20/2*

29.4   Manufacture of machine tools

29.40   Manufacture of machine tools

This class includes:
- manufacture of machine tools for working any material by removal of material including those working by laser, ultrasonic, electro-discharge processes:
  . lathes, boring machines, drills, etc.
- manufacture of machine tools for working any material without removing material:
  . forging or die-stamping machines, draw-benches, etc.
- manufacture of machines for nailing, stapling, gluing, etc.
- manufacture of welding, brazing or soldering machines
- manufacture of workholders, toolholders and special attachments for machine tools
- manufacture of hand tools with self-contained motor or with pneumatic drive

This class excludes:
- *manufacture of interchangeable tools for hand tools or machine tools cf. 28.62*
- *manufacture of machinery for metallurgy cf. 29.51*
- *manufacture of machinery for mining and quarrying cf. 29.52*

29.5   Manufacture of other special purpose machinery

29.51   Manufacture of machinery for metallurgy

This class includes:
- manufacture of machines and equipment for handling hot metals:
  . converters, ingot moulds, ladles, casting machines
- manufacture of metal-rolling mills and rolls for such mills

This class excludes:
- *manufacture of draw-benches cf. 29.40*
- *manufacture of moulding boxes and moulds (except ingot moulds) and of machines for forming foundry moulds cf. 29.56*

29.52 Manufacture of machinery for mining, quarrying and construction

29.52/1 Manufacture of machinery for mining

This subclass includes:
- manufacture of continuous-action elevators and conveyors for underground use
- manufacture of boring, cutting, sinking and tunnelling machinery
- manufacture of machinery for treating minerals by screening, sorting, separating, etc.

This subclass excludes:
- *manufacture of lifting and handling equipment cf. 29.22*

29.52/2 Manufacture of earth-moving equipment

This subclass includes:
- manufacture of earth moving machinery:
  . bulldozers, angle-dozers, graders, scrapers, levellers, mechanical shovels, shovel loaders, etc.
- manufacture of bulldozer and angle-dozer blades

This subclass excludes:
- *manufacture of lifting and handling equipment cf. 29.22*
- *manufacture of wheeled tractors cf. 29.31, 34.10*
- *manufacture of machine tools for working stone, including machines for splitting or clearing stone cf. 29.40*

29.52/3 Manufacture of equipment for concrete crushing and screening and roadworks

This subclass includes:
- manufacture of concrete and mortar mixers
- manufacture of pile-drivers and pile-extractors, mortar spreaders, bitumen spreaders, concrete surfacing machinery, etc.

This subclass excludes:
- *manufacture of lifting and handling equipment cf. 29.22*
- *manufacture of wheeled tractors cf. 29.31, 34.10*
- *manufacture of machine tools for working stone, including machines for splitting or clearing stone cf. 29.40*
- *manufacture of concrete-mixer lorries cf. 34.10*

29.53 Manufacture of machinery for food, beverage and tobacco processing

This class includes:
- manufacture of agricultural dryers
- manufacture of machinery for the dairy industry:
  . cream separators
  . milk processing machinery (homogenisers and irradiators)
  . milk converting machinery (butter churns, butter workers and moulding machines)
  . cheese-making machines (homogenisers, moulders, presses, etc.)
- manufacture of machinery for the grain milling industry:
  . winnowers, sieving belts, cyclone separators, aspirator separators, grain brushing machines and the like; grinding mills, "breading" rolls or mills, feeders, sifters, bran cleaners, blenders, rice hullers, pea splitters
- manufacture of presses, crushers, etc. used to make wine, cider, fruit juices, etc.
- manufacture of machinery for the bakery industry or for making macaroni, spaghetti or similar products:
  . manufacture of non-electric bakery ovens, dough mixers, dough-dividers, moulders, slicers, cake depositing machines, etc.
- manufacture of machines and equipment to process diverse food:
  . machinery to make confectionery, cocoa or chocolate; to manufacture sugar; for breweries; to process meat or poultry; to prepare fruit, nuts or vegetables; to prepare fish, shell fish or other sea-food; other

machinery for the industrial preparation or manufacture of food or drink
- manufacture of machinery for the extraction or preparation of animal or vegetable fats or oils
- manufacture of machinery for the preparation of tobacco and for the making of cigarettes or cigars, or for pipe or chewing tobacco or snuff
- manufacture of machinery for the preparation of food in hotels and restaurants

This class excludes:
- *manufacture of packing, wrapping and weighing machinery cf. 29.24*
- *manufacture of cleaning, sorting or grading machinery for eggs, fruit or other crops cf. 29.32*

29.54   Manufacture of machinery for textile, apparel and leather production

This class includes:
- manufacture of textile machinery:
  . machines for preparing, producing, extruding, drawing, texturing or cutting man-made textile fibres, materials or yarns
  . machines for preparing textile fibres: cotton gins, bale breakers, garnetters, cotton spreaders, wool scourers, wool carbonizers, combs, carders, roving frames, etc.
  . spinning machines
  . machines for preparing textile yarns: reelers, warpers and related machines
  . weaving machines (looms) including hand looms
  . knitting machines
  . machines for making knotted net, tulle, lace, braid, etc.
- manufacture of auxiliary machines or equipment for textile machinery:
  . Dobbies, Jacquards, automatic stop motions, shuttle changing mechanisms, spindles and spindle flyers, etc.
- manufacture of machinery for fabric processing:
  . machinery for washing, bleaching, dyeing, dressing, finishing, coating or impregnating textile fabrics
  . manufacture of machines for reeling, unreeling, folding, cutting or pinking textile fabrics
- manufacture of laundry machinery:
  . ironing machines including fusing presses
  . laundry-type washing and drying machines
  . dry cleaning machines
- manufacture of sewing machines, sewing machine heads and sewing machine needles
- manufacture of machines for producing or finishing felt or nonwovens
- manufacture of leather machines:
  . machinery for preparing, tanning or working hides, skins or leather
  . machinery for making or repairing footwear or other articles of hides, skins, leather or furskins

This class excludes:
- *manufacture of paper or paperboard cards for use on Jacquard machines cf. 21.25*
- *manufacture of ironing machines of the calender type cf. 29.24*
- *manufacture of machines used in bookbinding cf. 29.56*
- *manufacture of domestic washing and drying machines cf. 29.71*

29.55   Manufacture of machinery for paper and paperboard production

This class includes:
- manufacture of machinery for making paper pulp
- manufacture of paper and paperboard making machinery
- manufacture of machinery producing articles of paper or paperboard

29.56   Manufacture of other special purpose machinery not elsewhere classified

This class includes:
- manufacture of machinery for working soft rubber or plastics or for the manufacture of products of these materials:

. extruders, moulders, pneumatic tyre making or retreading machines and other machines for making a specific rubber or plastic product
- manufacture of printing and bookbinding machines
- manufacture of machinery for producing tiles, bricks, shaped ceramic pastes, pipes, graphite electrodes, blackboard chalk, foundry moulds, etc.
- manufacture of moulding boxes for any material; mould bases; moulding patterns; moulds
- manufacture of diverse special machinery and equipment: machines to assemble electric or electronic lamps, tubes (valves) or bulbs; machines for production or hot-working of glass or glassware, glass fibre or yarn; machinery or apparatus for isotopic separation; rope-making machinery, etc.
- manufacture of centrifugal clothes dryers
- manufacture of dryers for wood, paper pulp, paper or paperboard
- manufacture of industrial robots for multiple uses

This class excludes:
- *manufacture of mechanical manipulators and industrial robots specifically designed for lifting, handling, loading or unloading cf. 29.22*
- *manufacture of machinery or equipment to work hard rubber, hard plastics or cold glass cf. 29.40*
- *manufacture of household appliances cf. 29.7*

29.6   Manufacture of weapons and ammunition

29.60   Manufacture of weapons and ammunition

This class includes:
- manufacture of tanks and other fighting vehicles
- manufacture of artillery material and ballistic missiles
- manufacture of small arms
- manufacture of war ammunition

This class also includes:
- manufacture of explosive devices such as bombs, mines and torpedoes
- manufacture of hunting, sporting or protective firearms and ammunition

This class excludes:
- *manufacture of percussion caps, detonators or signalling flares cf. 24.61*
- *manufacture of cutlasses, swords, bayonets, etc. cf. 28.75*
- *manufacture of armoured vehicles for the transport of bank notes or valuables cf. 34.10*

29.7   Manufacture of domestic appliances not elsewhere classified

29.71   Manufacture of electric domestic appliances

This class includes:
- manufacture of domestic electric appliances: refrigerators and freezers, dishwashers, washing and drying machines, vacuum cleaners, floor polishers, waste disposers, grinders, blenders, juice squeezers, tin openers, electric shavers, electric tooth brushes, knife sharpeners, ventilating or recycling hoods
- manufacture of domestic electro-thermic appliances: electric water heaters; electric blankets, electric dryers, combs, brushes, curlers; electric smoothing irons; space heaters and household type fans; electric ovens, microwave ovens, cookers, hot plates, toasters, coffee or tea makers, frying pans, roasters, grills, electric heating resistors, etc.

This class excludes:
- *manufacture of sewing machines cf. 29.54*

29.72 Manufacture of non-electric domestic appliances

This class includes:
- manufacture of non-electric domestic cooking and heating equipment:
  . non-electric space heaters, cooking ranges, grates, stoves, water heaters, cooking appliances, plate warmers

This class excludes:
- *manufacture of machinery for the preparation of food in commercial kitchens cf. 29.53*

SUBSECTION DL MANUFACTURE OF ELECTRICAL AND OPTICAL EQUIPMENT

30 MANUFACTURE OF OFFICE MACHINERY AND COMPUTERS

30.0 Manufacture of office machinery and computers

30.01 Manufacture of office machinery

This class includes:
- manufacture of manual or electric typewriters
- manufacture of word-processing machines
- manufacture of hectograph or stencil duplicating machines, addressing machines and sheet fed office type offset printing machines
- manufacture of calculating machines, cash registers, postage franking machines, special terminals for issuing of tickets and reservations, etc.
- manufacture of diverse office machinery or equipment: machines that sort, wrap or count coins; automatic banknote dispensers; machines that stuff envelopes, sort mail; pencil sharpening machines; perforating or stapling machines, etc.

30.02 Manufacture of computers and other information processing equipment

This class includes:
- manufacture of automatic data processing machines including micro-computers:
  . digital machines
  . analogue machines
  . hybrid machines
- manufacture of peripheral units:
  . printers, terminals, etc.
  . magnetic or optical readers
  . machines for transcribing data onto data media in coded form

This class excludes:
- *manufacture of electronic parts found in computing machinery cf. 32.10*
- *manufacture of electronic games cf. 36.50*
- *repair and maintenance of computer systems cf. 72.50*

31 MANUFACTURE OF ELECTRICAL MACHINERY AND APPARATUS NOT ELSEWHERE CLASSIFIED

31.1 Manufacture of electric motors, generators and transformers

31.10 Manufacture of electric motors, generators and transformers

This class includes:
- manufacture of AC motors
- manufacture of AC generators
- manufacture of universal AC/DC motors
- manufacture of DC motors or generators
- manufacture of AC or DC generator sets
- manufacture of electric rotary or static converters
- manufacture of electrical transformers

This class excludes:
- *manufacture of vehicle generators and cranking motors cf. 31.61*
- *manufacture of diode valves cf. 32.10*

31.2 Manufacture of electricity distribution and control apparatus

31.20 Manufacture of electricity distribution and control apparatus

This class includes:
- manufacture of electrical apparatus for switching or protecting electrical circuits, or for making connections to or in electrical circuits: manufacture of switches, fuses, lightning arresters, voltage limiters, surge suppressors, plugs, junction boxes, relays, sockets, lamp holders
- manufacture of electric control or distribution boards, panels, consoles, desks, cabinets and other bases

This class excludes:
- *manufacture of fuse wire or strip cf. 27.4*
- *manufacture of carbon or graphite electrodes cf. 31.62*
- *manufacture of boards, panels, consoles, etc. for use in line telephony or line telegraphy cf. 32.20/1*

31.3 Manufacture of insulated wire and cable

31.30 Manufacture of insulated wire and cable

This class includes:
- manufacture of insulated wire, cable, strip and other insulated conductors whether or not fitted with connectors
- manufacture of optical fibre cables for coded data transmission: telecommunications, video, control, data, etc.

This class excludes:
- *manufacture of uninsulated non-ferrous metal wire cf. 27.4*
- *manufacture of uninsulated metal cable or insulated cable not capable of being used as a conductor of electricity cf. 28.73*
- *manufacture of wiring sets cf. 31.61*
- *manufacture of optical fibres and optical fibre cables for live transmission of images: endoscopy, lighting, live images cf. 33.40/1*

31.4 Manufacture of accumulators, primary cells and primary batteries

31.40 Manufacture of accumulators, primary cells and primary batteries

This class includes:
- manufacture of primary cells and primary batteries
- manufacture of electric accumulators, including parts thereof

31.5 Manufacture of lighting equipment and electric lamps

31.50   Manufacture of lighting equipment and electric lamps

This class includes:
- manufacture of electric filament or discharge lamps:
  . ultra-violet or infra-red lamps
  . arc lamps
  . flashbulbs, flashcubes, etc.
- manufacture of electric lamps and lighting fittings:
  . chandeliers, table, desk, bedside or floor-standing lamps, even non-electric
  . portable electric lamps
  . illuminated signs and name-plates, etc.
  . outdoor and road lighting
  . lighting sets of a kind used for Christmas trees

31.6   Manufacture of electrical equipment not elsewhere classified

31.61   Manufacture of electrical equipment for engines and vehicles not elsewhere classified

This class includes:
- manufacture of electrical ignition or starting equipment for internal combustion engines: ignition magnetos, magneto-dynamos, ignition coils, sparking plugs, glow plugs, starter motors, generators (dynamos, alternators), voltage regulators, etc.
- manufacture of electrical lighting and sound or visual signalling equipment for cycles and motor vehicles: lamps, horns, sirens, etc.
- manufacture of wiring sets
- manufacture of windscreen wipers and electrical defrosters and demisters
- manufacture of dynamos for cycles

31.62   Manufacture of other electrical equipment not elsewhere classified

This class includes:
- manufacture of electrical signalling, safety or traffic control equipment for motorways, roads or streets, railways and tramways, inland waterways, ports and harbours and airports
- manufacture of diverse electrical sound or visual signalling apparatus:
  . bells, sirens, indicator panels, burglar and fire alarms, etc.
- manufacture of electromagnets including electromagnetic or permanent magnet chucks, clutches, brakes, couplings, clamps or lifting heads
- manufacture of electrical insulators and insulating fittings, except of glass or ceramics
- manufacture of insulating fittings for electrical machines or equipment, except of ceramics or plastics
- manufacture of carbon or graphite electrodes
- manufacture of electrical conduit tubing and joints for such tubing, of base metal lined with insulating material
- manufacture of diverse electrical machines and apparatus: manufacture of particle accelerators, signal generators, mine detectors, electrical detonators, etc.

This class excludes:
- manufacture of glass envelopes for lamps cf. 26.15
- manufacture of hand-held electrically operated spray guns cf. 29.24
- manufacture of electric lawn mowers cf. 29.32
- manufacture of electric shavers cf. 29.71
- manufacture of electronic valves and tubes (including cold cathode valves) cf. 32.10
- manufacture of electrically operated hand-held medical or dental instruments cf. 33.10

32.1 Manufacture of electronic valves and tubes and other electronic components

32.10 Manufacture of electronic valves and tubes and other electronic components

This class includes:
- manufacture of thermionic, cold cathode or photo-cathode valves or tubes:
  . television picture tubes, television camera tubes, image converters and intensifiers, microwave tubes, receiver or amplifier valves or tubes, etc.
- manufacture of diodes, transistors and similar semi-conductor devices
- manufacture of photosensitive semi-conductor devices including photo-voltaic cells
- manufacture of mounted piezo-electric crystals
- manufacture of electronic integrated circuits and micro-assemblies:
  . monolithic integrated circuits, hybrid integrated circuits and electronic micro-assemblies of moulded module, micromodule or similar types
- manufacture of printed circuits
- manufacture of electrical capacitors (or condensers), including power capacitors
- manufacture of resistors including rheostats and potentiometers

This class excludes:
- *manufacture of heating resistors cf. 29.71*
- *manufacture of transformers cf. 31.10*
- *manufacture of switches cf. 31.20*

32.2 Manufacture of television and radio transmitters and apparatus for line telephony and line telegraphy

32.20 Manufacture of television and radio transmitters and apparatus for line telephony and line telegraphy

32.20/1 Manufacture of telegraph and telephone apparatus and equipment

This subclass includes:
- manufacture of apparatus for line telephony:
  . telephone sets, fax machines, automatic and non-automatic switchboards and exchanges, telex and teleprinter apparatus

This subclass excludes:
- *manufacture of electronic components cf. 32.10*

32.20/2 Manufacture of radio and electronic capital goods

This subclass includes:
- manufacture of apparatus for television transmission including manufacture of relay transmitters and television transmitters for industrial use
- manufacture of television cameras
- manufacture of transmission apparatus for radio-broadcasting
- manufacture of transmission apparatus for radio-telephony:
  . fixed transmitters and transmitter-receivers, radio-telephony apparatus for transport equipment, radio-telephones, other transponders, etc.
- manufacture of reception apparatus for radio-telephony

32.3 Manufacture of television and radio receivers, sound or video recording or reproducing apparatus and associated goods

32.30 Manufacture of television and radio receivers, sound or video recording or reproducing apparatus and associated goods

This class includes:
- manufacture of television receivers including video monitors and video projectors
- manufacture of video recording or reproducing apparatus including camcorders
- manufacture of radio-broadcasting receivers
- manufacture of magnetic tape recorders and other sound recording apparatus including telephone answering machines, cassette-type recorders, etc.
- manufacture of turn-tables (record decks), record players, cassette players, CD players, etc.
- manufacture of microphones, loudspeakers, headphones, earphones, amplifiers and sound amplifier sets
- manufacture of pick-ups, tone arms, sound-heads, tables for turn-tables, record cutters, aerials, aerial reflectors and aerial rotors, cable converters, TV decoders

This class also includes:
- manufacture of sound electro-acoustic apparatus including door intercoms, command transmitter intercoms, simultaneous interpretation apparatus, electronic voting systems, conference systems, paging devices, portable sound systems
- manufacture of furniture specially designed as parts of radios, tv-sets, loudspeakers, etc.

This class excludes:
- *publishing and reproduction of pre-recorded audio and video discs and tapes cf. 22.1, 22.3*
- *manufacture of prepared unrecorded media cf. 24.65*

33 MANUFACTURE OF MEDICAL, PRECISION AND OPTICAL INSTRUMENTS, WATCHES AND CLOCKS

33.1 Manufacture of medical and surgical equipment and orthopaedic appliances

33.10 Manufacture of medical and surgical equipment and orthopaedic appliances

This class includes:
- manufacture of instruments and appliances used for medical, surgical, dental or veterinary purposes:
  . electro-diagnostic apparatus such as electrocardiographs, ultrasonic diagnostic equipment, scintillation scanners, nuclear magnetic resonance apparatus, dental drill engines, sterilizers, ophthalmic instruments
- manufacture of syringes, needles used in medicine, mirrors, reflectors, endoscopes, etc.
- manufacture of apparatus based on the use of X-rays or alpha, beta or gamma radiation whether or not for use in human or animal medicine:
  . X-ray tubes, high tension generators, control panels, desks, screens, etc.
- manufacture of medical, surgical, dental or veterinary furniture:
  . operating tables, hospital beds with mechanical fittings, dentists' chairs
- manufacture of mechano-therapy appliances, massage apparatus, psychological testing apparatus, ozone therapy, oxygen therapy, artificial respiration apparatus, gas masks, etc.
- manufacture of orthopaedic appliances:
  . crutches, surgical belts and trusses, splints, artificial teeth, artificial limbs and other artificial parts of the body, hearing aids, pace-makers, etc.

This class excludes:
- *manufacture of cement used in dentistry cf. 24.42/2*
- *manufacture of thermometers cf. 33.20*
- *manufacture of corrective spectacle lenses and of their frames cf. 33.40/1, or of optical microscopes cf. 33.40/2*

33.2 Manufacture of instruments and appliances for measuring, checking, testing, navigating and other purposes, except industrial process control equipment

33.20 Manufacture of instruments and appliances for measuring, checking, testing, navigating and other purposes, except industrial process control equipment

33.20/1 Manufacture of electronic instruments and appliances for measuring, checking, testing, navigating and other purposes, except industrial process control equipment

This subclass includes:
- manufacture of laboratory type sensitive balances
- manufacture of apparatus for measuring and checking electrical quantities: oscilloscopes, spectrum analysers, cross-talk meters, instruments for checking current, voltage, resistance, etc.
- manufacture of navigational, meteorological, geophysical and related instruments and apparatus:
  . surveying instruments, oceanographic or hydrological instruments, seismometers, range-finders, automatic pilots, sextants, ultrasonic sounding instruments, air navigation instruments and systems
- manufacture of radar apparatus, radio remote control apparatus and radio navigational aid apparatus
- manufacture of electricity supply meters and supply meters for water, gas, petrol, etc.
- manufacture of machines and appliances for testing the mechanical properties of materials
- manufacture of instruments and apparatus for carrying out physical or chemical analyses:
  . polarimeters, photometers, refractometers, colorimeters, spectrometers, pH-meters, viscometers, surface tension instruments, etc.
- manufacture of instruments and apparatus for measuring or checking the flow, level, pressure or other variables of liquids or gases:
  . flow meters, level gauges, manometers, heat meters, etc.
- manufacture of diverse measuring, checking or testing instruments, apparatus or machines:
  . hydrometers, thermometers, barometers, revolution counters, taximeters, pedometers, tachometers, balancing machines, test benches, comparators, etc.

This subclass also includes:
- manufacture of optical type measuring and checking appliances and instruments

This subclass excludes:
- *manufacture of pumps incorporating measuring devices cf. 29.12/1*
- *manufacture of medical and surgical instruments cf. 33.10*
- *manufacture of industrial process control equipment cf. 33.30*
- *manufacture of optical microscopes cf. 33.40/2*

33.20/2 Manufacture of non-electronic instruments and appliances for measuring, checking, testing, navigating and other purposes, except industrial process control equipment

This subclass includes:
- manufacture of laboratory type sensitive balances
- manufacture of drawing, marking-out or mathematical calculating instruments:
  . measuring rods and tapes, micrometers, callipers and gauges, etc.
- manufacture of microscopes other than optical microscopes and diffraction apparatus
- manufacture of apparatus for measuring or checking non-electrical quantities:
  . radiation detectors and counters, apparatus for testing and regulating vehicle motors, etc.
- manufacture of navigational, meteorological, geophysical and related instruments and apparatus:
  . surveying instruments, oceanographic or hydrological instruments, seismometers, range-finders, automatic pilots, sextants, ultrasonic sounding instruments, air navigation instruments and systems

- manufacture of electricity supply meters and supply meters for water, gas, petrol, etc.
- manufacture of machines and appliances for testing the mechanical properties of materials
- manufacture of instruments and apparatus for carrying out physical or chemical analyses:
  . polarimeters, photometers, refractometers, colorimeters, spectrometers, pH-meters, viscometers, surface tension instruments, etc.
- manufacture of instruments and apparatus for measuring or checking the flow, level, pressure or other variables of liquids or gases:
  . flow meters, level gauges, manometers, heat meters, etc.
- manufacture of diverse measuring, checking or testing instruments, apparatus or machines:
  . hydrometers, thermometers, barometers, revolution counters, taximeters, pedometers, tachometers, balancing machines, test benches, comparators, etc.

This subclass also includes:
- manufacture of optical type measuring and checking appliances and instruments

This subclass excludes:
- *manufacture of pumps incorporating measuring devices cf. 29.12/1*
- *manufacture of medical and surgical instruments cf. 33.10*
- *manufacture of industrial process control equipment cf. 33.30*
- *manufacture of binoculars, monoculars and similar optical devices cf. 33.40/2*
- *manufacture of optical microscopes cf. 33.40/2*

33.3   Manufacture of industrial process control equipment

33.30   Manufacture of industrial process control equipment

33.30/1   Manufacture of electronic industrial process control equipment

This subclass includes:
- design and assembly of automated production plants consisting of various machines, handling devices and centralised controlling apparatus

33.30/2   Manufacture of non-electronic industrial process control equipment

This subclass includes:
- design and assembly of industrial continuous process control systems

33.4   Manufacture of optical instruments and photographic equipment

33.40   Manufacture of optical instruments and photographic equipment

33.40/1   Manufacture of spectacles and unmounted lenses

This subclass includes:
- manufacture of optical elements mounted or not:
  . spectacle lenses and contact lenses
  . spectacle frames and frames fitted with lenses whether or not the lenses are optically worked: sun-glasses, protective glasses, corrective glasses, etc.
  . unworked optical elements other than of glass
  . prisms, lenses, optical mirrors, colour filters, polarising elements, etc. of glass or other material
  . optical fibres and optical fibre cables for live transmission of images: endoscopy, lighting, live images

This subclass excludes:
- *manufacture of unworked glass optical elements cf. 26.15*
- *manufacture of optical fibre cables for coded data transmission cf. 31.30*

33.40/2   Manufacture of optical precision instruments

This subclass includes:
- manufacture of optical instruments:
  . optical microscopes, equipment for microphotography and microprojection, magnifying glasses, reading glasses, thread counters, etc.
  . binoculars, sight telescopes, telescopic sights and observation telescopes, astronomical equipment etc.
  . lasers, but excluding laser diodes etc.

This subclass excludes:
- *manufacture of microscopes other than optical cf. 33.20*
- *manufacture of optical type measuring and checking appliances and instruments cf. 33.20*

33.40/3   Manufacture of photographic and cinematographic equipment

This subclass includes:
- manufacture of photographic and cinematographic equipment:
  . cameras
  . image projectors, enlargers and reducers
  . discharge lamps ("electronic") and other flashlight apparatus
  . apparatus and equipment for photographic and cinematographic laboratories, apparatus for the projection of circuit patterns on sensitised semi-conductor materials, projection screens

This subclass excludes:
- *manufacture of photochemical products cf. 24.64*
- *manufacture of photographic flashbulbs cf. 31.50*
- *manufacture of television cameras cf. 32.20/2*

33.5   Manufacture of watches and clocks

33.50   Manufacture of watches and clocks

This class includes:
- manufacture of clocks and watches of all kinds, including instrument panel clocks; watch and clock cases, including cases of noble metals; movements of all kinds for watches and clocks
- manufacture of time recording equipment and equipment for measuring, recording and otherwise displaying intervals of time, e.g. parking meters, process timers, time switches and other releases
- manufacture of components for clocks and watches, such as springs, jewels, dials, hands, metal watch bands and bracelets, plates, bridges and other parts

This class excludes:
- *manufacture of non-metallic watch bands cf. 19.20*

SUBSECTION DM   MANUFACTURE OF TRANSPORT EQUIPMENT

34   MANUFACTURE OF MOTOR VEHICLES, TRAILERS AND SEMI-TRAILERS

34.1   Manufacture of motor vehicles

34.10   Manufacture of motor vehicles

This class includes:
- manufacture of passenger cars

- manufacture of commercial vehicles:
  . vans, lorries, over-the-road tractors for semi-trailers, dumpers for off road use, etc.
- manufacture of buses, trolley-buses and coaches
- manufacture of motor vehicle engines
- manufacture of chassis fitted with engines
- manufacture of other motor vehicles:
  . snow mobiles, golf carts, amphibious vehicles
  . fire engines, street sweepers, travelling libraries and banks, etc.

This class excludes:
- *manufacture of agricultural and industrial tractors cf. 29.31, 29.52/2*
- *manufacture of electrical parts for motor vehicles cf. 31.61*
- *manufacture of bodies for motor vehicles cf. 34.20/1*
- *manufacture of parts and accessories of motor vehicles cf. 34.30*
- *maintenance, repair and alteration of motor vehicles cf. 50.20*

34.2 Manufacture of bodies (coachwork) for motor vehicles; manufacture of trailers and semi-trailers

34.20 Manufacture of bodies (coachwork) for motor vehicles; manufacture of trailers and semi-trailers

34.20/1 Manufacture of bodies (coachwork) for motor vehicles (except caravans)

This subclass includes:
- manufacture of bodies including cabs for motor vehicles
- outfitting of all types of motor vehicles (except caravans)

34.20/2 Manufacture of trailers and semi-trailers

This subclass includes:
- manufacture of trailers and semi-trailers:
  . tankers
- manufacture of containers for carriage by one or more modes of transport

This subclass excludes:
- *manufacture of trailers and semi-trailers specially designed for use in agriculture cf. 29.32*

34.20/3 Manufacture of caravans

This subclass includes:
- manufacture of caravan trailers
- outfitting of caravans

34.3 Manufacture of parts and accessories for motor vehicles and their engines

34.30 Manufacture of parts and accessories for motor vehicles and their engines

This class includes:
- manufacture of diverse parts and accessories of motor vehicles:
  . brakes, gear boxes, axles, road wheels, suspension shock absorbers, radiators, silencers, exhaust pipes, catalyzers, clutches, steering wheels, steering columns and steering boxes
- manufacture of parts and accessories of bodies for motor vehicles:
  . safety belts, doors, bumpers

This class excludes:
- *manufacture of batteries for vehicles cf. 31.40*
- *manufacture of electrical equipment for motor vehicles cf. 31.61*
- *maintenance, repair and alteration of motor vehicles cf. 50.20*

35 MANUFACTURE OF OTHER TRANSPORT EQUIPMENT

35.1 Building and repairing of ships and boats

35.11 Building and repairing of ships

This class includes:
- building of commercial vessels: passenger vessels, ferry-boats, cargo ships, tankers, etc.
- building of warships
- building of fishing boats

This class also includes:
- construction of hovercraft
- construction of drilling platforms, floating or submersible
- construction of floating structures:
  . floating docks, pontoons, coffer-dams, floating landing stages, buoys, floating tanks, barges, lighters, etc.
- maintenance, repair or alteration of ships
- shipbreaking

This class excludes:
- *manufacture of ships' propellers cf. 28.75*
- *manufacture of marine engines cf. 29.11*
- *manufacture of navigational instruments cf. 33.20*
- *manufacture of amphibious motor vehicles cf. 34.10*
- *manufacture of inflatable boats or rafts cf. 35.12*

35.12 Building and repairing of pleasure and sporting boats

This class includes:
- building of inflatables
- building of sailboats with or without auxiliary motor
- building of motor boats
- building of other pleasure and sporting boats:
  . canoes, kayaks, skiffs

This class excludes:
- *manufacture of marine engines cf. 29.11*
- *manufacture of sailboards cf. 36.40*

35.2 Manufacture of railway and tramway locomotives and rolling stock

35.20 Manufacture of railway and tramway locomotives and rolling stock

This class includes:
- manufacture of electric and diesel rail locomotives
- manufacture of self-propelled railway or tramway coaches, vans and trucks, maintenance or service vehicles
- manufacture of railway or tramway rolling stock, not self-propelled:
  . passenger coaches, goods vans, tank wagons, self-discharging vans and wagons, and workshop vans, crane vans, tenders, etc.

- manufacture of specialised parts of railway or tramway locomotives or of rolling-stock:
  . bogies, axles and wheels, brakes and parts of brakes; hooks and coupling devices, buffers and buffer parts; shock absorbers; wagon and locomotive frames; bodies; corridor connections; etc.
- manufacture of mechanical and electro-mechanical signalling, safety or traffic control equipment for railways, tramways, roads, inland waterways, parking facilities, port installations or airfields:
  . signal box equipment, point locks, railbrakes, automatic fog-signalling apparatus, level crossing control gear, etc.

This class excludes:
- *manufacture of unassembled rails cf. 27.10*
- *manufacture of engines and turbines cf. 29.11*
- *manufacture of electric motors cf. 31.10*
- *manufacture of electrical signalling, safety or traffic control equipment cf. 31.62*

35.3　　Manufacture of aircraft and spacecraft

35.30　　Manufacture of aircraft and spacecraft

This class includes:
- manufacture of aeroplanes for the transport of goods or passengers, for use by the defence forces, for sport or other purposes
- manufacture of helicopters
- manufacture of gliders, hang gliders
- manufacture of dirigibles and balloons
- manufacture of spacecraft and spacecraft launch vehicles, satellites, planetary probes, orbital stations, shuttles
- manufacture of parts and accessories of the aircraft of this class:
  . major assemblies such as fuselages, wings, doors, control surfaces, landing gear, fuel tanks, nacelles, etc.
  . airscrews, helicopter rotors and propelled rotor blades
  . motors and engines of a kind typically found on aircraft
  . parts of turbo-jets and turbo-propellers
- manufacture of aircraft launching gear, deck arresters, etc.
- manufacture of ground flying trainers

This class excludes:
- *manufacture of parachutes cf. 17.40/2*
- *manufacture of military ballistic missiles cf. 29.60*
- *manufacture of ignition parts and other electrical parts for internal combustion engines cf. 31.61*
- *manufacture of instruments used on aircraft cf. 33.20*
- *manufacture of air navigation systems cf. 33.20*

35.4　　Manufacture of motorcycles and bicycles

35.41　　Manufacture of motorcycles

This class includes:
- manufacture of motorcycles, mopeds and cycles fitted with an auxiliary engine
- manufacture of engines for motorcycles
- manufacture of side-cars
- manufacture of parts and accessories for motorcycles

This class excludes:
- *manufacture of parts of motorcycle engines cf. 34.30*
- *manufacture of bicycles or invalid carriages cf. 35.42, 35.43*

35.42 Manufacture of bicycles

This class includes:
- manufacture of non-motorised bicycles and other cycles (including delivery tricycles)
- manufacture of parts and accessories of bicycles

This class excludes:
- *manufacture of bicycles with auxiliary motor cf. 35.41*
- *manufacture of children's cycles other than bicycles cf. 36.50/2*

35.43 Manufacture of invalid carriages

This class includes:
- manufacture of invalid carriages with or without motor
- manufacture of parts and accessories of invalid carriages

35.5 Manufacture of other transport equipment not elsewhere classified

35.50 Manufacture of other transport equipment not elsewhere classified

This class includes:
- manufacture of wheelbarrows, luggage trucks, hand-carts, etc.
- manufacture of vehicles drawn by animals

SUBSECTION DN MANUFACTURING NOT ELSEWHERE CLASSIFIED

36 MANUFACTURE OF FURNITURE; MANUFACTURING NOT ELSEWHERE CLASSIFIED

36.1 Manufacture of furniture

36.11 Manufacture of chairs and seats

This class includes:
- manufacture of chairs and seats for offices, workrooms and domestic premises, of any material
- manufacture of chairs and seats for theatres, cinemas and the like, of any material
- manufacture of chairs and seats for transport equipment, of any material

This class also includes:
- finishing such as upholstery of chairs and seats

This class excludes:
- *manufacture of medical, surgical, dental or veterinary furniture cf. 33.10*

36.12 Manufacture of other office and shop furniture

This class includes:
- manufacture of special furniture for shops: counters, display cases, shelves, etc.
- manufacture of furniture for workrooms, restaurants, schools, churches, etc.
- manufacture of office furniture

This class excludes:
- *manufacture of lighting fittings or lamps cf. 31.50*
- *manufacture of medical, surgical, dental or veterinary furniture cf. 33.10*

36.13   Manufacture of other kitchen furniture

This class includes:
- manufacture of fitted kitchen furniture

36.14   Manufacture of other furniture

This class includes:
- manufacture of furniture for bedrooms, living rooms, gardens, etc.

This class also includes:
- finishing of furniture such as spraying, painting, French polishing and upholstering

This class excludes:
- *manufacture of furniture specially designed as parts of refrigerators cf. 29.23 and 29.71, sewing machines cf. 29.54, radios, tv-sets, loudspeakers cf. 32.30, etc.*
- *manufacture of lighting fittings or lamps cf. 31.50*

36.15   Manufacture of mattresses

This class includes:
- manufacture of mattress supports
- manufacture of mattresses:
  . manufacture of mattresses fitted with springs or stuffed or internally fitted with a supporting material
  . manufacture of uncovered cellular rubber or plastic mattresses

This class excludes:
- *manufacture of pillows, pouffes, cushions cf. 17.40/1, and quilts and eiderdowns cf. 17.40/3*
- *manufacture of inflatable mattresses cf. 25.13*

36.2   Manufacture of jewellery and related articles

36.21   Striking of coins and medals

This class includes:
- manufacture of coins including coins for use as legal tender, medals and medallions, whether or not of precious metal

36.22   Manufacture of jewellery and related articles not elsewhere classified

This class includes:
- production of worked pearls
- production of precious and semi-precious stones in the worked state. Included is the working of industrial quality stones and synthetic or reconstructed precious or semi-precious stones
- working of diamonds
- manufacture of jewellery of precious metal or of base metals clad with precious metals, or precious or semi-precious stones, or of combinations of precious metal and precious or semi-precious stones or of other materials
- manufacture of goldsmiths' articles of precious metals or of base metals clad with precious metals:
  . dinnerware, flatware, hollowware, toilet articles, office or desk articles, articles for religious use, etc.

This class also includes:
- engraving on objects of precious metals

This class excludes:
- *manufacture of articles of base metal plated with precious metal cf. 28*
- *manufacture of watch cases and metal straps cf. 33.50*
- *manufacture of imitation jewellery cf. 36.61*

36.3   Manufacture of musical instruments

36.30   Manufacture of musical instruments

This class includes:
- manufacture of stringed instruments
- manufacture of keyboard stringed instruments, including automatic pianos
- manufacture of keyboard pipe organs including harmoniums and similar keyboard instruments with free metal
  reeds
- manufacture of accordions and similar instruments including mouth organs
- manufacture of wind instruments
- manufacture of percussion musical instruments
- manufacture of musical instruments, the sound of which is produced electronically
- manufacture of musical boxes, fairground organs, calliopes, etc.
- manufacture of instrument parts and accessories: metronomes, tuning forks, pitch pipes, cards, discs and
  rolls for automatic mechanical instruments, etc.

This class also includes:
- manufacture of whistles, call horns and other mouth blown sound signalling instruments

This class excludes:
- *publishing and reproduction of pre-recorded tapes and discs cf. 22.1, 22.3*
- *manufacture of microphones, amplifiers, loudspeakers, head-phones and similar components cf. 32.30*
- *manufacture of record players, tape recorders and the like cf. 32.30*
- *manufacture of toy instruments cf. 36.50/2*

36.4   Manufacture of sports goods

36.40   Manufacture of sports goods

This class includes:
- manufacture of articles and equipment for sports, outdoor and indoor games:
  . hard, soft and inflatable balls
  . rackets, bats and clubs
  . skis, bindings and poles
  . sailboards
  . requisites for sport fishing including landing nets
  . requisites for hunting, mountain climbing, etc.
  . leather sports gloves and sports headgear
  . basins for swimming and paddling pools, etc.
  . ice-skates, roller-skates, etc.
  . bows and crossbows
  . gymnasium or athletic equipment

This class excludes:
- *manufacture of boat sails cf. 17.40/2*
- *manufacture of sport clothing cf. 18*
- *manufacture of saddlery and harness cf. 19.20*
- *manufacture of sports footwear cf. 19.30*
- *manufacture of weapons and ammunition cf. 29.60*
- *manufacture of sports vehicles other than toboggans and the like cf. divisions 34-35*
- *manufacture of boats cf. 35.12*

- manufacture of billiard tables and bowling equipment cf. 36.50/1
- manufacture of whips and riding crops cf. 36.63/2

36.5   Manufacture of games and toys

36.50   Manufacture of games and toys

36.50/1   Manufacture of professional and arcade games and toys

This subclass includes:
- manufacture of pin-tables, coin-operated games, billiards, special tables for casino games, automatic bowling alley equipment, etc.
- manufacture of articles for funfair

This subclass excludes:
- manufacture of festive, carnival or other entertainment articles cf. 36.63/2

36.50/2   Manufacture of other games and toys not elsewhere classified

This subclass includes:
- manufacture of dolls and doll garments and accessories
- manufacture of toy animals
- manufacture of wheeled toys designed to be ridden including tricycles
- manufacture of toy musical instruments
- manufacture of domestic electronic games: video games, chess, etc.
- manufacture of articles for table or parlour games
- manufacture of playing cards
- manufacture of reduced-size ("scale") models and similar recreational models, electrical trains, construction sets, etc.
- manufacture of puzzles, etc.

This subclass excludes:
- manufacture of bicycles cf. 35.42
- manufacture of festive, carnival or other entertainment articles cf. 36.63/2

36.6   Miscellaneous manufacturing not elsewhere classified

36.61   Manufacture of imitation jewellery

36.62   Manufacture of brooms and brushes

This class includes:
- manufacture of brooms and brushes including brooms constituting parts of machines, hand operated mechanical floor sweepers, mops and feather dusters, paint brushes, paint pads and rollers, squeegees and other brushes, brooms, mops, etc.
- manufacture of shoe and clothes brushes

36.63   Other manufacturing not elsewhere classified

36.63/1   Manufacture of miscellaneous stationers' goods

This subclass includes:
- manufacture of pens and pencils of all kinds whether or not mechanical
- manufacture of pencil leads
- manufacture of date, sealing or numbering stamps, hand-operated devices for printing, or embossing labels, hand printing sets
- manufacture of prepared typewriter ribbons and inked pads

36.63/2   Other manufacturing not elsewhere classified

This subclass includes:
- manufacture of baby carriages
- manufacture of umbrellas, sun-umbrellas, walking-sticks, seat-sticks, whips, riding-crops, buttons, press-fasteners, snap-fasteners, press-studs, slide fasteners
- manufacture of cigarette lighters and matches
- manufacture of articles for personal use: smoking pipes, combs, hair slides, scent sprays, vacuum flasks and other vacuum vessels for personal or household use, wigs, false beards, eyebrows
- manufacture of roundabouts, swings, shooting galleries and other fairground amusements
- manufacture of linoleum and hard non-plastic surface floor coverings
- manufacture of miscellaneous articles: candles, tapers and the like, artificial flowers, fruit and foliage, jokes and novelties, hand sieves and hand riddles, tailors dummies, etc.
- taxidermy activities

This subclass excludes:
- *manufacture of lighter wicks cf. 17.54/2*
- *manufacture of glass inners for vacuum flasks and other vacuum vessels cf. 26.13*

37   RECYCLING

37.1   Recycling of metal waste and scrap

37.10   Recycling of metal waste and scrap

This class includes:
- processing of metal waste and scrap and of metal articles, whether or not used, into secondary raw material. Typical is that, in terms of commodities, input consists of waste and scrap, the input being sorted or unsorted but always unfit for further direct use in an industrial process whereas the output is made fit for further processing and is to be considered then as an intermediate good. A process is required, either mechanical or chemical

This class excludes:
- *manufacture of new products from secondary raw material cf. divisions 27-36*
- *wholesale in waste and scrap including collecting, sorting, packing, dealing, etc. without an industrial process cf. 51.57*
- *wholesale or retail trade in second hand goods cf. 51, 52.50*

37.2   Recycling of non-metal waste and scrap

37.20   Recycling of non-metal waste and scrap

This class includes:
- processing of non-metal waste and scrap and of non-metal articles, whether or not used, into secondary raw material. Typical is that, in terms of commodities, input consists of waste and scrap, the input being sorted or unsorted but always unfit for further direct use in an industrial process whereas the output is made fit for further processing and is to be considered then as an intermediate good. A process is required, either mechanical or chemical

This class excludes:
- *treatment of food, beverages' and tobacco waste cf. divisions 15-16*
- *production of new products from secondary raw material such as spinning of yarn from garnetted stock or making pulp from waste paper or retreading tyres should be classified in the appropriate class of manufacturing*
- *processing of depleted thorium or uranium cf. 23.30*
- *wholesale in waste and scrap including collecting, sorting, packing, dealing, etc. without an industrial process cf. 51.57*
- *wholesale or retail trade in second hand goods cf. 51, 52.50*

SECTION E   ELECTRICITY, GAS AND WATER SUPPLY

40   ELECTRICITY, GAS, STEAM AND HOT WATER SUPPLY

40.1   Production and distribution of electricity

40.10   Production and distribution of electricity

40.10/1   Electricity generation

This subclass includes:
- generation of electricity by all means including thermal, nuclear, hydroelectric, gas turbine, diesel and renewables (including generation by industrial, transport, etc. undertakings), where separately identifiable

40.10/2   Electricity transmission, distribution and supply

This subclass includes:
- transmission, distribution and supply of electricity

This subclass excludes:
- *retailing of appliances in electricity showrooms cf. 52.45*

40.2   Manufacture of gas; distribution of gaseous fuels through mains

40.20   Manufacture of gas; distribution of gaseous fuels through mains

This class includes:
- transportation, distribution and supply of gaseous fuels of all kinds through a system of mains
- manufacture of gaseous fuels with a specified calorific value, by purification, blending and other processes from gases of various types
- production of gas for the purpose of gas supply by carbonation of coal, from by-products of agriculture or from waste

This class excludes:
- *operation of coke ovens cf. 23.10*
- *manufacture of refined petroleum products cf. 23.20*
- *manufacture of technical gases cf. 24.11*
- *retailing of appliances in gas showrooms cf. 52.44*
- *transportation of gases by pipelines (other than mains) cf. 60.30*

40.3   Steam and hot water supply

40.30   Steam and hot water supply

This class includes:
- production, collection and distribution of steam and hot water for heating, power and other purposes

This class also includes:
- production and distribution of chilled water for cooling purposes

41.0   Collection, purification and distribution of water

41.00   Collection, purification and distribution of water

This class includes:
- collection, purification and distribution of water
- desalting of sea water to produce water as the principal product of interest

This class excludes:
- *irrigation system operation for agricultural purposes cf. 01.41*
- *treatment of waste water solely in order to prevent pollution cf. 90.00*

SECTION F   CONSTRUCTION

45   CONSTRUCTION

This division includes:
- new construction, restoration and ordinary repair

45.1   Site preparation

45.11   Demolition and wrecking of buildings; earth moving

This class includes:
- demolition or wrecking of buildings and other structures
- clearing of building sites
- earthmoving: excavation, landfill, levelling and grading of construction sites, trench digging, rock removal, blasting, etc.
- site preparation for mining: overburden removal and other development and preparation of mineral properties and sites

This class also includes:
- building site drainage
- drainage of agricultural or forestry land

45.12   Test drilling and boring

This class includes:
- test drilling, test boring and core sampling for construction, geophysical, geological or any other similar purpose

This class excludes:
- *drilling of production oil or gas wells cf. 11.20*
- *test drilling and boring incidental to petroleum and gas extraction cf. 11.20*
- *shaft sinking cf. 45.25*
- *water well drilling cf. 45.25*
- *oil and gas field exploration, geophysical, geological and seismic surveying cf. 74.20*

45.2   Building of complete constructions or parts thereof; civil engineering

45.21   General construction of buildings and civil engineering works

This class includes:
- construction of all types of buildings
- construction of civil engineering constructions:
  . bridges, including those for elevated highways, viaducts, tunnels and subways
  . long distance pipelines, communication and power lines
  . urban pipelines, urban communication and power lines; ancillary urban works
- assembly and erection of prefabricated constructions on the site

This class excludes:
- *service activities incidental to oil and gas extraction cf. 11.20*
- *erection of complete prefabricated constructions from self-manufactured parts not of concrete cf. divisions 20, 26 and 28*
- *construction work other than of buildings for stadiums, swimming pools, gymnasiums, tennis courts, golf courses and other sports installations cf. 45.23*
- *building installation cf. 45.3*

- *building completion cf. 45.4*
- *architectural and engineering activities cf. 74.20*
- *project management for construction cf. 74.20*

45.22   Erection of roof covering and frames

This class includes:
- erection of roofs
- roof covering
- waterproofing

45.23   Construction of highways, roads, airfields and sport facilities

This class includes:
- construction of highways, streets, roads, other vehicular and pedestrian ways
- construction of railways
- construction of airfield runways
- construction work other than of buildings for stadiums, swimming pools, gymnasiums, tennis courts, golf courses and other sports installations
- painting of markings on road surfaces and parking lots

This class excludes:
- *preliminary earth moving cf. 45.11*

45.24   Construction of water projects

This class includes:
- construction of:
  . waterways, harbour and river works, pleasure ports (marinas), locks, etc.
  . dams and dykes
- dredging
- sub-surface work

45.25   Other construction work involving special trades

This class includes:
- construction activities specialising in one aspect common to different kinds of structures, requiring specialised skills or equipment:
  . construction of foundations, including pile driving
  . water well drilling and construction, shaft sinking
  . erection of not self-manufactured steel elements
  . steel bending
  . brick laying and stone setting
  . scaffolds and work platform erecting and dismantling, including renting of scaffolds and work platforms
  . erection of chimneys and industrial ovens

This class excludes:
- *renting of scaffolds without erection and dismantling cf. 71.32*

45.3   Building installation

45.31   Installation of electrical wiring and fittings

This class includes:
- installation in buildings or other construction projects of:
  . electrical wiring and fittings

. telecommunication systems
. electrical heating systems
. lifts and escalators
. fire alarms
. burglar alarm systems
. residential antennas and aerials
. lightning conductors, etc.

45.32 Insulation work activities

This class includes:
- installation in buildings or other construction projects of thermal, sound or vibration insulation

This class excludes:
- *waterproofing cf. 45.22*

45.33 Plumbing

This class includes:
- installation in buildings or other construction projects of:
  . plumbing and sanitary equipment
  . gas fittings
  . heating, ventilation, refrigeration or air conditioning equipment and ducts
  . sprinkler systems

This class excludes:
- *installation of electrical heating systems cf. 45.31*

45.34 Other building installation

This class includes:
- installation of illumination and signalling systems for roads, railways, airports and harbours
- installation in buildings or other construction projects of fittings and fixtures not elsewhere classified

45.4 Building completion

45.41 Plastering

This class includes:
- application in buildings or other construction projects of interior and exterior plaster or stucco including related lathing materials

45.42 Joinery installation

This class includes:
- installation of not self-manufactured doors, windows, door and window frames, fitted kitchens, staircases, shop fittings and the like, of wood or other materials
- interior completion such as ceilings, wooden wall coverings, movable partitions, etc.

This class excludes:
- *laying of parquet and other wood floor coverings cf. 45.43*

45.43 Floor and wall covering

This class includes:
- laying, tiling, hanging or fitting in buildings or other construction projects of:

. ceramic, concrete or cut stone wall or floor tiles
. parquet and other wood floor coverings
. carpets and linoleum floor coverings including of rubber or plastic
. terrazzo, marble, granite or slate floor or wall coverings
. wallpaper

45.44   Painting and glazing

This class includes:
- interior and exterior painting of buildings
- painting of civil engineering structures
- installation of glass, mirrors, etc.

This class excludes:
- *installation of windows cf. 45.42*

45.45   Other building completion

This class includes:
- installation of private swimming pools
- steam cleaning, sandblasting and similar activities for building exteriors
- other building completion and finishing work not elsewhere classified

This class excludes:
- *interior cleaning of buildings and other structures cf. 74.70*

45.5   Renting of construction or demolition equipment with operator

45.50   Renting of construction or demolition equipment with operator

This class excludes:
- *renting of construction or demolition machinery and equipment without operators cf. 71.32*

SECTION G WHOLESALE AND RETAIL TRADE; REPAIR OF MOTOR VEHICLES, MOTORCYCLES AND PERSONAL AND HOUSEHOLD GOODS

50   SALE, MAINTENANCE AND REPAIR OF MOTOR VEHICLES AND MOTORCYCLES; RETAIL SALE OF AUTOMOTIVE FUEL

This division includes:
- all activities (except manufacture and renting) related to motor vehicles and motorcycles including lorries and trucks:
  . wholesale and retail sale of new and second hand vehicles
  . maintenance and repair
  . wholesale and retail sale of parts and accessories
  . activities of commission agents involved in wholesale or retail sale of vehicles
  . washing, polishing and towing of vehicles, etc.

This division also includes:
- retail sale of automotive fuel and lubricating or cooling products

This division excludes:
- *renting of motor vehicles cf. 71.10*
- *renting of motorcycles cf. 71.21*

50.1   Sale of motor vehicles

50.10   Sale of motor vehicles

This class includes:
- wholesale and retail sale of new and used vehicles:
  . passenger motor vehicles including specialised passenger motor vehicles such as ambulances and minibuses, etc.
  . lorries, trailers and semi-trailers
  . camping vehicles such as caravans and motorhomes

This class also includes:
- wholesale and retail sale of off-road motor vehicles (jeeps, etc.)
- wholesale and retail sale by commission agents

This class excludes:
- *wholesale and retail sale of parts and accessories for motor vehicles cf. 50.30*

50.2   Maintenance and repair of motor vehicles

50.20   Maintenance and repair of motor vehicles

This class includes:
- maintenance and repair of motor vehicles:
  . mechanical repairs
  . electrical repairs
  . ordinary servicing
  . bodywork repair
  . repair of motor vehicle parts
  . washing, polishing, etc.
  . spraying and painting
  . repair of screens and windows
- tyre and tube repair, fitting or replacement

- anti-rust treatment
- towing
- installation of parts and accessories
- roadside assistance

This class excludes:
- retreading and rebuilding of tyres cf. 25.12
- maintenance and repair of caravans cf. 34.20

50.3   Sale of motor vehicle parts and accessories

50.30   Sale of motor vehicle parts and accessories

50.4   Sale, maintenance and repair of motorcycles and related parts and accessories

50.40   Sale, maintenance and repair of motorcycles and related parts and accessories

This class includes:
- wholesale and retail sale of motorcycles including mopeds
- wholesale and retail sale of parts and accessories for motorcycles
- activities of commission agents
- maintenance and repair of motorcycles

This class excludes:
- sale, maintenance and repair of bicycles and related parts and accessories cf. 51.18, 51.47/2, 52.48/3, 52.74

50.5   Retail sale of automotive fuel

50.50   Retail sale of automotive fuel

This class includes:
- retail sale of fuel for motor vehicles and motorcycles

This class also includes:
- retail sale of lubricating products and cooling products for motor vehicles

This class excludes:
- wholesale of fuels cf. 51.51

51   WHOLESALE TRADE AND COMMISSION TRADE, EXCEPT OF MOTOR VEHICLES AND MOTORCYCLES

This division includes:
- re-sale (sale without transformation) of new and used goods to retailers, to industrial, commercial, institutional or professional users; or to other wholesalers; or acting as agents in buying merchandise for, or selling merchandise to, such persons or companies:
  . activities of wholesale merchants, jobbers, industrial distributors, exporters, importers, co-operative buying associations, merchandise and commodity brokers, commission merchants and agents and assemblers, buyers and co-operative associations engaged in the marketing of farm products

This division also includes:
- the usual manipulations involved in wholesaling such as assembling, sorting and grading of goods in large lots, break bulks, re-packing and bottling, redistribution in smaller lots e.g. pharmaceuticals; storage, refrigeration, delivery and installation of goods on own account

This division excludes:
- *wholesale of motor vehicles, caravans and motorcycles cf. 50.10, 50.40*
- *wholesale of motor accessories cf. 50.30*
- *renting and leasing of goods cf. 71*

51.1 Wholesale on a fee or contract basis

This group includes:
- activities of commission agents, commodity brokers and all other wholesalers who trade on behalf and on the account of others
- activities of those involved in bringing sellers and buyers together or undertaking commercial transactions on behalf of a principal

This group excludes:
- *activities of commission agents serving sales of motor vehicles and motorcycles cf. 50.10, 50.40*
- *wholesale trade in own name cf. 51.2-51.7*
- *retail sale by agents cf. 52*
- *activities of insurance agencies cf. 67.20*
- *activities of real estate agents cf. 70.3*

51.11 Agents involved in the sale of agricultural raw materials, live animals, textile raw materials and semi-finished goods

51.12 Agents involved in the sale of fuels, ores, metals and industrial chemicals

51.13 Agents involved in the sale of timber and building materials

51.14 Agents involved in the sale of machinery, industrial equipment, ships and aircraft

This class also includes:
- agents involved in the sale of agricultural machinery
- agents involved in the sale of office machinery

51.15 Agents involved in the sale of furniture, household goods, hardware and ironmongery

51.16 Agents involved in the sale of textiles, clothing, footwear and leather goods

This class also includes:
- agents involved in the sale of fur

51.17 Agents involved in the sale of food, beverages and tobacco

51.18 Agents specialising in the sale of particular products or ranges of products not elsewhere classified

This class also includes:
- agents involved in the sale of bicycles

51.19 Agents involved in the sale of a variety of goods

51.2-51.7

These groups include:
- **only** wholesale on own account

51.2 Wholesale of agricultural raw materials and live animals

51.21   Wholesale of grain, seeds and animal feeds

This class also includes:
- wholesale of seed potatoes
- wholesale of tulip bulbs
- wholesale of feed for farm animals

51.22   Wholesale of flowers and plants

This class excludes:
- *wholesale of textile fibres cf. 51.56*

51.23   Wholesale of live animals

51.24   Wholesale of hides, skins and leather

51.25   Wholesale of unmanufactured tobacco

51.3   Wholesale of food, beverages and tobacco

51.31   Wholesale of fruit and vegetables

This class includes:
- wholesale of unprocessed fruit and vegetables including potatoes
- wholesale of herbs

51.32   Wholesale of meat and meat products

This class includes:
- wholesale of meat, poultry meat, game meat, processed meat and meat products

51.33   Wholesale of dairy produce, eggs and edible oils and fats

This class includes:
- wholesale of dairy produce
- wholesale of eggs and egg products
- wholesale of edible oils and fats of animal and vegetable origin

51.34   Wholesale of alcoholic and other beverages

This class also includes:
- buying of wine in bulk and bottling without transformation
- buying of wine in bulk with blending, purification, bottling and resale

51.35   Wholesale of tobacco products

51.36   Wholesale of sugar and chocolate and sugar confectionery

51.37   Wholesale of coffee, tea, cocoa and spices

51.38   Wholesale of other food including fish, crustaceans and molluscs

This class also includes:
- wholesale of potato products
- wholesale of food for pet animals

51.39   Non-specialised wholesale of food, beverages and tobacco

51.4 Wholesale of household goods

51.41 Wholesale of textiles

This class includes:
- wholesale of yarn
- wholesale of fabrics
- wholesale of household linen, etc.
- wholesale of haberdashery: needles, sewing thread, etc.

This class excludes:
- *wholesale of textile fibres cf. 51.56*

51.42 Wholesale of clothing and footwear

This class includes:
- wholesale of clothing including sports clothes
- wholesale of clothing accessories such as gloves, ties and braces
- wholesale of fur articles
- wholesale of footwear

This class excludes:
- *wholesale of umbrellas, jewellery and leather goods cf. 51.47/2*

51.43 Wholesale of electrical household appliances and radio and television goods

This class also includes:
- wholesale of gramophone records, tapes, CDs and videos
- wholesale of lighting equipment
- wholesale of wire and switches and other installation equipment for domestic use

51.44 Wholesale of china and glassware, wallpaper and cleaning materials

51.45 Wholesale of perfume and cosmetics

51.46 Wholesale of pharmaceutical goods

This class also includes:
- wholesale of instruments and devices for doctors and hospitals
- wholesale of orthopaedic goods

51.47 Wholesale of other household goods

51.47/1 Wholesale of furniture

This subclass excludes:
- *wholesale of office furniture cf. 51.64*

51.47/2 Wholesale of other household goods not elsewhere classified

This subclass includes:
- wholesale of carpets and other floor coverings and non-electrical household appliances
- wholesale of stationery, books, magazines and newspapers, photographic and optical goods, leather goods and travel accessories, watches, clocks and jewellery, musical instruments, games and toys, sport goods, bicycles and their parts and accessories, umbrellas, wooden ware, wickerwork and cork ware, etc.

51.5   Wholesale of non-agricultural intermediate products, waste and scrap

51.51   Wholesale of solid, liquid and gaseous fuels and related products

51.51/1   Wholesale of petroleum and petroleum products

This subclass includes:
- wholesale of automotive fuels

51.51/2   Wholesale of other fuels and related products

This subclass includes:
- wholesale of greases, lubricants, oils, etc.

51.52   Wholesale of metals and metal ores

This class includes:
- wholesale of ferrous and non-ferrous metal ores
- wholesale of ferrous and non-ferrous metals in primary forms
- wholesale of gold and other precious metals

This class excludes:
- *wholesale of waste and scrap cf. 51.57*

51.53   Wholesale of wood, construction materials and sanitary equipment

This class includes:
- wholesale of paint and varnish
- wholesale of wood in the rough
- wholesale of products of primary processing of wood
- wholesale of construction materials:
  . sand, gravel
- wholesale of flat glass
- wholesale of sanitary equipment:
  . baths, washbasins, toilets and other sanitary porcelain

51.54   Wholesale of hardware, plumbing and heating equipment and supplies

This class also includes:
- wholesale of sanitary installation equipment:
  . tubes, pipes, fittings, taps, t-pieces, connections, rubber pipes, etc.
- wholesale of tools such as hammers, saws, screwdrivers and other hand tools

51.55   Wholesale of chemical products

This class includes:
- wholesale of industrial chemicals:
  . aniline, printing ink, essential oils, industrial gases, chemical glues, colouring matter, synthetic resin,
    methanol, paraffin, scents and flavourings, soda, industrial salt, acids and sulphurs, starch derivates, etc.
- wholesale of fertilizers and agro-chemical products
- wholesale of plastic materials in primary forms
- wholesale of rubber

51.56 Wholesale of other intermediate products

This class also includes:
- wholesale of textile fibres, etc.
- wholesale of paper in bulk

51.57 Wholesale of waste and scrap

This class includes:
- wholesale of metal and non-metal waste and scrap and materials for recycling

51.6 Wholesale of machinery, equipment and supplies

51.61 Wholesale of machine tools

This class also includes:
- wholesale of computer controlled machine tools

51.62 Wholesale of construction machinery

51.63 Wholesale of machinery for the textile industry, and of sewing and knitting machines

This class also includes:
- wholesale of computer controlled machinery for the textile industry and of computer controlled sewing and knitting machines

51.64 Wholesale of office machinery and equipment

This class includes:
- wholesale of computers and peripheral equipment
- wholesale of other office machinery and equipment such as typewriters, adding machines, etc.
- wholesale of office furniture

51.65 Wholesale of other machinery for use in industry, trade and navigation

This class includes:
- wholesale of transport equipment except motor vehicles, motorcycles and bicycles
- wholesale of production line robots
- wholesale of wires and switches and other installation equipment for industrial use
- wholesale of other electrical material such as electrical motors and transformers as well as electronic components
- wholesale of other machinery not elsewhere classified for use in industry, trade and navigation and other services

This class also includes:
- wholesale of measuring instruments and equipment

This class excludes:
- wholesale of motor vehicles, trailers and caravans cf. 50.10
- wholesale of motor vehicle parts cf. 50.30
- wholesale of motorcycles cf. 50.40
- wholesale of bicycles cf. 51.47/2

51.66   Wholesale of agricultural machinery and accessories and implements, including tractors

This class also includes:
- wholesale of lawn mowers however operated

51.7   Other wholesale

51.70   Other wholesale

This class includes:
- specialised wholesale not covered in one of the previous categories
- wholesale of a variety of goods without any particular specialisation

52   RETAIL TRADE, EXCEPT OF MOTOR VEHICLES AND MOTOR-CYCLES; REPAIR OF PERSONAL AND HOUSEHOLD GOODS

This division includes:
- re-sale (sale without transformation) of new and used goods to the general public for personal or household consumption or utilisation, by shops, department stores, stalls, mail-order houses, hawkers and peddlers, consumer co-operatives, etc.

This division also includes:
- repair and installation of personal or household goods whether or not done in combination with retail sale
- retail sale by commission agents

This division excludes:
- *sale of motor vehicles, motorcycles and their parts and of fuel for these articles cf. 50*
- *trade in cereals, grains, ores, crude petroleum, industrial chemicals, iron and steel and industrial machinery and equipment cf. 51*
- *sale of food and drinks for consumption on the premises and sale of take-away food cf. 55.30, 55.40, 55.51*
- *renting and hiring of personal and household goods to the general public cf. 71.40*

52.1   Retail sale in non-specialised stores

52.11   Retail sale in non-specialised stores with food, beverages or tobacco predominating

This class includes:
- retail sale of a large variety of goods of which, however, food products, beverages or tobacco should be predominant:
  . activities of general stores which have, apart from their main sales of food products, beverages or tobacco, several other lines of merchandise such as wearing apparel, furniture, appliances, hardware, cosmetics, etc.

52.12   Other retail sale in non-specialised stores

This class includes:
- retail sale of a large variety of goods of which food products, beverages or tobacco should not be predominant
- activities of department stores carrying a general line of merchandise including wearing apparel, furniture, appliances, hardware, cosmetics, jewellery, toys, sporting goods, etc.

52.2   Retail sale of food, beverages and tobacco in specialised stores

52.21   Retail sale of fruit and vegetables

52.22   Retail sale of meat and meat products

This class also includes:
- retail sale of poultry and game

52.23   Retail sale of fish, crustaceans and molluscs

52.24   Retail sale of bread, cakes, flour confectionery and sugar confectionery

52.25   Retail sale of alcoholic and other beverages

52.26   Retail sale of tobacco products

52.27   Other retail sale of food, beverages and tobacco in specialised stores

This class also includes:
- retail sale of dairy produce, eggs and edible oils and fats

52.3   Retail sale of pharmaceutical and medical goods, cosmetic and toilet articles

52.31   Dispensing chemists

52.32   Retail sale of medical and orthopaedic goods

52.33   Retail sale of cosmetic and toilet articles

52.4   Other retail sale of new goods in specialised stores

52.41   Retail sale of textiles

This class includes:
- retail sale of fabrics
- retail sale of knitting yarn
- retail sale of basic materials for rug, tapestry or embroidery making
- retail sale of household textiles such as sheets, table-cloths, towels
- retail sale of haberdashery: needles, sewing thread, etc.

52.42   Retail sale of clothing

This class includes:
- retail sale of:
  . articles of clothing
  . articles of fur
  . clothing accessories such as gloves, ties, braces, etc.

52.43   Retail sale of footwear and leather goods

This class includes:
- retail sale of:
  . footwear
  . leather goods
  . travel accessories of leather and leather substitutes

52.44   Retail sale of furniture, lighting equipment and household articles not elsewhere classified

This class includes:
- retail sale of:
  . furniture
  . articles for lighting
  . non-electrical household appliances
  . household utensils and cutlery, crockery, glassware, china and pottery
  . curtains, net curtains and other household furnishing articles of textile materials
  . wood, cork goods and wickerwork goods
  . household articles and equipment not elsewhere classified

This class excludes:
- *retail sale of cork floor tiles cf. 52.48/1*
- *retail sale of antiques cf. 52.50*

52.45   Retail sale of electrical household appliances and radio and television goods

This class includes:
- retail sale of:
  . household appliances
  . radio and television goods and other household audio/visual equipment
  . musical records and audio/visual tapes, CDs and cassettes
  . musical instruments and scores

This class excludes:
- *renting of tapes and records cf. 71.40/1*

52.46   Retail sale of hardware, paints and glass

This class includes:
- retail sale of:
  . do-it-yourself material and equipment
  . lawn mowers however operated
  . hardware
  . paints, varnishes and lacquers
  . flat glass
  . other building material such as bricks, wood, sanitary equipment

52.47   Retail sale of books, newspapers and stationery

This class also includes:
- retail sale of office supplies such as pens, pencils, paper, etc.

This class excludes:
- *retail sale of second hand or antique books cf. 52.50*

52.48   Other retail sale in specialised stores

52.48/1   Retail sale of floor coverings

This subclass includes:
- specialised retail sale of floor coverings

52.48/2 Retail sale of photographic, optical and precision equipment, office supplies and equipment (including computers, etc.)

This subclass includes:
- specialised retail sale of:
  . photographic, optical and precision equipment
  . office equipment, computers and non-customised software

52.48/3 Other retail sale in specialised stores not elsewhere classified

This subclass includes:
- specialised retail sale of:
  . wallpaper
  . watches, clocks and jewellery
  . sports goods, fishing gear, camping goods, boats and bicycles
  . games and toys
  . flowers, plants, seeds, fertilizers, pet animals and pet foods
  . souvenirs, craftwork and religious articles
  . household fuel oil, bottled gas, coal and wood
  . weapons and ammunition
  . stamps and coins
  . non-food products not elsewhere classified

52.5 Retail sale of second-hand goods in stores

52.50 Retail sale of second-hand goods in stores

This class includes:
- retail sale of second-hand books
- retail sale of other second-hand goods
- retail sale of antiques

This class excludes:
- *retail sale of second-hand motor vehicles cf. 50.10*

52.6 Retail sale not in stores

52.61 Retail sale via mail order houses

This class includes:
- retail sale of any kind of product by mail order. Goods are sent to the buyer, who made his choice on the basis of advertisements, catalogues, models or any other means of advertising

This class also includes:
- direct sale via television, radio and telephone

52.62 Retail sale via stalls and markets

This class includes:
- retail sale of any kind of product in a usually movable stall either along a public road or on a fixed market place

52.63 Other non-store retail sale

This class includes:
- retail sale of any kind of product in any way which is not included in previous classes:

. by door-to-door sales persons
. by vending machines, etc.
. by mobile sellers

52.7   Repair of personal and household goods

This group includes:
- repair of personal and household goods when not done in combination with manufacture, wholesale or retail sale of these goods. If done in combination the repair is included in the retailing, wholesaling or manufacturing activity

This group excludes:
- repair of motor vehicles and motorcycles cf. 50

52.71   Repair of boots, shoes and other articles of leather

This class also includes:
- repair of boots, shoes, luggage and the like of other materials

52.72   Repair of electrical household goods

52.73   Repair of watches, clocks and jewellery

52.74   Repair not elsewhere classified

This class also includes:
- repair of bicycles
- repair and alteration of clothing

This class excludes:
- repair of wearing apparel when done in connection with cleaning cf. 93.01

SECTION H   HOTELS AND RESTAURANTS

55   HOTELS AND RESTAURANTS

55.1   Hotels

This group includes:
- provision of short-stay lodging in:
  . hotels, motels and inns
  . hotels with conference facilities

This group also includes:
- restaurant facilities operated in connection with the provision of lodging

This group excludes:
- *rental of long-stay accommodation cf. 70.20/2*
- *timeshare operations cf. 70.20/2*

55.11   Hotels and motels, with restaurant

55.11/1   Licensed hotels and motels

55.11/2   Unlicensed hotels and motels

55.12   Hotels and motels, without restaurant

55.2   Camping sites and other provision of short-stay accommodation

This group includes:
- provision mainly of short-stay lodging in:
  . holiday centres and villages, chalets and flats
  . camping space and camping facilities
  . other short-stay lodging facilities such as guest houses, farmhouses, inns with letting rooms, youth hostels, mountain refuges (shelters), etc.

This group excludes:
- *rental of long-stay accommodation cf. 70.20/2*

55.21   Youth hostels and mountain refuges

55.22   Camping sites, including caravan sites

55.23   Other provision of lodgings not elsewhere classified

55.23/1   Holiday centres and holiday villages

This subclass includes:
- provision of short-stay lodging in:
  . holiday chalets, cottages and flats in holiday centres and holiday villages

55.23/2   Other self-catering holiday accommodation

This subclass includes:
- provision of short-stay lodging in:
  . holiday chalets, cottages, flats, etc., other than in holiday centres and holiday villages

55.23/3   Other tourist or short-stay accommodation

This subclass includes:
- provision of short-stay lodging in:
  . guest houses, farmhouses, inns with letting rooms
  . other facilities not elsewhere classified

55.3   Restaurants

55.30   Restaurants

55.30/1   Licensed restaurants

This subclass includes:
- sale of meals for consumption generally on the premises, as well as sale of alcoholic drinks accompanying the meals, possibly accompanied by some form of entertainment, by:
  . restaurants
  . self-service restaurants such as cafeterias
  . dining car activities of railway companies and other passenger transport facilities

This subclass excludes:
- *the above mentioned activities carried out in connection with the provision of lodging cf. 55.1, 55.2*

55.30/2   Unlicensed restaurants and cafes

This subclass includes:
- sale of meals for consumption generally on the premises, with sale of only non-alcoholic drinks accompanying the meals, possibly accompanied by some form of entertainment, by:
  . restaurants
  . self-service restaurants such as cafeterias
  . fast-food outlets such as burger bars (with restaurant)

This subclass excludes:
- *the above mentioned activities carried out in connection with the provision of lodging cf. 55.1, 55.2*

55.30/3   Take-away food shops

This subclass includes:
  . fast-food outlets such as burger bars (without restaurant)
  . take away outlets such as sandwich bars
  . fish and chip stands and the like
  . ice cream parlours

This subclass excludes:
- *sale through vending machines cf. 52.63*

55.4   Bars

55.40   Bars

55.40/1   Licensed clubs with entertainment

This subclass includes:
- sale of drinks for consumption generally on the premises, accompanied by some form of entertainment, by:
  . nightclubs

This subclass excludes:
- *the above mentioned activities carried out in connection with the provision of lodging cf. 55.1, 55.2*

55.40/2 Public houses and bars

This subclass includes:
- sale of drinks for consumption generally on the premises, by:
  . public houses, bars, beer halls, etc.

This subclass excludes:
- *sale through vending machines cf. 52.63*
- *the above mentioned activities carried out in connection with the provision of lodging cf. 55.1, 55.2*

55.5 Canteens and catering

55.51 Canteens

This class includes:
- sale of meals and drinks, usually at reduced prices to groups of clearly defined persons who are mostly linked by ties of a professional nature:
  . activities of sport, factory or office canteens
  . activities of school canteens and kitchens
  . activities of university dining halls
  . activities of messes and canteens for members of the armed forces, etc.

55.52 Catering

This class includes:
- activities of contractors supplying meals prepared in a central food preparation unit for consumption on other premises such as the supply of prepared meals to:
  . airlines
  . "meals on wheels"
  . banquets, corporate hospitality
  . weddings, parties and other celebrations or functions

SECTION I   TRANSPORT, STORAGE AND COMMUNICATION

This section includes:
- activities related to providing passenger or freight transport, whether scheduled or not, by rail, pipeline, road, water or air
- supporting activities such as terminal and parking facilities, cargo handling, storage, etc.
- postal activities and telecommunication
- renting of transport equipment with driver or operator

This section excludes:
- *major repair or alteration of transport equipment except motor vehicles cf. 35*
- *construction, maintenance and repair of roads, railroads, harbours, airfields cf. 45*
- *maintenance and repair of motor vehicles cf. 50.20*
- *renting of transport equipment without driver or operator cf. 71.1 and 71.2*

60   LAND TRANSPORT; TRANSPORT VIA PIPELINES

60.1   **Transport via railways**

60.10   **Transport via railways**

60.10/1   **Inter-city services**

This subclass includes:
- passenger transport by inter-city rail services

This subclass excludes:
- *passenger terminal activities cf. 63*

60.10/2   **Other transport via railways**

This subclass includes:
- passenger and freight transport by interurban railways, other than inter-city services

This subclass excludes:
- *passenger and freight terminal activities, cargo handling, storage and other auxiliary activities cf. 63*
- *maintenance and minor repair of rolling stock cf. 63.21*

60.2   **Other land transport**

60.21   **Other scheduled passenger land transport**

60.21/1   **Inter-city coach services**

This subclass includes:
- activities providing interurban transport of passengers on scheduled routes following normally a fixed time schedule, picking up and setting down passengers at normally fixed stops

60.21/2   **Other scheduled passenger land transport not elsewhere classified**

This subclass includes:
- activities providing urban or suburban transport of passengers on scheduled routes following normally a fixed time schedule, picking up and setting down passengers at normally fixed stops. They may be carried out with motor bus, tramway, street car, trolley bus, underground and elevated railways, etc.

This subclass also includes:
- operation of school buses, town-to-airport or town-to-station lines, funicular railways, aerial cable-ways, etc.

60.22   Taxi operation

This class also includes:
- other rental of private cars with operator

60.23   Other passenger land transport

This class includes:
- other non-scheduled passenger road transport:
  . charters, excursions and other occasional coach services, sight-seeing buses

This class excludes:
- *ambulance transport cf. 85.14*

60.24   Freight transport by road

This class includes:
- freight transport operation by road:
  . logging haulage
  . stock haulage
  . refrigerated haulage
  . heavy haulage
  . bulk haulage including haulage in tanker trucks
  . haulage of automobiles

This class also includes:
  . furniture removal
  . renting of trucks with driver
  . freight transport by animal drawn vehicles

This class excludes:
- *operation of terminal facilities for handling freight cf. 63*

60.3   Transport via pipelines

60.30   Transport via pipelines

This class includes:
- transport of gases, liquids, slurry and other commodities via pipelines
- operation of pump stations

This class excludes:
- *distribution of natural or manufactured gas, water or steam cf. 40.20, 40.30, 41.00*

61   WATER TRANSPORT

61.1   Sea and coastal water transport

61.10   Sea and coastal water transport

61.10/1   Passenger sea and coastal water transport

This subclass includes:
- transport of passengers over water, whether scheduled or not
- operation of excursion, cruise or sightseeing boats
- operation of ferries, water taxis, etc.
- rental of ships and boats with crew for passenger conveyance

This subclass excludes:
- *restaurant and bar activities on board ships, cf. 55.3, 55.4*
- *harbour operation and other auxiliary activities such as docking, pilotage, vessel salvage cf. 63*

61.10/2   Freight sea and coastal water transport

This subclass includes:
- transport of freight over water, whether scheduled or not
- transport by towing or pushing of barges, oil-rigs, etc.
- rental of ships and boats with crew for transport of freight

This subclass excludes:
- *cargo handling, storage of freight, harbour operation and other auxiliary activities such as docking, pilotage, lighterage, vessel salvage cf. 63*

61.2   Inland water transport

61.20   Inland water transport

61.20/1   Passenger inland water transport

This subclass includes:
- transport of passengers via rivers, canals, lakes and other inland waterways including inside harbours and docks

61.20/2   Other inland water transport

This subclass includes:
- transport of freight via rivers, canals, lakes and other inland waterways including inside harbours and docks

62   AIR TRANSPORT

This division includes:
- transport of passengers or freight by air or via space

This division excludes:
- *crop spraying cf. 01.41*
- *overhaul of aircraft or aircraft engines cf. 35.30*
- *aerial advertising cf 74.40*
- *aerial photography cf 74.81*

62.1   Scheduled air transport

62.10   Scheduled air transport

62.10/1   Scheduled passenger air transport

This subclass includes:
- transport of passengers by air over regular routes and on regular schedules

This subclass excludes:
- regular charter flights cf. 62.20

62.10/2 Other scheduled air transport

This subclass includes:
- transport of freight by air over regular routes and on regular schedules

This subclass excludes:
- regular charter flights cf. 62.20

62.2 Non-scheduled air transport

62.20 Non-scheduled air transport

62.20/1 Non-scheduled passenger air transport

This subclass includes:
- non-scheduled transport of passengers by air

This subclass also includes:
- regular passenger charter flights

62.20/2 Other non-scheduled air transport

This subclass includes:
- non-scheduled transport of freight by air

This subclass also includes:
- regular freight charter flights

62.3 Space transport

62.30 Space transport

This class includes:
- launching of satellites and space vehicles
- space transport of physical goods and passengers

63 SUPPORTING AND AUXILIARY TRANSPORT ACTIVITIES; ACTIVITIES OF TRAVEL AGENCIES

63.1 Cargo handling and storage

63.11 Cargo handling

This class includes:
- loading and unloading of goods or passengers' luggage irrespective of the mode of transport used for transportation
- stevedoring

This class excludes:
- operation of terminal facilities cf. 63.2

63.12   Storage and warehousing

This class includes:
- operation of storage and warehouse facilities for all kinds of goods:
  . operation of grain silos, general merchandise warehouses, refrigerated warehouses, storage tanks, etc.

This class excludes:
- *parking facilities for motor vehicles cf. 63.21*

63.2   Other supporting transport activities

63.21   Other supporting land transport activities

This class includes:
- activities related to land transport of passengers, animals or freight:
  . operation of terminal facilities such as railway stations, bus stations, stations for the handling of goods
  . operation of roads, bridges, tunnels, parking lots or garages, bicycle parkings
  . winter storage of caravans

63.22   Other supporting water transport activities

This class includes:
- activities related to water transport of passengers, animals or freight:
  . operation of terminal facilities such as harbours and piers
  . operation of waterway locks, etc.
  . navigation, pilotage and berthing activities
  . lighterage, salvage activities
  . lighthouse activities

63.23   Other supporting air transport activities

This class includes:
- activities related to air transport of passengers, animals or freight:
  . operation of terminal facilities such as airway terminals, etc.
  . airport and air traffic control activities
  . ground service activities on airfields, etc.
  . activities of flying schools for commercial airline pilots

This class excludes:
- *operation of flying schools except for professional certificates cf. 80.41*

63.3   Activities of travel agencies and tour operators; tourist assistance activities not elsewhere classified

63.30   Activities of travel agencies and tour operators; tourist assistance activities not elsewhere classified

63.30/1   Activities of travel agencies

This subclass includes:
- travel agency activities:
  . furnishing of travel information, advice and planning
  . arranging of made to measure tours, accommodation and transportation for travellers and tourists
  . furnishing of tickets, sale of packaged tours, etc.

63.30/2   Activities of travel organisers

This subclass includes:
- activities of tour operators

63.30/3 Activities of tour guides

This subclass includes:
- activities of tourist guides

63.30/4 Other tourist assistance activities not elsewhere classified

63.4 Activities of other transport agencies

63.40 Activities of other transport agencies

This class includes:
- forwarding of freight
- arranging or carrying out of transport operations by road, sea or air
- receipt of group and individual consignments (including pick-up of goods and grouping of consignments)
- issue and procurement of transport documents and way-bills
- organisation of group consignments by road, rail, air or sea (including collection and distribution of goods)
- activities of customs agents
- activities of sea freight forwarders and air cargo agents
- goods handling operations, e.g. temporary crating for the sole purpose of protecting the goods during transit, uncrating, sampling, weighing of goods

This class excludes:
- *courier activities cf. 64.12*
- *activities related to the arrangement of freight insurance cf. 67.20*

64 POST AND TELECOMMUNICATIONS

64.1 Post and courier activities

64.11 National post activities

This class includes:
- pick-up, transport and delivery (domestic or international) of mail and parcels
- collection of mail and parcels from public letter boxes or from post offices
- distribution and delivery of mail and parcels
- mailbox rental, poste restante, etc.

64.12 Courier activities other than national post activities

This class includes:
- pick-up, transport and delivery of letters and mail-type parcels and packages by firms other than national post. Either only one kind of transport or more than one mode of transport may be involved and the activity may be carried out with either self-owned (private) transport media or via public transport

64.2 Telecommunications

64.20 Telecommunications

This class includes transmission of sound, images, data or other information via cables, broadcasting, relay or satellite:
- telephone, telegraph and telex communication
- maintenance of the network
- transmission (transport) of radio and television programmes

This class excludes:
- *telephone answering activities cf. 74.83*
- *production of radio and television programmes even if in connection with broadcasting cf. 92.20*

SECTION J   FINANCIAL INTERMEDIATION

65   FINANCIAL INTERMEDIATION, EXCEPT INSURANCE AND PENSION FUNDING

This division includes:
- the activity of obtaining and redistributing funds other than for the purpose of insurance or pension funding or compulsory social security

Note:
- Credit card activities are classified according to type of operator

65.1   Monetary intermediation

This group includes:
- the obtaining of funds in the form of transferable deposits

65.11   Central banking

This class includes:
- monetary intermediation of the Bank of England

65.12   Other monetary intermediation

65.12/1   Banks

This subclass includes:
- monetary intermediation of banks other than the Bank of England

This subclass also includes:
- monetary intermediation of discount houses
- monetary intermediation of the National Savings Bank

65.12/2   Building societies

This subclass includes:
- monetary intermediation of building societies

This subclass excludes:
- activities of specialist mortgage finance companies cf. 65.22/3
- activities of housing associations cf. 70.11

65.2   Other financial intermediation

This group includes:
- financial intermediation other than that conducted by banks and building societies

65.21   Financial leasing

This class includes:
- leasing where the term approximately covers the expected life of the asset and the lessee acquires substantially all the benefits of its use and takes all the risks associated with its ownership, and the lessee's rental payments virtually cover the whole of the purchase price of the asset. The asset may or may not eventually be transferred

This class excludes:
- operating leasing cf. 71 according to type of goods leased

65.22 Other credit granting

65.22/1 Credit granting by non-deposit taking finance houses and other specialist consumer credit grantors

This subclass includes:
- activities of non-deposit taking finance houses
- activities of hire purchase and loan companies not in the UK banking sector
- activities of check traders
- activities of money lenders
- pawnbroking where the primary activity is in lending money
- activities of building societies' personal finance subsidiaries
- other consumer credit granting where the main business is the direct financing (other than finance leasing) of instalment credit sales mainly to persons, together with farm, industrial and building plant equipment to unincorporated businesses

This subclass excludes:
- *activities of pawn shops where the primary activity is in dealing in second-hand goods cf. 52.50*
- *financial leasing cf. 65.21*
- *operating leasing cf. 71*

65.22/2 Factoring

This subclass includes:
- activities of companies specialising in debt factoring and invoice discounting

65.22/3 Activities of mortgage finance companies

This subclass includes:
- activities of specialist mortgage finance companies other than banks and building societies

65.22/4 Other credit granting not elsewhere classified

This subclass includes:
- activities of banking institutions in the Channel Islands and the Isle of Man not included in the UK banking sector
- activities of other institutions not in the UK banking sector whose main activity is to extend credit abroad
- activities of other special finance agencies and export credit companies

65.23 Other financial intermediation not elsewhere classified

This class includes:
- other financial intermediation primarily concerned with distributing funds other than by making loans

65.23/1 Activities of investment trusts

This subclass includes:
- activities of investment trust companies recognised as such by the Inland Revenue for tax purposes
- activities of investment funds authorised by the Channel Islands and the Isle of Man authorities

65.23/2 Activities of unit trusts and property unit trusts

This subclass includes:
- activities of unit trusts authorised by the Securities and Investment Board under the terms of the Financial Services Act 1986

- activities of property unit trusts
- activities of open-ended unit trusts authorised by the Channel Islands and the Isle of Man authorities
- activities of unauthorised unit trusts such as "in-house" trusts (ie funds run on unit trust lines by, for example, stockbrokers and merchant banks which are designed for their own clients)

65.23/3   Security dealing on own account

This subclass includes:
- dealing for own account by securities dealers
- activities of gilt-edged market makers
- activities of Stock Exchange money brokers
- activities of inter-dealer brokers
- dealing in financial futures, options and other derivatives for own account

This subclass excludes:
- *security and other dealing on behalf of others cf. 67.12*

65.23/4   Activities of bank holding companies

This subclass includes:
- activities of holding companies which are not themselves part of the UK banking sector and whose main subsidiaries are UK banks

This subclass excludes:
- *activities of other financial holding companies cf 65.23/6*
- *activities of non-financial holding companies cf. 74.15*

65.23/5   Activities of venture and development capital companies

This subclass includes:
- activities of venture and development capital companies and funds

65.23/6   Financial intermediation not elsewhere classified

This subclass includes:
- activities of non-specific financial holding companies

This subclass excludes:
- *trade, leasing and renting of property cf. 70*

66   INSURANCE AND PENSION FUNDING, EXCEPT COMPULSORY SOCIAL SECURITY

66.0   Insurance and pension funding, except compulsory social security

This group includes:
- long and short term risk spreading with or without a savings element

66.01   Life insurance

This class includes:
- life insurance and life reinsurance, with or without a substantial savings element, including life insurance undertaken by corporate and quasi-corporate insurers such as Lloyd's underwriting syndicates

66.02   Pension funding

This class includes:
- the provision of retirement incomes

This class excludes:
- *non-contributory schemes where the funding is largely derived from public sources cf. 75.12*
- *compulsory social security schemes cf. 75.30*

66.03   Non-life insurance

This class includes:
- insurance and reinsurance of non-life business, including non-life insurance undertaken by corporate insurers and quasi-corporate insurers such as Lloyd's underwriting syndicates:
  - . accident, fire
  - . health
  - . property
  - . motor, marine, aviation, transport
  - . pecuniary loss and liability insurance

67   ACTIVITIES AUXILIARY TO FINANCIAL INTERMEDIATION

This division includes:
- provision of services involved in or closely related to financial intermediation, but not themselves involving financial intermediation

67.1   Activities auxiliary to financial intermediation, except insurance and pension funding

67.11   Administration of financial markets

This class includes:
- operation and supervision of financial markets other than by public authorities:
  - . activities of stock exchanges
  - . activities of other bodies that regulate or supervise the financial markets, including exchanges for commodity future contracts

67.12   Security broking and fund management

67.12/1   Fund management activities

This subclass includes:
- portfolio management services provided by fund managers on behalf of clients, including decisions about the content of the portfolios

This subclass excludes:
- *dealing in markets on own account cf. 65.23/3*

67.12/2   Security broking and related activities

This subclass includes:
- dealing in financial markets on behalf of others (e.g. stock broking) and related activities other than fund management

This subclass excludes:
- dealing in markets on own account cf. 65.23/3

67.13 Activities auxiliary to financial intermediation not elsewhere classified

This class includes:
- activities auxiliary to financial intermediation not elsewhere classified:
  . mortgage brokers
  . bureaux de change, etc.

67.2 Activities auxiliary to insurance and pension funding

67.20 Activities auxiliary to insurance and pension funding

This class includes:
- activities involved in or closely related to insurance and pension funding other than financial intermediation:
  . activities of insurance agents
  . activities of insurance brokers
  . activities of insurance risk and damage evaluators
  . activities of Lloyd's underwriting brokers; and of managing and underwriting agents of Lloyd's syndicates

SECTION K   REAL ESTATE, RENTING AND BUSINESS ACTIVITIES

70   REAL ESTATE ACTIVITIES

70.1   Real estate activities with own property

70.11   Development and selling of real estate

This class includes:
- development of real estate projects:
  . bringing together financial, technical and physical means to realise real estate projects for later sale, whether for residential buildings or other real estate

This class excludes:
- *development and construction work of real estate projects by construction units cf. 45.2*

70.12   Buying and selling of own real estate

This class includes:
- buying and selling of self-owned real estate:
  . apartment buildings and dwellings
  . non-residential buildings
  . land

70.2   Letting of own property

70.20   Letting of own property

70.20/1   Letting of conference and exhibition centres`

This subclass includes:
- letting of exhibition halls

70.20/2   Other letting of own property

This subclass includes:
- letting and operating of self-owned real estate such as:
  . apartment buildings and dwellings
  . other non-residential buildings
  . land

This subclass also includes:
- timeshare operations

This subclass excludes:
- *operation of hotels, rooming houses, camps, trailer camps and other non-residential or short stay lodging places cf. 55*

70.3   .Real estate activities on a fee or contract basis

70.31   Real estate agencies

This class includes:
- intermediation in buying, selling, renting and appraising real estate

70.32   Management of real estate on a fee or contract basis

This class also includes:
- rent collecting agencies

71   RENTING OF MACHINERY AND EQUIPMENT WITHOUT OPERATOR AND OF PERSONAL AND HOUSEHOLD GOODS

71.1   Renting of automobiles

71.10   Renting of automobiles

This class includes:
- renting and operating leasing of self-drive private cars and light vans up to 3.5 tonnes

This class excludes:
- *financial leasing cf. 65.21*

71.2   Renting of other transport equipment

71.21   Renting of other land transport equipment

71.21/1   Renting of passenger land transport equipment

This subclass includes:
- renting and operating leasing of passenger land transport equipment without drivers except automobiles:
  . railroad passenger vehicles
  . motorcycles, caravans, campers, etc.

This subclass excludes:
- *renting or leasing of passenger vehicles with driver cf. 60.2*
- *financial leasing cf. 65.21*

71.21/2   Renting of other land transport equipment

This subclass includes:
- renting and operating leasing of other land transport equipment without drivers except automobiles:
  . trucks, haulage tractors, trailers and semi-trailers
  . railroad freight vehicles

This subclass also includes:
- renting of containers

This subclass excludes:
- *renting or leasing of freight vehicles or trucks with driver cf. 60.24*
- *financial leasing cf. 65.21*
- *renting of bicycles cf. 71.40/1*

71.22   Renting of water transport equipment

71.22/1   Renting of passenger water transport equipment

This subclass includes:
- renting and operating leasing of passenger water transport equipment such as commercial boats and ships, without operator

This subclass excludes:
- renting of passenger water transport equipment with operator cf. 61
- financial leasing cf. 65.21
- renting of pleasure-boats cf. 71.40/1

71.22/2   Renting of other water transport equipment

This subclass includes:
- renting and operating leasing of other water transport equipment such as commercial boats and ships, without operator

This subclass excludes:
- renting of other water transport equipment with operator cf. 61
- financial leasing cf. 65.21

71.23   Renting of air transport equipment

71.23/1   Renting of passenger air transport equipment

This subclass includes:
- renting and operating leasing of passenger air transport equipment without operator

This subclass excludes:
- renting of passenger air transport equipment with operator cf. 62
- financial leasing cf. 65.21

71.23/2   Renting of other air transport equipment

This subclass includes:
- renting and operating leasing of other air transport equipment without operator

This subclass excludes:
- renting of other air transport equipment with operator cf. 62
- financial leasing cf. 65.21

71.3   Renting of other machinery and equipment

71.31   Renting of agricultural machinery and equipment

This class includes:
- renting and operating leasing of agricultural and forestry machinery and equipment without operator:
  . renting of products produced by Group 29.3, such as agricultural tractors, etc.

This class excludes:
- renting of this machinery or equipment with operator cf. 01.41
- financial leasing cf. 65.21

71.32   Renting of construction and civil engineering machinery and equipment

This class includes:
- renting and operating leasing of construction and civil engineering machinery and equipment without operator
- renting of scaffolds and work platforms without erection and dismantling

This class excludes:
- renting of this machinery or equipment with operator cf. 45.50
- financial leasing cf. 65.21

71.33   Renting of office machinery and equipment including computers

This class includes:
- renting and operating leasing of office machinery and equipment including computers, without operator:
  . computing machinery and equipment
  . duplicating machines, typewriters and word processing machines
  . accounting machinery and equipment

This class excludes:
- *financial leasing cf. 65.21*

71.34   Renting of other machinery and equipment not elsewhere classified

This class includes:
- renting and operating leasing of other machinery and equipment not elsewhere classified, without operator:
  . engines and turbines, machine tools
  . mining and oil field equipment
  . professional radio, television and communication equipment
  . measuring and controlling equipment
  . other scientific, commercial and industrial machinery

This class excludes:
- *financial leasing cf. 65.21*
- *renting of agricultural machinery and equipment cf. 71.31*
- *renting of construction and civil engineering machinery and equipment cf. 71.32*
- *renting of office machinery and equipment including computers cf. 71.33*

71.4   Renting of personal and household goods not elsewhere classified

71.40   Renting of personal and household goods not elsewhere classified

71.40/1   Renting of sporting and recreational equipment

This subclass includes the renting of sporting and recreational goods to households or industries:
- pleasure-craft
- bicycles
- sports equipment
- musical instruments, scenery and costumes
- books, journals and magazines
- video tapes, records, etc.
- do-it-yourself machinery and equipment

This subclass excludes:
- *renting of passenger cars and small vans, motorcycles, caravans and trailers cf. 71.1 and 71.2*
- *renting of books, journals, magazines, video tapes and records by libraries cf. 92.51*

71.40/2   Renting of other personal and household goods not elsewhere classified

This subclass includes the renting of other good, to households or industries:
- textiles, wearing apparel and footwear
- furniture, pottery and glass, kitchen and tableware, electrical appliances and housewares
- flowers and plants
- jewellery

This subclass excludes:
- *renting of linens, work uniforms and related items by laundries cf. 93.01*

72 COMPUTER AND RELATED ACTIVITIES

72.1 Hardware consultancy

72.10 Hardware consultancy

This class includes:
- consultancy on type and configuration of hardware and associated software application:
  . analysing the users' needs and problems and presenting the best solution

This class excludes:
- *hardware consultancy carried out by computer producing or selling units cf. 30.02, 51.64, 52.48/2*

72.2 Software consultancy and supply

72.20 Software consultancy and supply

This class includes:
- analysis, design and programming of systems ready to use:
  . analysis of the user's needs and problems, consultancy on the best solution
  . development, production, supply and documentation of order-make software based on orders from specific users
  . development, production, supply and documentation of ready-made (non-customised) software
  . writing of programs following directives of the user

This class excludes:
- *reproduction of non-customised software cf. 22.33*
- *software consultancy related to hardware consultancy cf. 72.10*

72.3 Data processing

72.30 Data processing

This class includes:
- processing of data employing either the customer's or a proprietary program:
  . complete processing of data
  . data entry services
- management and operation on a continuing basis of data processing facilities belonging to others

72.4 Data base activities

72.40 Data base activities

This class includes data base related activities:
- data base development: assembly of data from one or more sources
- data storage: preparation of a computer record for such information in a predetermined format
- data base availability: provision of data in a certain order or sequence, by on-line data retrieval or accessibility (computerised management) to everybody or to limited users, sorted on demand

72.5 Maintenance and repair of office, accounting and computing machinery

72.50 Maintenance and repair of office, accounting and computing machinery

72.6 Other computer related activities

72.60   Other computer related activities

73   RESEARCH AND DEVELOPMENT

This division includes three types of research and development:
- basic research:
  . experimental or theoretical work undertaken primarily to acquire new knowledge of the underlying foundations of phenomena and observable facts, without particular application or use in view
- applied research:
  . original investigation undertaken in order to acquire new knowledge, directed primarily towards a specific practical aim or objective
- experimental development:
  . systematic work, drawing on existing knowledge gained from research and/or practical experience, directed to producing new materials, products and devices, to installing new processes, systems and services, and to improving substantially those already produced or installed

73.1   Research and experimental development on natural sciences and engineering

73.10   Research and experimental development on natural sciences and engineering

This class includes:
- systematic studies and creative efforts in the three types of research and development defined above, in natural sciences (mathematics, physics, astronomy, chemistry, life sciences, medical sciences, earth sciences, agriculture, etc.). They are intended to increase the stock of knowledge and to improve the use of this stock of knowledge

73.2   Research and experimental development on social sciences and humanities

73.20   Research and experimental development on social sciences and humanities

This class includes:
- systematic studies and creative efforts in the three types of research and development defined above, in social sciences and humanities (economics, psychology, sociology, legal sciences, linguistics and languages, arts, etc.). They are intended to increase the stock of knowledge and to improve the use of this stock of knowledge

This class excludes:
- market research cf. 74.13

74   OTHER BUSINESS ACTIVITIES

74.1   Legal, accounting, book-keeping and auditing activities; tax consultancy; market research and public opinion polling; business and management consultancy; holdings

74.11   Legal activities

This class includes:
- legal representation of one party's interest against another party, whether or not before courts or other judicial bodies by, or under supervision of, persons who are members of the bar:
  . advice and representation in civil cases
  . advice and representation in criminal actions
- advice and representation in connection with labour disputes
- general counselling and advising, preparation of legal documents:

. articles of incorporation, partnership agreements or similar documents in connection with company formation
. patents and copyrights
. preparation of deeds, wills, trusts, etc.
- activities of notary public, notaries, bailiffs, arbitrators, examiners and referees

This class excludes:
- *arbitration and conciliation between labour and management cf. 74.14*
- *law court activities cf. 75.23*

74.12   Accounting, book-keeping and auditing activities; tax consultancy

This class includes:
- recording of commercial transactions from businesses or others
- preparation of financial accounts, examination of such accounts and certification of their accuracy
- preparation of personal and business income tax returns
- advisory activities and representation (other than legal representation) on behalf of clients before tax authorities

This class excludes:
- *data processing and tabulation activities even for accounting purposes cf. 72.30*
- *management consultancy such as design of accounting systems, cost accounting programmes, budgetary control procedures cf. 74.14*
- *bill collection cf. 74.84*

74.13   Market research and public opinion polling

This class includes:
- investigation into market potential, acceptance and familiarity of products and buying habits of consumers for the purpose of sales promotion and development of new products including statistical analyses of the results
- investigation into collective opinions of the public about political, economic and social issues and statistical analysis thereof

74.14   Business and management consultancy activities

This class includes:
- provision of advice, guidance or operational assistance to businesses and the public service:
  . public relations and communication
  . design of accounting systems, cost accounting programmes, budgetary control procedures
  . advice and help to businesses and public services in planning, organisation, efficiency and control, management information, etc.
  . management consultancy such as by agronomists and agricultural economists to farms, etc.
  . arbitration and conciliation between management and labour

74.15   Management activities of holding companies

74.2   Architectural and engineering activities and related technical consultancy

74.20   Architectural and engineering activities and related technical consultancy

This class includes:
- consulting architectural activities:
  . building design and drafting
  . supervision of construction
  . town and city planning and landscape architecture

- machinery and industrial plant design
- engineering, project management and technical activities:
  . projects involving civil engineering, hydraulic engineering, traffic engineering
  . projects elaboration and realisation relative to electrical and electronic engineering, mining engineering, chemical engineering, mechanical, industrial and systems engineering, safety engineering
- elaboration of projects using air-conditioning, refrigerating, sanitary and pollution control engineering, acoustical engineering, etc.
- geological and prospecting activities:
  . surface measurements and observations designed to yield information on sub-surface structure and the location of petroleum, natural gas and mineral deposits and of ground water
- weather forecasting activities
- geodetic surveying activities:
  . land surveying activities
  . hydrographic surveying activities
  . sub-surface surveying activities
  . boundary surveying activities
  . cartographic and spatial information activities including aerial photography thereof
  . industrial and engineering surveying activities

This class excludes:
- *production drilling and boring in connection with petroleum and gas extraction cf. 11.20*
- *test drilling and testhole boring incidental to petroleum and gas extraction cf. 11.20*
- *other test drilling and testhole boring cf. 45.12*
- *research and development activities cf. 73*
- *technical testing cf. 74.30*
- *interior decorating cf. 74.84*

74.3   Technical testing and analysis

74.30   Technical testing and analysis

This class includes:
- measuring related to cleanness of water or air, measuring of radioactivity and the like; analysis of potential pollution such as smoke or waste water
- testing activities in the field of food hygiene
- strength and failure testing
- testing of calculations for building elements
- certification of ships, aircraft, motor vehicles, pressurised containers, nuclear plant, etc.
- periodic road safety testing of motor vehicles

74.4   Advertising

74.40   Advertising

This class includes:
- creation and realisation of advertising campaigns
- creating and placing of outdoor advertising, e.g. billboards, panels, bulletins and frames, window dressing, showroom design, car and bus carding, etc.
- media representation, i.e. sale of time and space for various media soliciting advertising
- aerial advertising
- distribution or delivery of advertising material or samples
- provision of spaces for advertising

This class excludes:
- *printing of advertising material cf. 22.22*
- *market research cf. 74.13*

- public relations activities cf. 74.14
- advertising photography cf. 74.81
- direct mailing activities cf. 74.83
- production of commercial messages for radio, television and film cf. 92

74.5 Labour recruitment and provision of personnel

74.50 Labour recruitment and provision of personnel

This class includes:
- personnel search, selection referral and placement in connection with employment supplied to the potential employer or to the prospective employee:
  . formulation of job descriptions
  . screening and testing of applicants
  . investigation of references, etc.
- executive search and placement activities (headhunters)
- labour contracting activities:
  . supply to others, chiefly on a temporary basis, of personnel hired by, and whose emoluments are paid by, the agency

This class excludes:
- activities of farm labour contractors cf. 01.4
- activities of personal theatrical or artistic agents cf. 74.84
- motion picture, television and other theatrical casting activities cf. 92.72

74.6 Investigation and security activities

74.60 Investigation and security activities

This class includes:
- investigation activities
- activities of private investigators
- surveillance, guard and other protective activities:
  . transport of valuables
  . bodyguard activities
  . street patrol, guard and watchman activities for apartment buildings, offices, factories, construction sites, hotels, theatres, dance halls, etc.
  . store detective activities
  . monitoring by mechanical or electrical protective devices
- consultancy in the field of industrial, household and public service security
- training of dogs for security reasons

This class excludes:
- installation of alarm systems cf. 45.31
- investigation in connection with insurance cf. 67.20

74.7 Industrial cleaning

74.70 Industrial cleaning

This class includes:
- interior cleaning of buildings of all types, including offices, factories, shops, institutions and other business and professional premises and multi-unit residential buildings
- window cleaning
- chimney cleaning and cleaning of fire-places, stoves, furnaces, incinerators, boilers, ventilation ducts and exhaust units

This class also includes:
- disinfecting and exterminating activities for buildings, ships, trains, etc.
- cleaning of trains, buses, planes, etc.

This class excludes:
- *agricultural pest control cf. 01.41*
- *steam cleaning, sand blasting and similar activities for building exteriors cf. 45.45*
- *cleaning of new buildings after construction cf. 45.45*
- *carpet and rug shampooing, drapery and curtain cleaning cf. 93.01*
- *activities of domestics cf. 95.00*

74.8 Miscellaneous business activities not elsewhere classified

74.81 Photographic activities

This class includes:
- commercial and consumer photograph production:
  . portrait photography for passports, school, weddings, etc.
  . photography for commercials, publishers, fashion, real estate or tourism purposes
  . aerial photography
- film processing:
  . developing, printing and enlarging from client-taken negatives or cine films
  . mounting of slides
  . copying and restoring or transparency retouching in connection with photographs

This class also includes:
- operation of photo coin-operated machines

This class excludes:
- *cartographic and spatial information activities including aerial photography thereof cf. 74.20*
- *processing motion picture film related to the motion picture and television industries cf. 92.11*

74.82 Packaging activities

This class includes:
- packaging activities, whether or not this involves an automated process:
  . filling of aerosols
  . bottling of liquids, including beverages and food
  . packaging of solids (blister packaging, foil covered, etc.)
  . labelling, stamping and imprinting
  . parcel packing and gift wrapping

This class excludes:
- *packing activities incidental to transport cf. 63.40*

74.83 Secretarial and translation activities

This class includes:
- stenographic and mailing activities:
  . typing
  . other secretarial activities such as transcribing from tapes, discs, etc.
  . copying, blue printing, multigraphing and similar activities
- envelope addressing, stuffing, sealing and mailing, mailing list compilation, etc., including for advertising material
- translation and interpretation

This class also includes:
- proof-reading

This class excludes:
- *database activities cf. 72.40*
- *bookkeeping activities cf. 74.12*

74.84   Other business activities not elsewhere classified

This class includes:
- bill collecting, credit rating in connection with an individual's or firm's credit-worthiness or business practices
- business brokerage activities, i.e. arranging for the purchase and sale of small and medium-sized businesses, including professional practices
- appraisal activities other than for real estate and insurance
- fashion design related to textiles, wearing apparel, shoes, jewellery, furniture and other interior decoration and other fashion goods as well as other personal or household goods
- trading stamp activities
- activities of interior decorators
- activities of fair, exhibition and congress organisers
- activities of stand designers

This class also includes:
- activities carried on by agents and agencies on behalf of individuals usually involving the obtaining of engagements in motion pictures, theatrical productions or other entertainment or sports attractions and the placement of books, plays, artworks, photographs, etc., with publishers, producers, etc.

This class excludes:
- *credit card activities cf. 65*
- *machinery and industrial plant design cf. 74.20*
- *display of advertisements and other advertising design cf. 74.40*

SECTION L   PUBLIC ADMINISTRATION AND DEFENCE; COMPULSORY SOCIAL SECURITY

75   PUBLIC ADMINISTRATION AND DEFENCE; COMPULSORY SOCIAL SECURITY

75.1   Administration of the State and the economic and social policy of the community

75.11   General (overall) public service activities

This class includes:
- executive and legislative administration of central, regional and local bodies
- administration and supervision of fiscal affairs:
  . operation of taxation schemes
  . duty/tax collection on goods and tax violation investigation
  . customs administration
- budget implementation and management of public funds and public debt:
  . raising and receiving of moneys and control of their disbursement
- administration and operation of overall economic and social planning and statistical and sociological services at the various levels of government

75.12   Regulation of the activities of agencies that provide health care, education, cultural services and other social services excluding social security

This class includes:
- public administration of programmes aimed to increase personal well-being: health, education, culture, sport, recreation, environment, housing, social services, etc.

This class excludes:
- *compulsory social security activities cf. 75.30*
- *education activities cf. 80*
- *human health related activities cf. 85.1*
- *sewage and refuse disposal and sanitation cf. 90.00*
- *activities of libraries, public archives, museums and other cultural institutions cf. 92.5*
- *sporting or other recreational activities cf. 92.6, 92.7*

75.13   Regulation of and contribution to more efficient operation of business

This class includes:
- public administration and regulation of different economic sectors: agriculture, land use, energy and mining resources, infrastructure, transport, communication, hotels and tourism
- administration of general labour affairs
- implementation of regional development policy

75.14   Supporting service activities for the government as a whole

This class includes:
- general personnel and other general service activities:
  . administration and operation of general personnel services, whether or not connected with a specific function
  . development and implementation of general personnel policies and procedures covering selection and promotion, rating methods, job description, evaluation and classification, administration of civil service regulations, etc.
- administration, operation and support of overall general services:
  . centralised supply and purchasing services
  . maintenance and storage of government records and archives

. operation of government owned or occupied buildings

. operation of central offices and other general services not connected with a specific function

This class excludes:
- *activities of historical archives cf. 92.51*

75.2 Provision of services to the community as a whole

75.21 Foreign affairs

This class includes:
- administration and operation of the ministry of foreign affairs and diplomatic and consular missions stationed abroad or at offices of international organisations
- administration, operation and support for information and cultural services intended for distribution beyond national boundaries
- aid to foreign countries whether or not routed through international organisations
- provision of military aid to foreign countries
- management of foreign trade, international financial and foreign technical affairs
- international assistance, e.g. refugee or hunger relief programmes

75.22 Defence activities

This class includes:
- administration, supervision and operation of military defence affairs and land, sea, air and space defence forces such as:
  . combat forces of army, navy and air force
  . engineering, transport, communications, intelligence, material, personnel and other non-combat forces and commands
  . reserve and auxiliary forces
  . provision of equipment, structures, supplies, etc.
  . health activities for military personnel in the field
- administration, operation and support of civil defence forces
- support for the working out of contingency plans and the carrying out of exercises in which civilian institutions and populations are involved

This class excludes:
- *provision of military aid to foreign countries cf. 75.21*
- *activities of military tribunals cf. 75.23*
- *provision of supplies for domestic emergency use in case of peace-time disasters cf. 75.24*
- *educational activities of military schools, colleges and academies cf. 80*
- *activities of military hospitals cf. 85.11*

75.23 Justice and judicial activities

This class includes:
- administration and operation of administrative civil and criminal law courts, military tribunals and the judicial system
- prison administration and provision of correctional services

This class also includes:
- rehabilitation services

This class excludes:
- *advice and representation in civil, criminal and other cases cf. 74.11*
- *activities of prison schools cf. 80*
- *activities of prison hospitals cf. 85.11*

75.24   Public security, law and order activities

This class includes:
- administration and operation of regular and auxiliary police forces supported by public authorities and of port, border, coast guards and other special police forces including traffic regulation, alien registration, operation of police laboratories and maintenance of arrest records
- provision of supplies for domestic emergency use in case of peace-time disasters

This class excludes:
- *administration and operation of military armed forces cf. 75.22*

75.25   Fire service activities

This class includes:
- fire-fighting and fire-prevention:
  . administration and operation of regular and auxiliary fire brigades supported by public authorities in fire prevention, fire fighting, rescue of persons and animals, assistance in civic disasters, floods, road accidents, etc.

This class also includes:
- marine fireboat services

This class excludes:
- *forestry fire protection services cf. 02.02*
- *private firefighting and fire prevention services in factories cf. Section D*
- *firefighting and fire prevention services at airports cf. 63.23*
- *firefighting and fire prevention services at defence establishments cf. 75.22*

75.3   Compulsory social security activities

75.30   Compulsory social security activities

This class includes:
- administration of compulsory social security:
  . sickness, work-accident and unemployment insurance
  . retirement pensions

This class excludes:
- *non-compulsory social security cf. 66.0*
- *provision of welfare services and social work cf. 85.3*

SECTION M   EDUCATION

80   EDUCATION

This division includes:
- public as well as private education at any level or for any profession, oral or written as well as by radio and television

It includes both education by the different institutions in the regular school system at its different levels as well as adult education, literacy programmes, etc. For each level of initial education the classes include special education for physically or mentally handicapped pupils

The levels and stages referred to in the explanatory notes to this division are those of the International Standard Classification of Education (ISCED)

This division also includes:
- other education such as driving schools

This division excludes:
- *education primarily concerned with recreation such as bridge or golf cf. 92*

80.1   Primary education

80.10   Primary education

This class includes:
- pre-primary education (education preceding the first level)
- primary education (education at the first level)

This class excludes:
- *provision of literacy programmes for adults cf. 80.42/2*
- *child day-care activities cf. 85.32*

80.2   Secondary education

80.21   General secondary education

This class includes:
- general school education in the first stage of the secondary level corresponding more or less to the period of compulsory school attendance
- general school education in the second stage of the secondary level giving in principle access to higher education

Subject specialisation at this level often begins to have some influence even on the educational experience of those pursuing a general programme. Such programmes are designated to qualify students either for technical and vocational education or for higher education entrance without any special subject prerequisite

This class excludes:
- *adult education as defined in class 80.42*

80.22   Technical and vocational secondary education

This class includes:
- technical and vocational education (mainly that usually referred to as further education in the UK) below the level of higher education as defined in Class 80.30

Typically, the programmes emphasise a subject-matter specialisation and instruction of both theoretical background and practical skills generally associated with present or prospective employment. The aim of a programme can vary from preparation for a general field of employment to a very specific job

This class excludes:
- *technical and vocational education at post-secondary and university levels cf. 80.30*

80.3   Higher education

80.30   Higher education

A great variety of subject-matter programmes is offered at this level, some emphasising more theoretical instruction and some more practical instruction

80.30/1   Sub-degree level higher education

This subclass includes:
- education at the third level (post-secondary) of the type that leads to an award below first degree level or equivalent

This includes education for nursing and most education leading to professional qualifications

80.30/2   First-degree level higher education

This subclass includes:
- education of the type that leads to an award of first degree or equivalent either at University or other institute which provides such study

This subclass also includes:
- education leading to some professional qualifications
- study leading to a one year Post Graduate Certificate of Education (PGCE)

80.30/3   Post-graduate level higher education

This subclass includes:
- education that leads to a post-graduate degree or equivalent (e.g. Ph.D, M.A., M.Sc.) either in University or other institute which provides such study

80.4   Adult and other education

80.41   Driving school activities

This class also includes:
- tuition for flying certificates and ship licences other than for commercial certificates and permits

80.42   Adult and other education not elsewhere classified

80.42/1   Activities of private training providers

This subclass includes:
- the provision of training and enterprise by training and enterprise councils and local enterprise companies
- private companies advising on training, designing/delivering training courses or involved in the preparation of training materials for people in the Youth and Employment Training Schemes

80.42/2 Other adult and other education not elsewhere classified

This subclass includes:
- other adult education, i.e. education for people who are not in the regular school and university system. Instruction may be given in day or evening classes in schools or in special institutions providing for adults
- all instruction through radio and television broadcasts, or by correspondence
- education which is not definable by level

This subclass excludes:
- *higher education cf. 80.30*
- *activities of dance schools cf. 92.34*
- *instruction in sport and games cf. 92.62*

SECTION N   HEALTH AND SOCIAL WORK

85   HEALTH AND SOCIAL WORK

85.1   Human health activities

85.11   Hospital activities

This class includes:
- hospitalisation activities such as:
  . medical and surgical technical care activities such as diagnosis, treatment, operations, analyses, emergency activities, etc.
  . accommodation activities such as boarding, meals, etc.

This includes short or long term hospital activities of general and specialised hospitals, sanatoria, preventoria, medical nursing homes, asylums, mental hospital institutions, rehabilitation centres, leprosaria and other health institutions which have accommodation facilities, including military base and prison hospitals

The activities are chiefly directed to in-patients and carried out under the direct supervision of medical doctors

This class excludes:
- *health activities for military personnel in the field cf. 75.22*
- *private consultants' services to in-patients cf. 85.12*
- *dental activities without accommodation cf. 85.13*
- *ambulance and rescue activities cf. 85.14*

85.12   Medical practice activities

This class includes:
- medical consultation and treatment in the field of general and specialised medicine by general practitioners and medical specialists and surgeons

The activities can be carried out in private practice, group practices and in hospital out-patient clinics

Included are private consultants' activities in hospitals as well as activities carried-out in clinics such as those attached to firms, schools, homes for the aged, labour organisations and fraternal organisations as well as in patients' homes. Patients are usually ambulatory and can be referred to specialists by general practitioners

This class excludes:
- *para-medical activities such as those of midwives, nurses and physiotherapists cf. 85.14*

85.13   Dental practice activities

This class includes:
- dental practice activities of a general or specialised nature
- orthodontic activities

They can be carried out in private practice or in out-patient clinics including clinics attached to firms, schools, etc., as well as in operating rooms

This class excludes:
- *production of artificial teeth, denture and prostatic appliances by dental technicians who do not fit them cf. 33.10*

85.14   Other human health activities

This class includes:
- activities for human health not performed by hospitals or by medical doctors but by para-medical practitioners legally recognized to treat patients

This class may include activities of nurses, midwives, physiotherapists or others in the field of optometry, hydrotherapy, medical massage, occupational therapy, speech therapy, chiropody, homoepathy, chiropractice, acupuncture, etc.

These activities may be carried out in health clinics such as those attached to firms, schools, homes for the aged, labour organisations and fraternal organisations, in residential health facilities other than hospitals, as well as in own consulting rooms, patients' homes or elsewhere

This class also includes:
- activities of dental para-medical personnel such as dental therapists, school dental nurses and dental hygienists
- activities of medical laboratories
- activities of blood banks, sperm banks, transplant organ banks, etc.
- ambulance transport of patients

This class excludes:
- *production of artificial teeth, denture and prostatic appliances by dental technicians who do not fit them cf. 33.10*
- *testing activities in the field of food hygiene cf. 74.30*

85.2   Veterinary activities

85.20   Veterinary activities

This class includes:
- animal health care and control activities for farm animals
- animal health care and control activities for pet animals

These activities are carried out by qualified veterinarians in veterinary hospitals as well as when visiting farms, kennels or homes, in own consulting and surgery rooms or elsewhere

This class also includes:
- animal ambulance activities

This class excludes:
- *animal boarding activities without health care cf. 01.42*

85.3   Social work activities

85.31   Social work activities with accommodation

This class includes:
- activities provided on a round-the-clock basis directed to provide social assistance to children, the aged and special categories of persons with some limits on ability for self-care, but where medical treatment or education are not important elements:
  . activities provided by orphanages, children's boarding homes and hostels, residential nurseries, homes for the aged, homes for the physically or mentally handicapped including the blind, deaf and dumb, rehabilitation homes (without medical treatment) for people addicted to drugs or alcohol, homes for the homeless, institutions that take care of unmarried mothers and their children, etc.

This class excludes:
- *adoption activities cf. 85.32*
- *short term shelter activities for disaster victims cf. 85.32*

85.32 Social work activities without accommodation

This class includes:
- social, counselling, welfare, refugee, referral and similar activities, the services of which are delivered to individuals and families in their homes or elsewhere and carried out by government offices or by private organisations, disaster relief organisations and national or local self-help organisations and by specialists providing counselling services:
  - . welfare and guidance activities for children and adolescents
  - . adoption activities, activities for the prevention of cruelty to children and others
  - . eligibility determination in connection with welfare aid, rent supplements, etc.
  - . old age and sick visiting
  - . household budget counselling, marriage and family guidance
  - . guidance delivered to persons on parole or probation
  - . community and neighbourhood activities
  - . activities for disaster victims, refugees, immigrants, etc., including temporary or extended shelter for them
  - . vocational rehabilitation and habilitation activities for handicapped or unemployed persons provided that the education component is limited
- child day-care activities (creches), including day-care activities for the handicapped children
- day care activities for handicapped adults
- day facilities for homeless and other socially weak groups
- charitable activities like fund raising or other supporting activities aimed at social work

This class excludes:
- *activities typically included in compulsory social security schemes cf. 75.30*

SECTION O OTHER COMMUNITY, SOCIAL AND PERSONAL SERVICE ACTIVITIES

90   SEWAGE AND REFUSE DISPOSAL, SANITATION AND SIMILAR ACTIVITIES

90.0   Sewage and refuse disposal, sanitation and similar activities

90.00   Sewage and refuse disposal, sanitation and similar activities

This class includes:
- treatment of solid waste:
  . collection of garbage, trash, rubbish and waste
  . waste transportation:
    . removal of building debris
  . waste disposal by incineration or by other means:
    . waste reduction
    . dumping of refuse on land or in water, burial or ploughing-under of refuse
    . treatment and destruction of toxic waste including the cleaning of polluted soil
- treatment of liquid waste:
  . sewage removal, whether via drains, sewers or by other means, of human waste products and their treatment and disposal
  . disposal of sewage by dilution, screening and filtering, sedimentation, chemical precipitation, activated sludge treatment and other processes
  . maintenance of sewers and drains
  . emptying and cleaning of cesspools and septic tanks, servicing of chemical toilets
  . treatment of waste water from swimming pools and from industries

This class also includes:
- collection of refuse in litter boxes in public places
- outdoor sweeping and watering of streets, paths, parking lots, etc.
- snow and ice cleaning on highways and airport runways, including spreading of salt or sand, etc.

This class excludes:
- *pest control in connection with agriculture cf. 01.41*
- *recycling of refuse or waste cf. 37*
- *collection, purification and distribution of water cf. 41.00*
- *construction and repair of sewage systems cf. 45.21*
- *disinfecting and exterminating activities in buildings cf. 74.70*

91   ACTIVITIES OF MEMBERSHIP ORGANISATIONS NOT ELSEWHERE CLASSIFIED

91.1   Activities of business, employers and professional organisations

91.11   Activities of business and employers organisations

This class includes:
- activities of organisations whose members' interests centre on the development and prosperity of enterprises in a particular line of business or trade including farming, or on the economic growth and climate of a particular geographical area or political subdivision without regard for line of business. Included are activities of federations of such associations. The main services supplied involve dissemination of information, representation before government agencies, public relations and labour negotiations:
  . activities of chambers of commerce, guilds and similar organisations

91.12   Activities of professional organisations

This class includes:
- activities of organisations whose members' interests centre chiefly on a particular scholarly discipline or professional practice or technical field. Included are activities of associations of specialists engaged in scientific, academic or cultural activities such as writers, painters, performers of various kinds, journalists, etc. The main services supplied involve the dissemination of information, the establishment and supervision of standards of practice, representation before government agencies and public relations

This class also includes:
- activities of learned societies

91.2   Activities of trade unions

91.20   Activities of trade unions

This class includes:
- activities of associations whose members are employees interested chiefly in the representation of their views concerning the salary and work situation and in concerted action through organisation. This involves the activities of single plant unions, of unions composed of affiliated branches and of labour organisations composed of affiliated unions on the basis of trade, region, organisational structure or other criteria

91.3   Activities of other membership organisations

91.31   Activities of religious organisations

This class includes:
- activities of religious or similar organisations
- activities of organisations furnishing monastery and convent services

This class excludes:
- *education provided by such organisations cf. 80*
- *health activities by such organisations cf. 85.1*
- *social work activities by such organisations cf. 85.3*

91.32   Activities of political organisations

This class includes:
- activities of political organisations and auxiliary organisations such as young people's auxiliaries, associated with a political party. These organisations chiefly engage in influencing decision-taking in public governing bodies by placing members of the party or those sympathetic to the party in political office and involve the dissemination of information, public relations, fund raising, etc.

91.33   Activities of other membership organisations not elsewhere classified

This class includes:
- activities of organisations not directly affiliated to a political party but furthering a public cause or issue by means of public education, political influence, fund raising, etc.:
  . citizens initiative or protest movements
  . environmental and ecological movements
  . organisations supporting community and educational facilities not elsewhere classified
  . organisations for the protection and betterment of special groups, e.g. ethnic and minority groups
  . associations for patriotic purposes including war veterans' associations
- special interest groups such as touring clubs and automobile associations and consumer associations
- associations for the purpose of social acquaintanceship such as rotary clubs, lodges, etc.

- associations of youth, young persons' associations, student associations, clubs and fraternities, etc.
- associations for the pursuit of a cultural or recreational activity or hobby (other than sports or games), e.g.
  poetry, literature and book clubs, historical, gardening, film and photo, music and art, craft and collectors'
  clubs, social clubs, carnival clubs, etc.
- associations for the protection of animals

This class excludes:
- *activities of professional associations cf. 91.12*
- *associations for practising or promoting artistic activities cf. 92.31*

92   RECREATIONAL, CULTURAL AND SPORTING ACTIVITIES

92.1   Motion picture and video activities

92.11   Motion picture and video production

This class includes:
- production of theatrical and non-theatrical motion pictures whether on film or on video tape for direct
  projection in theatres or for broadcasting on television:
  . production in a motion picture studio, or in special laboratories for animated films or cartoons, of full-
    length films, documentaries, shorts, etc., for public entertainment, promotion, education or training
- supporting activities such as dubbing, etc.

This class excludes:
- *film duplicating as well as audio and video tape reproduction from master copies cf. 22.3*
- *film processing other than for the motion picture industry cf. 74.81*
- *agency activities cf. 74.84*
- *production of films or tapes normally produced in television studios cf. 92.20*
- *activities of own account actors, cartoonists, directors, consultants and other technical specialists cf. 92.31*

92.12   Motion picture and video distribution

This class includes:
- distribution of motion pictures and video tapes to other industries but not to the general public . This
  involves the sale or rental of movies or tapes to other industries, as well as activities allied to the distribution
  of films and video tapes such as film and tape booking, delivery, storage, etc.
- buying and selling of motion picture and video distribution rights

This class excludes:
- *film duplicating as well as audio and video tape reproduction from master copies cf. 22.3*
- *retail trade of tapes cf. 52.1, 52.4*
- *renting of tapes to the general public cf. 71.40/1*

92.13   Motion picture projection

This class includes:
- motion picture or video tape projection in cinemas, in the open air or in other projection facilities

This class also includes:
- activities of cine-clubs

92.2   Radio and television activities

92.20 Radio and television activities

This class includes:
- broadcasting of radio and television programmes
- production of radio and television programmes whether or not combined with broadcasting

The programmes produced and broadcast may be for entertainment, promotion, education or training or news dissemination. The production of programmes may result in a permanent tape which may be sold, rented or stored for broadcast or re-broadcast

This class excludes:
- *radio and television transmission via cable networks cf. 64.20*
- *radio and television transmission by relay or satellite cf. 64.20*
- *production of movies and video tapes which are normally produced in movie studios cf. 92.11*
- *press agencies cf. 92.40*

92.3 Other entertainment activities

92.31 Artistic and literary creation and interpretation

92.31/1 Live theatrical presentations

This subclass includes:
- production of live theatrical presentations, concerts and opera or dance productions and other stage productions:
  . activities of groups or companies, orchestras or bands
- activities of individual artists such as actors, directors, musicians, stage set designers and builders, etc.

92.31/2 Other artistic and literary creation and interpretation

This subclass includes:
- activities of individual artists such as authors, lecturers or speakers, sculptors, painters, cartoonists, engravers, etchers, etc.
- restoring works of art such as paintings

This subclass excludes:
- *restoring of furniture cf. 36.1*
- *restoring of buildings cf. 45*

92.32 Operation of arts facilities

This class includes:
- operation of concert and theatre halls and other arts facilities
- operation of ticket agencies including those operated by local tourist information centres
- activities of sound recording studios

This class excludes:
- *operation of cinemas cf. 92.13*

92.33 Fair and amusement park activities

This class also includes:
- operation of theme parks and preserved railways

92.34 Other entertainment activities not elsewhere classified

This class includes:
- production of entertainment not elsewhere classified:
  . activities of dancing schools and dance instructors
  . circus production
  . puppet shows, rodeos, activities of shooting galleries, etc.

This class excludes:
- other recreational activities cf. 92.72

92.4   News agency activities

92.40   News agency activities

This class includes:
- news syndicates and news agency activities furnishing news, pictures and features to the media
- activities of journalists and press photographers

92.5   Library, archives, museums and other cultural activities

92.51   Library and archives activities

This class includes:
- activities of libraries of all kinds, reading, listening and viewing rooms, public archives providing service to the general public or to a special clientele, such as students, scientists, staff, members:
  . organisation of a collection whether specialised or not
  . making catalogues
  . lending and storage of books, maps, periodicals, films, records, tapes, works of art, etc.
  . retrieval activities in order to comply with information requests, etc.

This class excludes:
- renting of video tapes cf. 71.40/1
- data base activities cf. 72.40

92.52   Museum activities and preservation of historical sites and buildings

This class includes:
- operation of museums of all kinds:
  . art museums, museums of jewellery, furniture, costumes, ceramics, silverware
  . natural history, science and technological museums, historical museums including military museums and historic houses
  . other specialised museums
  . open air museums
- preservation or reconstruction of historical sites and buildings

92.53   Botanical and zoological gardens and nature reserves activities

This class includes:
- operation of botanical and zoological gardens including children's zoos
- operation of nature reserves including wildlife preservation, etc.

92.6   Sporting activities

92.61   Operation of sports arenas and stadiums

This class includes:
- operation of the facilities for outdoor or indoor sports events:

. football stadiums
. swimming pools and stadiums
. golf courses
. boxing arenas
. winter sport arenas and stadiums
. field and track stadiums, etc.
. private and local authority owned leisure centres

The facilities may be enclosed or covered and may have provision for spectator seating or viewing

This class excludes:
- *rental of sporting equipment cf. 71.40/1*
- *park and beach activities cf. 92.72*

92.62 Other sporting activities

This class includes:
- organisation and operation of sports events, outdoor or indoor, for professionals or amateurs by
  organisations with or without own facilities:
   . football clubs, bowling clubs, swimming clubs, golf clubs, boxing, wrestling, health or body building clubs,
      winter sport clubs, chess, draughts, domino or card clubs, field and track clubs, shooting clubs
- activities related to promotion and production of sporting events
- activities of individual own-account sportsmen and athletes, judges, timekeepers, instructors, teachers,
  coaches, etc.
- activities of sport and game schools
- activities of racing stables, kennels and garages
- activities of riding academies
- activities of marinas
- hunting for sport or recreation
- related service activities

This class excludes:
- *rental of sporting equipment cf. 71.40/1*
- *park and beach activities cf. 92.72*

92.7 Other recreational activities

92.71 Gambling and betting activities

This class also includes:
- sale of lottery tickets

92.72 Other recreational activities not elsewhere classified

This class includes:
- activities related to recreation not classified elsewhere in this division:
   . activities of recreation parks and beaches including renting of facilities such as bath houses, lockers, chairs, etc.
   . activities related to recreational fishing
   . recreational transport facilities such as pedalos, riding stables, etc.
   . training of pet animals
   . motion picture, television and other theatrical casting activities

This class excludes:
- *personal theatrical or artistic agency activities cf. 74.84*
- *other entertainment activities, e.g. circus production or activities of dancing schools cf. 92.34*

93   OTHER SERVICE ACTIVITIES

93.0   Other service activities

93.01   Washing and dry cleaning of textile and fur products

This class includes:
- laundering and dry cleaning, pressing, etc., of all kinds of clothing (including fur) and textiles, provided by mechanical equipment, by hand or by self-service coin-operated machines whether for the general public or for industrial or commercial clients
- laundry collection and delivery
- carpet and rug shampooing and drapery and curtain cleaning
- renting of linens, work uniforms and related items by laundries

This class also includes:
- repair and minor alteration of garments or other textile articles when done in connection with cleaning

This class excludes:
- *repair and alteration of clothing, etc., as an independent activity cf. 52.74*
- *renting of clothing other than work uniforms, even if cleaning of these goods is an integral part of the activity cf. 71.40/2*

93.02   Hairdressing and other beauty treatment

This class includes:
- hair washing, trimming and cutting, setting, dyeing, tinting, waving, straightening and similar activities for men and women as well as shaving and beard trimming
- facial massage, manicure and pedicure, make-up, etc.

This class excludes:
- *manufacture of wigs cf. 36.63/2*

93.03   Funeral and related activities

This class includes:
- burial and incineration of human or animal corpses and related activities:
  . preparing the dead for burial or cremation and embalming and undertakers' services
  . providing burial or cremation services
  . rental of equipped space in funeral parlours
  . rental or sale of graves

This class excludes:
- *religious funeral service activities cf. 91.31*

93.04   Physical well-being activities

This class includes:
- activities related to physical well-being and comfort such as delivered by Turkish baths, sauna and steam baths, solariums, spas, reducing and slendering salons, massage salons, fitness centres, etc.

93.05   Other service activities not elsewhere classified

This class includes:
- astrological and spiritualists' activities
- social activities such as escort services, dating services, services of marriage bureaux
- genealogical organisations
- shoe shiners, porters, valet car parkers, etc.

SECTION P PRIVATE HOUSEHOLDS WITH EMPLOYED PERSONS

95 PRIVATE HOUSEHOLDS WITH EMPLOYED PERSONS

95.0 Private households with employed persons

95.00 Private households with employed persons

This class includes:
- activities of private households employing domestic personnel such as maids, cooks, waiters, valets, butlers, laundresses, gardeners, gatekeepers, stable-lads, chauffeurs, caretakers, governesses, baby-sitters, tutors, secretaries, etc.

SECTION Q   EXTRA-TERRITORIAL ORGANISATIONS AND BODIES

99   EXTRA-TERRITORIAL ORGANISATIONS AND BODIES

99.0   Extra-territorial organisations and bodies

99.00   Extra-territorial organisations and bodies

This class includes:
- activities of international organisations such as the United Nations and its specialised agencies, regional bodies, etc., European Communities, European Free Trade Association, Organisation for Economic Co-operation and Development, Customs Co-operation Council, Organisation of Oil Producing and Exporting Countries, International Monetary Fund, World Bank, etc.

This class also includes:
- activities of diplomatic and consular missions when being counted by the country of their location rather than being counted by the country they represent

This class excludes:
- *administration and operation of diplomatic and consular missions stationed abroad or at offices of international organisations cf. 75.21*

INDEX

A

electronic, manufacture of	33.20/1
non-electronic, manufacture of	33.20/2
air traffic control activities	63.23
air transport activities	63.23
air, measuring related to cleanness of	74.30
air-conditioning machines, manufacture of	29.23
aircraft	
agents involved in the sale of	51.14
certification of	74.30
manufacture of	35.30
airfield runways, construction of	45.23
airfields	
ground service activities on	63.23
mechanical and electro-mechanical signalling, safety or	
traffic control equipment for, manufacture of	35.20
airforce combat forces, administration, supervision and operation of	75.22
airline catering	55.52
airport activities	63.23
airport runways, snow and ice cleaning on	90.00
airscrews on aircraft, manufacture of	35.30
air transport equipment	
freight, without operator, renting of	71.23/2
passenger, without operator, renting of	71.23/1
airway terminals, operation of	63.23
albums, printing of	22.22
alcoholic and other beverages, wholesale of	51.34
alcoholic beverages	
distilled potable, manufacture of	15.91
retail sale of	52.25
algae, gathering of	05.01
alien registration, administration and operation of	75.24
alkalis, manufacture of	24.13
alkyd resins, manufacture of	24.16
aluminium	
alloys, production of	27.42
from alumina, production of	27.42
oxide (alumina), production of	27.42
products, casting of	27.53
semi-manufactures, production of	27.42
aluminous cement, manufacture of	26.51
ambulance transport of patients	85.14
ambulances, wholesale and retail sale of	50.10
ammonia, manufacture of	24.15
ammonium chloride, manufacture of	24.15
ammunition	
manufacture of	29.60
retail sale of	52.48/3
amphibious vehicles, manufacture of	34.10
amplifiers and sound amplifier sets, manufacture of	32.30
amusement park activities	92.33
analogue machines, manufacture of	30.02
andouillettes, production of	15.13/2
angle-dozers, manufacture of	29.52/2
anhydrite, mining of	14.12
aniline, wholesale of	51.55

animal ambulance activities	85.20
animal boarding and care	01.42
animal fats or oils, machinery for the extraction or preparation of, manufacture of	29.53
animal feed supplements, manufacture of	15.71
animal feeds, wholesale of	51.21
animal husbandry services	01.42
animal offal, processing of	15.11/2
animal oils and fats, non-edible, production of	15.41
animals	
farming of	01.2
hunting and trapping of	01.50
raising of	01.2
toy, manufacture of	36.50/2
animated films, production of	92.11
antiques, retail sale of	52.50
anti-freeze preparations, manufacture of	24.66
anti-knock preparations, manufacture of	24.66
anti-rust treatment of motor vehicles	50.20
anti-sera and other blood fractions, manufacture of	24.42/1
anti-sprouting products, manufacture of	24.20
anvils, manufacture of	28.62
apartment buildings	
buying and selling of	70.12
letting of	70.20/2
apparel production machinery, manufacture of	29.54
apparel	
plastic articles of, manufacture of	25.24
rubber, articles of, manufacture of	25.13
apples, production of	01.13
apricots, production of	01.13
arbitrators, activities of	74.11
arc lamps, manufacture of	31.50
architectural activities and related technical consultancy	74.20
archives activities	92.51
armoured doors, manufacture of	28.75
arms, manufacture of	29.60
army combat forces, administration, supervision and operation of	75.22
aromatic distilled waters, manufacture of	24.63
aromatic products, extracts of, manufacture of	24.63
art museums, operation of	92.52
art	
restoration of	92.31/2
works of, lending and storage of	92.51
articles of paper and paperboard n.e.c., manufacture of	21.25
articulated link chain, manufacture of	29.14
artificial flowers, fruit and foliage, manufacture of	36.63/2
artificial fur and articles thereof, manufacture of	18.30
artificial insemination, activities related to, (fee or contract basis)	01.42
artificial limbs, manufacture of	33.10
artificial respiration apparatus, manufacture of	33.10
artificial teeth, manufacture of	33.10
artillery material, manufacture of	29.60
arts facilities, operation of	92.32
asbestos, mining and quarrying of	14.50

ash dischargers, mechanical, manufacture of	29.21
asphalt, natural, mining and quarrying of	14.50
aspirator separators, manufacture of	29.53
asses, farming and breeding of	01.22
astrological activities	93.05
astronomical equipment, manufacture of	33.40/2
asylums, activities of	85.11
athletes, activities of	92.62
athletic equipment, manufacture of	36.40
atlases, printing of	22.22
audio/visual equipment, household, retail sale of	52.45
auditing activities	74.12
authors, activities of	92.31/2
automatic pilots	
electronic, manufacture of	33.20/1
non-electronic, manufacture of	33.20/2
automatic stop motions, manufacture of	29.54
automobile associations, activities of	91.33
automobiles, renting of	71.10
auxiliary plant for use with steam generators, manufacture of	28.30
aviation insurance	66.03
axles, manufacture of	34.30

B

babies garments, manufacture of	18.24/2
baby carriages	
manufacture of	36.63/2
retail sale of	52.48/3
baby foods, manufacture of	15.88
baby-sitters, employment of by private households	95.00
bacon, production of	15.13/1
badges, manufacture of	17.54/2
bags, plastic, manufacture of	25.22
bailiffs, activities of	74.11
bakery industry, machinery for, manufacture of	29.53
bakery ovens, non-electric, manufacture of	29.53
balancing machines	
electronic, manufacture of	33.20/1
non-electronic, manufacture of	33.20/2
bale breakers, manufacture of	29.54
ball bearings, manufacture of	29.14
ballistic missiles, manufacture of	29.60
balloons, manufacture of	35.30
balls, hard, soft and inflatable, manufacture of	36.40
balsams, gathering of	02.01
bandages, manufacture of	24.42/2
bands	
activities of	92.31/1
plaited metal, manufacture of	28.73
bank holding companies, activities of	65.23/4
banking, central	65.11
banking institutions in Channel Islands and Isle of Man, not in UK	
banking sector, activities of	65.22/4
banks, other than central banks, monetary intermediation of	65.12/1
banknote dispensers, automatic, manufacture of	30.01

banners, manufacture of	17.40/2
banquet catering	55.52
barbed wire, manufacture of	28.73
barges, construction of	35.11
barges, transport by towing or pushing of	61.10/2
barium sulphate, natural, mining of	14.30
barley, growing of	01.11
barometers	
electronic, manufacture of	33.20/1
non-electronic, manufacture of	33.20/2
barrels, wooden, manufacture of	20.40
bars, activities of	55.40/2
bas- and haut-reliefs, concrete, plaster, cement or	
artificial stone, manufacture of	26.66
base metal articles, manufacture of	28.75
basil, growing of	01.13
basins for swimming and paddling pools, manufacture of	36.40
basins, fibre-cement, manufacture of	26.65
basket ware, manufacture of	20.52
bast fibres, preparatory operations and spinning of	17.17
bath salts, manufacture of	24.52
baths	
metal, manufacture of	28.75
plastic, manufacture of	25.23/2
bats, manufacture of	36.40
bay, growing of	01.13
bayonets, manufacture of	28.75
beaches, activities of, including renting of facilities	92.72
beams, manufacture of	20.30
beans, growing of	01.12
beard trimming	93.02
beards, false, manufacture of	36.63/2
bearing housings, manufacture of	29.14
bearings, manufacture of	29.14
beauty and make-up preparations, manufacture of	24.52
beauty treatment activities	93.02
bed and breakfast, provision of, short-stay lodging facilities	55.2
bed linen, manufacture of	17.40/3
bedspreads, manufacture of	17.40/3
bee keeping	01.25
bee-keeping machinery, manufacture of	29.32
beer halls, activities of	55.40/2
beer, manufacture of	15.96
beets, thinning of, (fee or contract basis)	01.41
belting, rubber, manufacture of	25.13
belts, clothing accessories, manufacture of	18.24/2
berries, production of	01.13
berthing activities	63.22
beryllium products, casting of	27.53
betting activities	92.71
beverage processing machinery, manufacture of	29.53
beverages	
agents involved in the sale of	51.17
bottling of	74.82
fermented, fruit, manufacture of	15.94/2

non-distilled fermented, manufacture of	15.95
non-specialised wholesale of	51.39
retail sale of	52.25
bicycle parkings, operation of	63.21
bicycles and their parts and accessories, wholesale of	51.47/2
bicycles	
non-motorised, and parts and accessories, manufacture of	35.42
renting of	71.40/1
repair of	52.74
retail sale of	52.48/3
bill collecting	74.84
billiards, manufacture of	36.50/1
binoculars, manufacture of	33.40/2
bird skins, production of	01.50
biscuits, manufacture of	15.82
bitumen spreaders, manufacture of	29.52/3
bitumen, mining and quarrying of	14.50
bituminous shale and sand, extraction of	11.10
blackboard chalk, machinery for producing, manufacture of	29.56
blacksmiths' tools, manufacture of	28.62
blankets including travelling rugs, manufacture of	17.40/3
blankets, electric, manufacture of	29.71
blasting	45.11
blenders, manufacture of	
domestic	29.71
non-domestic	29.53
blinds	
canvas, manufacture of	17.40/2
plastic, manufacture of	25.23/2
soft furnishing, manufacture of	17.40/1
blockboard, manufacture of	20.20
blocks, plastic, manufacture of	25.21
blood banks, activities of	85.14
blood, processing of	24.41
blouses, made-up, women's, manufacture of	18.23/2
boards	
concrete, manufacture of	26.61
plaster, manufacture of	26.62
boats with crew, rental of, for passenger conveyance	61.10/1
boats with crew, rental of, for transport of freight	61.10/2
boats	
commercial, freight, without operator, renting of	71.22/2
commercial, passenger, without operator, renting of	71.22/1
excursion, cruise or sightseeing, operation of	61.10/1
pleasure and sporting, building and repairing of	35.12
retail sale of	52.48/3
bobbins	
paper and paperboard, manufacture of	21.25
wooden, manufacture of	20.51
bodies (coachwork) for motor vehicles, manufacture of	34.20/1
body building clubs, organisation and operation of	92.62
bodyguard activities	74.60
bodywork repair of motor vehicles	50.20
bogies, manufacture of	35.20
boiled ham, production of	15.13/1

manufacture of	34.10
business activities n.e.c.	74.84
business consultancy activities	74.14
business forms	
finishing of	22.23
printing of	22.22
business organisations, activities of	91.11
butane, production of	23.20/1
butlers, employment of by private households	95.00
butter churns, manufacture of	29.53
butter workers, manufacture of	29.53
butter, production of	15.51/2
buttons, manufacture of	36.63/2

C

cabbages, growing of	01.12
cable-drums, wooden, manufacture of	20.40
cable-ways, aerial, operation of	60.21/2
cabs for motor vehicles, manufacture of	34.20/1
cafeteria meals	
with alcoholic drinks, sale of	55.30/1
without alcoholic drinks, sale of	55.30/2
cake depositing machines, manufacture of	29.53
cakes	
manufacture of	15.81
preserved, manufacture of	15.82
retail sale of	52.24
calculating instruments, manufacture of	33.20/2
calculating machines, manufacture of	30.01
calendars	
finishing of	22.23
printing of	22.22
calendering or other rolling machines, manufacture of	29.24
calliopes, manufacture of	36.30
callipers, manufacture of	33.20/2
cam shafts, manufacture of	29.14
camel back strips for retreading tyres, manufacture of	25.11
cameras	
manufacture of	33.40/3
television, manufacture of	32.20/2
campers, (transport) renting of	71.21/1
camping goods	
manufacture of	17.40/2
retail sale of	52.48/3
camping sites	55.22
camping space and camping facilities	55.2
camping vehicles, wholesale and retail sale of	50.10
canals, transport of freight via	61.20/2
canals, transport of passengers via	61.20/1
candles, manufacture of	36.63/2
canoes, building of	35.12
cans for food products, manufacture of	28.72
cans, steel, manufacture of,	28.71
canteens, factory or office, activities of	55.51
canvas goods, made-up, manufacture of	17.40/2

canvas prepared for use by painters, manufacture of		17.54/3
capers, growing of		01.12
capstans, manufacture of		29.22
caravan sites		55.22
caravan trailers, manufacture of		34.20/3
caravans		
	renting of	71.21/1
	wholesale and retail sale of	50.10
	winter storage of	63.21
carbon or graphite electrodes, manufacture of		31.62
carbon paper ready for use, manufacture of		21.23
carbonate (barytes and witherite), mining of		14.30
carboys, plastic, manufacture of		25.22
car covers, loose, manufacture of		17.40/2
card clubs, organisation and operation of		92.62
carders, manufacture of		29.54
cardigans, manufacture of		17.72
cards for automatic mechanical instruments, manufacture of		36.30
caretakers, employment of by private households		95.00
cargo handling		63.11
cargo ships, building of		35.11
carpet shampooing		93.01
carpets		
	laying	45.43
	other than woven or tufted, manufacture of	17.51/3
	tufted, manufacture of	17.51/2
	wholesale of	51.47/2
	woven, manufacture of	17.51/1
carrots, growing of		01.12
cars with operator, rental of		60.22
cars		
	manufacture of	34.10
	self-drive private, renting of	71.10
cartographic and spatial information activities		74.20
cartoonists, activities of		92.31/2
cartoon films, production of		92.11
casein, production of		15.51/3
cases, plastic, manufacture of		25.22
cash registers, manufacture of		30.01
cassette players, manufacture of		32.30
cassette-type recorders, manufacture of		32.30
cassettes, audio/visual, retail sale of		52.45
cast iron products, malleable, casting of		27.51
cast iron tubes and fittings, manufacture of		27.21
casting for motion pictures, television and other theatrical		92.72
casting machines, manufacture of		29.51
castings		
	heavy metal and precious metal, casting of	27.54
	iron, grey, casting of	27.51
	light metals, casting of	27.53
	steel, casting of	27.52
catalogues for advertising, printing of		22.22
catalysts, manufacture of		24.66
catalyzers, manufacture of		34.30
catering		55.52

cattle, farming of		01.21
caulking compounds and similar non-refractory filling or surfacing		
preparations, manufacture of		24.30/3
caviar, production of		15.20/2
caviar substitutes, production of		15.20/2
CD players, manufacture of		32.30
CDs		
	retail sale of	52.45
	wholesale of	51.43
ceiling coverings, plastic, manufacture of		25.23/2
ceilings, installation of		45.42
cellulose fibre-cement, articles of, manufacture of		26.65
cellulose wadding products, manufacture of		21.22
cellulose		
	manufacture of	24.16
	webs of, manufacture of	21.12
cement		
	articles of, for use in construction, manufacture of	26.61
	manufacture of	26.51
	other articles of, manufacture of	26.66
	prepared additives for, manufacture of	24.66
cemeteries, activities of		93.03
central heating radiators and boilers, manufacture of		28.22
centrifugal clothes dryers, manufacture of		29.56
centrifuges, manufacture of		29.24
ceramic goods, refractory, manufacture of		26.26
ceramic pastes, shaped, machinery for producing, manufacture of		29.56
ceramic products		
	other manufacture of	26.25
	technical, manufacture of	26.24
cereal breakfast foods, manufacture of		15.61/2
cereal grains		
	growing of	01.11
	production of flour, groats, meal or pellets	15.61/1
cesspools, emptying and cleaning of		90.00
chain, manufacture of		28.74
chainsaw blades, manufacture of		28.62
chairs, manufacture of		36.11
chalets, short-stay lodging in		55.23
chalk, mining of		14.12
chambers of commerce, activities of		91.11
chamois dressed leather, manufacture of		19.10
charcoal, manufacture of		24.14
charitable activities		85.32
charts, publishing of		22.11
chassis fitted with engines, manufacture of		34.10
chauffeurs, employment of by private households		95.00
checking instruments and appliances		
	electronic, manufacture of	33.20/1
	non-electronic, manufacture of	33.20/2
check traders, activities of		65.22/1
cheese, production of		15.51/2
cheese-making machines, manufacture of		29.53
chemical contraceptive products, manufacture of		24.42/1
chemical elements except metals, manufacture of		24.13

chemical minerals, mining of	14.30
chemical preparations for photographic uses, manufacture of	24.64
chemical products n.e.c., manufacture of	24.66
chemical products, wholesale of	51.55
chemical toilets, servicing of	90.00
chemically pure sugars, manufacture of	24.41
chemicals, industrial, agents involved in the sale of	51.12
chemists, dispensing	52.31
chenille fabrics, manufacture of	17.21
cheques, printing of	22.22
cherries, production of	01.13
chervil, growing of	01.12
chess clubs, organisation and operation of	92.62
chess, electronic, manufacture of	36.50/2
chewing gum, manufacture of	15.84/2
chewing tobacco, manufacture of	16.00
child day-care activities	85.32
children's boarding homes and hostels, activities provided by	85.31
children's zoos, operation of	92.53
chimney cleaning	74.70
chimney-pots, manufacture of	26.40
chimneys, erection of	45.25
china	
retail sale of	52.44
wholesale of	51.44
chocolate	
manufacture of	15.84/1
wholesale of	51.36
Christmas trees, growing of	02.01
chrome	
mining and preparation of	13.20
production of	27.45
cider, manufacture of	15.94/1
cigarette lighters, manufacture of	36.63/2
cigarettes, manufacture of	16.00
cigars, manufacture of	16.00
cine-clubs, activities of	92.13
cinematographic equipment, manufacture of	33.40/3
circular sawblades, manufacture of	28.62
circus production	92.34
civil defence forces, administration, operation and support of	75.22
civil engineering construction	45.21
civil engineering machinery and equipment without operator, renting of	71.32
civil engineering structures, painting of	45.44
clamps, manufacture of	28.62
clasps, manufacture of	28.75
clay building materials, non-refractory, manufacture of	26.40
clays for brick, pipe and tile making, extraction of	14.22
clays, mining of	14.22
cleaning and polishing preparations, manufacture of	24.51/2
cleaning materials, wholesale of	51.44
cleansing tissues, manufacture of	21.22
clinics, private consultants activities in	85.12
clinkers and hydraulic cements, manufacture of	26.51

clock glasses, manufacture of	26.15
clocks	
manufacture of	33.50
repair of	52.73
retail sale of	52.48/3
wholesale of	51.47/2
cloth made of wire, manufacture of	28.73
clothes brushes, manufacture of	36.62
clothes hangers, manufacture of	20.51
clothing accessories	
manufacture of	18.24/2
retail sale of	52.42
clothing including sports clothes, wholesale of	51.42
clothing	
agents involved in the sale of	51.16
asbestos, manufacture of	26.82/1
retail sale of	52.42
repair and alteration of	52.74
washing and dry cleaning of	93.01
clubs	
activities of	91.33
manufacture of	36.40
clutches, for motor vehicles, manufacture of	34.30
clutches, other than for motor vehicles, manufacture of	29.14
co-operative buying associations, activities of	51
coach services, non-scheduled	60.23
coaches, manufacture of	34.10
coaches of sport, activities of	92.62
coal, hard	
deep mined, cleaning, sizing, grading, pulverising of	10.10/1
opencast, cleaning, sizing, grading, pulverising of	10.10/2
recovery of from tips	10.10/2
surface mining of	10.10/2
underground mining of	10.10/1
retail sale of	52.48/3
coal tar, distillation of	24.14
coast guards, administration and operation of	75.24
coastal water transport	61.10
coat and hat racks, manufacture of	20.51
coats	
men's, manufacture of	18.22/1
women's, manufacture of	18.22/2
cobalt, mining and preparation of	13.20
cocoa	
products, manufacture of	15.84/1
wholesale of	51.37
coffee or tea makers, electric, manufacture of	29.71
coffee substitutes, manufacture of	15.86/2
coffee	
processing of	15.86/2
products, production of	15.86/2
wholesale of	51.37
coffer-dams, construction of	35.11
coin-operated games, manufacture of	36.50/1
coins	

copper, production of	27.44
copper, mining and preparation of	13.20
coppice and pulpwood, growing of	02.01
cops	
paper and paperboard, manufacture of	21.25
wooden, manufacture of	20.51
copyrights, preparation of	74.11
cord, asbestos, manufacture of	26.82/1
cordage, manufacture of	17.52
core sampling	45.12
coriander, growing of	01.13
cork goods, retail sale of	52.44
cork	
articles of natural agglomerated, manufacture of	20.52
processing	20.52
wholesale of goods of	51.47/2
corn oil, manufacture of	15.62
corporate hospitality catering	55.52
corpses, human or animal, burial and incineration of	93.03
corrective glasses, manufacture of	33.40/1
corrugated paper and paperboard, manufacture of	21.21/1
corrugated sheets, fibre-cement, manufacture of	26.65
corsets, women's manufacture of	18.23/2
corundum, artificial, manufacture of	26.81
cosmetics	
retail sale of	52.33
wholesale of	51.45
cost accounting programmes, design of	74.14
costumes, renting of	71.40/1
cottages	
in holiday centres and holiday villages, provision of short-stay lodging in	55.23/1
other than in holiday centres and holiday villages, provision of short-stay lodging in	55.23/2
cotton gins, manufacture of	29.54
cotton seed oil, production of	15.41
cotton spreaders, manufacture of	29.54
cotton-type fabrics, manufacture of	17.21
cotton-type fibres, preparation and spinning of	17.11
cotton-type weaving	17.21
cotton-type yarn, manufacture of	17.11
counters for shops, manufacture of	36.12
coupling devices, manufacture of	35.20
courgettes, growing of	01.12
courier activities other than national post activities	64.12
couscous, manufacture of	15.85
coverings, rubber roller, manufacture of	25.13
cows' milk, production of	01.21
craftwork, retail sale of	52.48/3
crane vans, manufacture of	35.20
cranes, manufacture of	29.22
crank shafts, manufacture of	29.14
cranks, manufacture of	29.14
crates, wooden, manufacture of	20.40
cravats, manufacture of	18.24/2
cream separators, manufacture of	29.53

cream, production of	15.51/1
credit card activities	65
credit granting	65.22
credit rating	74.84
cremation services	93.03
creped paper, manufacture of	21.12
cress, growing of	01.12
crinkled paper, manufacture of	21.12
crocheted fabrics, manufacture of	17.60
crockery, retail sale of	52.44
cromite, articles containing, manufacture of	26.26
crop growing in combination with farming of livestock	01.30
crop spraying, (fee or contract basis)	01.41
crops	
growing of	01.11
harvesting and preparation of	01.41
treatment of, (fee or contract basis)	01.41
cross-talk meters, manufacture of	33.20/1
crossbows, manufacture of	36.40
crucibles, refractory ceramic, manufacture of	26.26
crude coal tar, production of	23.10
crude gaseous hydrocarbon (natural gas), production of	11.10
crude glycerol, manufacture of	24.51/1
crude petroleum, extraction of	11.10
crude vegetable oils, production of	15.41
crustacean and mollusc products, production of	15.20/2
crustaceans	
preservation of, by freezing	15.20/1
preservation of, other than by freezing	15.20/2
retail sale of	52.23
wholesale distribution of	51.38
crutches, manufacture of	33.10
crystal articles, manufacture of	26.13
cucumbers, growing of	01.12
culture programmes, public administration of	75.12
cupboards, kitchen, manufacture of	36.13
cups, paper, manufacture of	21.22
curd, production of	15.51/2
curlers, electric, manufacture of	29.71
current checking instruments, manufacture of	33.20/1
curtain cleaning	93.01
curtains	
manufacture of	17.40/1
retail sale of	52.44
cushions, manufacture of	17.40/1
custom tailoring	
men's	18.22/1
women's	18.22/2
customs administration	75.11
customs agents, activities of	63.40
Customs Co-operations Council, activities of	99.00
cutlasses, manufacture of	28.75
cutlery	
manufacture of	28.61
retail sale of	52.44

cutting blades for machines or for mechanical appliances, manufacture of	28.62
cutting machinery, manufacture of	29.52/1
cycles fitted with an auxiliary engine, manufacture of	35.41
cyclic alcohols, manufacture of	24.14
cyclic hydrocarbons, saturated and unsaturated, manufacture of	24.14
cyclone separators, manufacture of	29.53

D

dairy farming	01.21
dairy industry machinery, manufacture of	29.53
dairy produce, wholesale of	51.33
dairy products, retail sale of	52.27
damage evaluators, activities of	67.20
dams, construction of	45.24
dance productions	92.31/1
dancing schools and dance instructors, activities of	92.34
data base activities	72.40
data on discs and tapes, reproduction from master copies of	22.33
data processing	72.30
data, transmission of via cables, broadcasting, relay or satellite	64.20
date stamps, manufacture of	36.63/1
dating services	93.05
day care activities for the handicapped	85.32
DC motors or generators, manufacture of	31.10
dead, preparing for burial or cremation	93.03
dealing in financial markets on behalf of others (e.g. stock broking) and related activities other than fund management	67.12/2
deck arresters, aircraft, manufacture of	35.30
deeds, preparation of	74.11
defence activities	75.22
defrosters, electrical, manufacture of	31.61
demisters, electrical, manufacture of	31.61
demolition equipment with operator, renting of	45.50
dental drill engines, manufacture of	33.10
dental fillings, manufacture of	24.42/2
dental practice activities	85.13
dentifrices, manufacture of	24.52
dentist's chairs, manufacture of	33.10
denture fixative preparations, manufacture of	24.52
deodorants, manufacture of	24.52
deodorisers, manufacture of	24.51/2
department stores, activities of	52.12
depilatories, manufacture of	24.52
derrick erection in situ	11.20
derricks, manufacture of	29.22
detergents, manufacture of	24.51/1
detonators, electrical, manufacture of	31.62
diagnostic or laboratory reagents, composite, manufacture of	24.66
diamonds, working of	36.22
diaries, printing of	22.22
dictionaries, publishing of	22.11
die-stamping machines, manufacture of	29.40
dies, interchangeable tools for, manufacture of	28.62
dietetic food, manufacture of	15.88

digital data related to printing, preparation of	22.25
digital machines, manufacture of	30.02
dining car activities of railway companies and other passenger transport facilities	55.30/1
dining halls, university, activities of	55.51
diodes, manufacture of	32.10
diplomatic missions, activities of	99.00
diplomatic offices stationed abroad, administration and operation of	75.21
direct mailing	74.83
directors, activities of	92.31/1
dirigibles, manufacture of	35.30
discharge lamps, manufacture of	33.40/3
discount houses, monetary intermediation of	65.12/1
discs for automatic mechanical instruments, manufacture of	36.30
dish-cloths and similar articles, manufacture of	17.40/3
dish-washing preparations, manufacture of	24.51/1
dishes, paper, manufacture of	21.22
dishwashers, manufacture of	29.71
disinfectants, manufacture of	24.20
display cases for shops, manufacture of	36.12
distilling or rectifying plant, manufacture of	29.24
do-it-yourself machinery and equipment, renting of	71.40/1
do-it-yourself material and equipment, retail sale of	52.46
documents of title, printing of	22.22
Dobbies, manufacture of	29.54
dolls and doll garments and accessories, manufacture of	36.50/2
dolomite, articles containing, manufacture of	26.26
domestic appliances	
electric, manufacture of	29.71
non-electric, manufacture of	29.72
domino clubs, organisation and operation of	92.62
door hardware for buildings, furniture, vehicles, manufacture of	28.63
door-frames, wooden, installation of	45.42
door-to-door sales persons, retail sale by	52.63
doors for motor vehicles, manufacture of	34.30
doors on aircraft, manufacture of	35.30
doors	
manufacture of	20.30
metal, manufacture of	28.12
plastic, manufacture of	25.23/2
dough mixers, manufacture of	29.53
dough-dividers, manufacture of	29.53
down, production of	15.12
drains, maintenance of	90.00
drapery cleaning	93.01
draughts clubs, organisation and operation of	92.62
draw-benches, manufacture of	29.40
drawing instruments, manufacture of	33.20/2
dredging	45.24
dressers, kitchen, manufacture of	36.13
dresses, women's, manufacture of	18.22/2
dressing gowns	
men's, manufacture of	18.23/1
women's, manufacture of	18.23/2
dressings, manufacture of	24.42/2

dried leguminous vegetables, growing of	01.11
dried meat, production of	15.13/2
dried milk, production of	15.51/3
drilling platforms, construction of	35.11
drills	
interchangeable tools for, manufacture of	28.62
manufacture of	29.40
drinking glasses, manufacture of	26.13
driving elements, manufacture of	29.14
driving school activities	80.41
droving services	01.42
drums and similar packings of wood, manufacture of	20.40
drums, steel, manufacture of	28.71
dry bakery products, manufacture of	15.82
dry-cleaning machines, manufacture of	29.54
dryers	
agricultural, manufacture of	29.53
electric, manufacture of	29.71
wood, paper pulp, paper or paperboard, manufacture of	29.56
drying machines, laundry-type, manufacture of	29.54
dumpers for off road use, manufacture of	34.10
dummies, reprographic, production of	22.25
duplicating machines	
renting and operating leasing of	71.33
printing by	22.22
duplicator stencils ready for use, manufacture of	21.23
dust-cloths, manufacture of	17.40/3
dusters, feather, manufacture of	36.62
duty/tax collection on goods	75.11
dwellings	
buying and selling of	70.12
letting of	70.20/2
dyes and pigments from any source in basic form or	
as concentrate, manufacture of	24.12
dykes, construction of	45.24
dynamos for cycles, manufacture of	31.61

E

earphones, manufacture of	32.30
earth colours and fluorspar, mining of	14.30
earth moving	45.11
earth moving machinery, manufacture of	29.52/2
ecological movements, activities of	91.33
economic sectors, public administration and regulation of	75.13
economizers, manufacture of	28.30
edible fats of animal origin, rendering of	15.11/2
edible nuts, flour or meal of, production of	15.61/2
edible seaweeds, growing of	05.02
education programmes, public administration of	75.12
education	
higher, sub degree level	80.30/1
higher, first degree level	80.30/2
higher, post-graduate level	80.30/3
other adult and other, n.e.c.	80.42/2
primary and pre-primary	80.10

secondary level	80.21
technical and vocational	80.22
eel grass, gathering of	02.01
egg-plants, growing of	01.12
eggs and egg products, wholesale of	51.33
eggs	
machines for cleaning, sorting or grading, manufacture of	29.32
powdered or reconstituted, manufacture of	15.89/2
production of	01.24
egg-trays and other moulded pulp packaging products,	
manufacture of	21.25
eiderdowns, manufacture of	17.40/3
electric accumulators including parts thereof, manufacture of	31.40
electric control or distribution boards, manufacture of	31.20
electric light fittings, manufacture of	31.50
electric or electronic lamps, machinery for producing, manufacture of	29.56
electrical apparatus for switching or protecting electrical	
circuits, manufacture of	31.20
electrical appliances, renting of	71.40/2
electrical capacitors (or condensers), manufacture of	32.10
electrical conduit tubing, manufacture of	31.62
electrical equipment for engines and vehicles, manufacture of	31.61
electrical heating systems, installation of	45.31
electrical household goods, repair of	52.72
electrical insulators and insulating fittings, manufacture of	31.62
electrical wiring and fittings, installation of	45.31
electricity distribution and control apparatus, manufacture of	31.20
electricity	
generation of	40.10/1
transmission, distribution and supply of	40.10/2
electro-cardiographs, manufacture of	33.10
electro-diagnostic apparatus, manufacture of	33.10
electro-thermic appliances, domestic, manufacture of	29.71
electromagnets, manufacture of	31.62
electronic components	
manufacture of	32.10
wholesale of	51.65
electronic games, domestic, manufacture of	36.50/2
electronic integrated circuits, manufacture of	32.10
electronic micro-assemblies of moulded module, micromodule or	
similar types, manufacture of	32.10
elemental gases, manufacture of	24.11
elevated highways, construction of	45.21
elevators	
continuous-action for underground use, manufacture of	29.52/1
manufacture of	29.22
embossers, printing by	22.22
embossing labels, hand-operated devices for, manufacture of	36.63/1
embroidery making materials, retail sale of	52.41
employers organisations, activities of	91.11
employment of by private households	
baby-sitters	95.00
butlers	95.00
chauffeurs	95.00
cooks	95.00

gatekeepers	95.00
governesses	95.00
maids	95.00
secretaries	95.00
tutors	95.00
valets	95.00
waiters	95.00
enamels, manufacture of	24.30/1
encyclopaedias, publishing of	22.11
endoscopes, manufacture of	33.10
engineering, research and experimental development on	73.10
engineering activities and related technical consultancy	74.20
engines	
motorcycle, manufacture of	35.41
aircraft, manufacture of	35.30
renting and operating leasing of	71.34
vehicle, motor, manufacture of	34.10
engravers, activities of	92.31/2
enlargers, manufacture of	33.40/3
ensembles, clothing, manufacture of	18.22/2
entertainment activities n.e.c.	92.34
envelopes and letter-cards, manufacture of	21.23
environment programmes, public administration of	75.12
environmental movements, activities of	91.33
epoxide resins, manufacture of	24.16
escalators	
installation of	45.31
maintenance of	29.22
manufacture of	29.22
escort services	93.05
essential oils, manufacture of	24.63
etchers, activities of	92.31/2
ethane, production of	23.20/1
ethyl alcohol, production of	15.92
ethylene, manufacture of	24.16
European Communities, activities of	99.00
European Free Trade Association, activities of	99.00
examiners (legal), activities of	74.11
excavation	45.11
exchanges, telephone, manufacture of	32.20/1
exfoliated vermiculite, manufacture of	26.82/2
exhaust pipes, manufacture of	34.30
exhaust units, cleaning of	74.70
exhaust valves of internal combustion engines, manufacture of	29.11
exhibition halls, letting of	70.20/1
expanded clay, manufacture of	26.82/2
explosives, manufacture of	24.61
exporters, activities of	51
extruders, rubber or plastics, manufacture of	29.56
eyebrows, false, manufacture of	36.63/2

F

fabric processing machinery, manufacture of	29.54
fabric, asbestos, manufacture of	26.82/1
fabrics coated with gum or amylaceous substances, manufacture of	17.54/3

fabrics impregnated, coated, covered or laminated with plastics, manufacture of	17.54/3
fabrics	
retail sale of	52.41
rubberised, manufacture of	25.13
wholesale of	51.41
facial massage	93.02
factice, manufacture of	24.17
factoring debt	65.22/2
fairground activities	92.33
fairground amusements, manufacture of	36.63/2
fairground organs, manufacture of	36.30
fans, household type electric, manufacture of	29.71
fans, non-domestic, manufacture of	29.23
farinaceous products, manufacture of	15.85
farmhouses, provision of short-stay lodging in	55.23/3
fashion design related to textiles	74.84
fasteners, manufacture of	28.74
fats, edible, manufacture of	15.43
fax machines, manufacture of	32.20/1
feathers, production of	15.12
feeders, manufacture of	29.53
feeds, prepared, for farm animals,	
manufacture of	15.71
wholesale of	51.21
feldspar, mining and quarrying of	14.50
fellmongery	15.11/3
felt or nonwovens, machines for producing or finishing,	
manufacture of	29.54
felt	
asbestos, manufacture of	26.82/1
manufacture of	17.54/3
fencing, wire, manufacture of	28.73
fennel, growing of	01.12
ferries, operation of	61.10/1
ferro alloys (ECSC), manufacture of	27.10
ferro-alloys except high carbon ferro-manganese, production of	27.35
ferro-phosphor, production of	27.35
ferrous products by reduction of iron ore, production of	27.10
ferry-boats, building of	35.11
fertilizer minerals, mining of	14.30
fertilizers	
manufacture of	24.15
retail sale of	52.48/3
wholesale of	51.55
fibre board, manufacture of	20.20
fibre cement, manufacture of	26.65
field and track clubs, organisation and operation of	92.62
field and track stadiums, operation of	92.61
fields, preparation of, (fee or contract basis)	01.41
filament tow, manufacture of	24.70
film processing	74.81
film, plastic, manufacture of	25.21
films	
lending and storage of	92.51

flashlight apparatus, manufacture of	33.40/3
flat glass, retail sale of	52.46
flat ware, base metal, manufacture of	28.75
flats	
in holiday centres and holiday villages, provision of short-stay lodging in	55.23/1
other than in holiday centres and holiday villages, provision of short-stay lodging in	55.23/2
flavourings, wholesale of	51.55
flax-type yarns, manufacture of	17.14
flax-type fibres, preparation and spinning of	17.14
flexographic printing	22.22
flights, regular charter	62.20
floating docks, construction of	35.11
floating landing stages, construction of	35.11
floating tanks, construction of	35.11
floor covering	45.43
floor coverings	
hard surface, manufacture of	36.63/2
plastic, manufacture of	25.23/1
retail sale of	52.48/1
rubber, manufacture of	25.13
wholesale of	51.47/2
floor polishers, electric, manufacture of	29.71
floor sweepers, hand operated mechanical, manufacture of	36.62
flooring blocks in baked clay, manufacture of	26.40
flour	
confectionery, retail sale of	52.24
of cereal grains, production of	15.61/1
of dried leguminous vegetables, production of	15.61/2
flours and meals of meat, production of	15.11/2
fluorspar, mining of	14.30
flow meters	
electronic, manufacture of	33.20/1
non-electronic, manufacture of	33.20/2
flowerpots, concrete, plaster, cement or artificial stone, manufacture of	26.66
flowers	
growing of	01.12
retail sale of	52.48/3
wholesale of	51.22
fluid power equipment, manufacture of	29.12/2
fluorescent brightening agents, manufacture of	24.12
flushing cisterns, plastic, manufacture of	25.23/2
flying certificates, tuition for	80.41
flying schools for commercial airline pilots, activities of	63.23
flywheels, manufacture of	29.14
fodder preparing equipment, manufacture of	29.32
fog-signalling apparatus, manufacture of	35.20
foil, plastic, manufacture of	25.21
folding paperboard containers, manufacture of	21.21/2
follow-up milk, manufacture of	15.88
food hygiene, testing activities in the field of	74.30
food in hotels and restaurants, manufacture of machinery for the preparation of	29.53
food processing machinery, manufacture of	29.53

food

agents involved in the sale of	51.17
bottling and packaging of	74.82
for pet animals, wholesale of	51.38
non-specialised wholesale of	51.39

foods for particular nutritional uses, manufacture of   15.88
football clubs, organisation and operation of   92.62
football stadiums, operation of   92.61
footwear, of any material, manufacture of   19.30
footwear of textile material without applied soles,
    manufacture of   18.24/2
footwear

agents involved in the sale of	51.16
asbestos, manufacture of	26.82/1
machinery for making or repairing, manufacture of	29.54
parts of, manufacture of	19.30
renting of	71.40/2
retail sale of	52.43
wholesale of	51.42

forage plant seeds, production of   01.11
foreign affairs   75.21
foreign trade, management of   75.21
forest tree nurseries, operation of   02.01
forestry inventories   02.02
forestry land, drainage of   45.11
forestry machinery and equipment without operator, renting of   71.31
forestry machinery, manufacture of   29.32
forestry service activities   02.02
forests and timber tracts, planting, replanting, transplanting,
    thinning of, conserving of   02.01
forges, manufacture of   28.62
forging machines, manufacture of   29.40
forks, manufacture of   28.61
forms, publishing of   22.15
foundations, construction of   45.25
foundry moulds, machinery for producing, manufacture of   29.56
frames, plastic, manufacture of   25.23/2
fraternities, activities of   91.33
freezers, manufacture of   29.71
freight by air or via space, transport of   62
freight by air, non-scheduled transport of   62.20/2
freight over water, transport of   61.10/2
freight transport by interurban railways   60.10/2
freight transport operation by road   60.24
freight

forwarding of	63.40
scheduled air transport	62.10

fresh poultry, production of   15.12
fresh water, fish farming in   05.02
friction material, non-metallic mineral, manufacture of   26.82/2
frozen poultry, production of   15.12
fruit drinks, production of   15.98
fruit juice, manufacture of   15.32
fruit or vegetable food products, manufacture of   15.33
fruit trees and vines, trimming of, (fee or contract basis)   01.41

fruit beverages, fermented, other, manufacture of	15.94/2
fruit	
machines and equipment to process, manufacture of	29.53
machines for cleaning, sorting or grading, manufacture of	29.32
preserving in sugar of	15.84/2
preserving of	15.33
production of	01.13
retail sale of	52.21
unprocessed, wholesale of	51.31
fruit-peels, preserving in sugar of	15.84/2
frying pans, electric, manufacture of	29.71
frying pans, manufacture of	28.75
fuel elements for nuclear reactors, production of	23.30
fuel for motor vehicles and motorcycles, retail sale of	50.50
fuel oil, household, retail sale of	52.48/3
fuel, production of	23.20/1
fuel tanks on aircraft, manufacture of	35.30
fuel wood, production of	02.01
fuels	
agents involved in the sale of	51.12
other than petroleum, wholesale of	51.51/2
fund management activities	67.12/1
funds in the form of deposits, obtaining of	65.1
funeral and related activities	93.03
funfair articles, manufacture of	36.50/1
fungicides, manufacture of	24.20
fur animals, raising of	01.25
fur articles, wholesale of	51.42
fur products, washing and cleaning of	93.01
fur wearing apparel and clothing accessories, manufacture of	18.30
fur	
agents involved in the sale of	51.16
articles of, retail sale of	52.42
furnaces and furnace burners, manufacture of	29.21
furnaces, cleaning of	— 74.70
furnishing articles, made-up, manufacture of	17.40/1
furniture fittings, plastic, manufacture of	25.24
furniture	
for bedrooms, living rooms, gardens, manufacture of	36.14
for shops, manufacture of	36.12
for workrooms, manufacture of	36.12
furniture covers, manufacture of	17.40/1
furniture removal by road	60.24
furniture	
agents involved in the sale of	51.15
concrete, plaster, cement or artificial stone, manufacture of	26.66
finishing of	36.14
fibre-cement, manufacture of	26.65
medical, surgical, dental or veterinary, manufacture of	33.10
office, manufacture of	36.12
renting of	71.40/2
retail sale of	52.44
wholesale of	51.47/1
furskin articles , manufacture of	18.30
furskins and hides with the hair on, dressing and dyeing of	18.30

furskins

assemblies of	18.30
production of	01.50
fuselages on aircraft, manufacture of	35.30
fuses, manufacture of	31.20

G

gaiters, manufacture of	19.30
galantines, production of	15.13/2
gambling activities	92.71
game meat, wholesale of	51.32
game, propagation of	01.50
games and toys, retail sale of	52.48/3

games

professional and arcade, manufacture of	36.50/1
wholesale of	51.47/2
garages, operation of	63.21
garbage, collection of	90.00
gardeners, employment of by private households	95.00
gardens and sport installations, planting and maintenance of, (fee or contract basis)	01.41
garnetters, manufacture of	29.54
gas desulphurisation	11.10

gas extraction

natural gas	11.10
service activities	11.20
gas fittings, installation of	45.33
gas for the purpose of gas supply, production of	40.20
gas generators, manufacture of	29.24
gas mantles and tubular gas mantle fabric, manufacture of	17.54/3
gas masks, manufacture of	33.10
gas turbines, manufacture of	29.11

gas

bottled, retail sale of	52.48/3
manufacture of	40.20

gaseous fuels

other than petroleum, wholesale of	51.51/2
petroleum, wholesale of	51.51/1
through mains, distribution of	40.20

gases

industrial, wholesale of	51.55
transport via pipelines of	60.30
gaskets, manufacture of	29.24
gatekeepers, employment of by private households	95.00
gates, metal, manufacture of	28.12
gauges, manufacture of	33.20/2

gauze

pharmaceutical, manufacture of	24.42/2
woven in bulk, manufacture of	17.21
gear boxes, other than for motor vehicles, manufacture of	29.14
gear boxes, for motor vehicles, manufacture of	34.30
gearing, manufacture of	29.14
gears, manufacture of	29.14
gelatine, manufacture of	24.62
gem stones, mining and quarrying of	14.50

genealogical organisations, services of	93.05
general stores, activities of	52.11
generators (dynamos, alternators), manufacture of	31.61
generators, electric, manufacture of	31.10
geodetic surveying activities	74.20
geological and prospecting activities	74.20
geological test drilling, test boring and core sampling	45.12
geophysical instruments and appliances	
electronic, manufacture of	33.20/1
non-electronic, manufacture of	33.20/2
geophysical test drilling, test boring and core sampling	45.12
gilt-edged market makers, activities of	65.23/3
gin, manufacture of	15.91
glands, processing of	24.41
glass envelopes, manufacture of	26.15
glass fibres, manufacture of	26.14
glass inners for vacuum flasks and other vacuum vessels, manufacture of	26.13
glass, glassware or glass fibre or yarn,	
machinery for producing, manufacture of	29.56
glass or glassware production machines, manufacture of	29.56
glass wool, manufacture of	26.14
glass	
flat, manufacture of	26.11
flat, wholesale of	51.53
hollow, manufacture of	26.13
installation of	45.44
renting of	71.40/2
retail sale of	52.46
shaping and processing of	26.12
glassware, laboratory, hygienic or pharmaceutical, manufacture of	26.15
glassware	
retail sale of	52.44
technical, manufacture of	26.15
wholesale of	51.44
glazes and engobes and similar preparations, manufacture of	24.30/1
glazing	45.44
gliders, manufacture of	35.30
gloves	
manufacture of	18.24/2
leather, sports, manufacture of	36.40
wholesale of	51.42
glow plugs, manufacture of	31.61
glucose syrup, manufacture of	15.62
glucose, manufacture of	15.62
glues	
chemical, wholesale of	51.55
manufacture of	24.62
gluing machines, manufacture of	29.40
gluten, manufacture of	15.62
gluten-free foods, manufacture of	15.88
goat milk, production of	01.22
goats, farming of	01.22
gold rolled onto base metals or silver, production of	27.41
gold, mining and preparation of	13.20
goldsmiths' articles, manufacture of	36.22

golf carts, manufacture of	34.10
golf clubs, organisation and operation of	92.62
golf courses	
construction of	45.23
operation of	92.61
goods handling operations	63.40
goods vans, railway, manufacture of	35.20
goods vending machines, manufacture of	29.24
governesses, employment of by private households	95.00
government, supporting service activities for	75.14
graders, manufacture of	29.52/2
grain brushing machines, manufacture of	29.53
grain milling	15.61/1
grain milling industry machinery, manufacture of	29.53
grain silos, operation of	63.12
grain	
machines for cleaning, sorting or grading, manufacture of	29.32
wholesale of	51.21
gramophone records	
publishing of	22.14
reproduction from master copies of	22.31
wholesale of	51.43
granite, quarrying, rough trimming and sawing of	14.11
grapes, production of	01.13
graphic activities, other	22.25
graphite electrodes, machinery for producing, manufacture of	29.56
graphite iron castings, spheroidal, casting of	27.51
graphite	
manufacture of	26.82/2
natural, mining of	14.50
grates, mechanical, manufacture of	29.21
grates, non-electric domestic, manufacture of	29.72
gravel and sand pits, operation of	14.21
gravel	
breaking and crushing of	14.21
wholesale of	51.53
graves, sale of	93.03
greases	
other than at petroleum refineries, manufacture of	23.20/2
wholesale of	51.51/2
green areas for sport installations, planting and maintenance of,	
(fee or contract basis)	01.41
grill made of wire, manufacture of	28.73
grills, electric, manufacture of	29.71
grinders, electric, manufacture of	29.71
grinding mills, manufacture of	29.53
groats, production of	15.61/1
ground flying trainers, manufacture of	35.30
guard activities	74.60
guest houses, provision of short-stay lodging in	55.23/3
guilds, activities of	91.11
gummed paper ready for use, manufacture of	21.23
gymnasium equipment, manufacture of	36.40
gypsum, mining of	14.12

H

haberdashery		
retail sale of		52.41
wholesale of		51.41
hair clippers, manufacture of		28.61
hair lacquers, manufacture of		24.52
hair nets, manufacture of		18.24/2
hair slides, manufacture of		36.63/2
hairdressing activities		93.02
ham, production of		15.13/1
hammers, wholesale of		51.54
hand printing sets, manufacture of		36.63/1
hand riddles, manufacture of		36.63/2
hand sieves, manufacture of		36.63/2
hand tools		
manufacture of		28.62
with self contained motor or pneumatic drive, manufacture of		29.40
wholesale of		51.54
hand-carts, manufacture of		35.50
handbags, leather, manufacture of		19.20
handkerchiefs, paper, manufacture of		21.22
handles and bodies for tools, wooden, manufacture of		20.51
handles and bodies for brooms, wooden, manufacture of		20.51
handles and bodies for brushes, wooden, manufacture of		20.51
hang gliders, manufacture of		35.30
harbours, construction of		45.24
harbours, operation of		63.22
hard coal		
agglomeration of		10.10
mining of		10.10
hardware equipment and supplies, wholesale of		51.54
hardware		
agents involved in the sale of		51.15
computer, consultancy on		72.10
retail sale of		52.46
harmoniums, manufacture of		36.30
harness, manufacture of		19.20
harrows, manufacture of		29.32
harvesters, manufacture of		29.32
hats and caps, manufacture of		18.24/1
haulage in tanker trucks by road		60.24
haulage of automobiles by road		60.24
haulage tractors, renting of		71.21/2
headgear of furskins, manufacture of		18.24/1
headgear		
asbestos, manufacture of		26.82/1
plastic, manufacture of		25.24
sports, manufacture of		36.40
headphones, manufacture of		32.30
health clubs, organisation and operation of		92.62
health institutions, activities of		85.11
health insurance		66.03
health programmes, public administration of		75.12
hearing aids, manufacture of		33.10
hearth or wall tiles, non-refractory ceramic, manufacture of		26.30

heat exchangers, manufacture of		29.23
heat meters		
	electronic, manufacture of	33.20/1
	non-electronic, manufacture of	33.20/2
heat-insulating ceramic goods of siliceous fossil meals,		
	manufacture of	26.26
heat-insulating materials, manufacture of		26.82/2
heating equipment and supplies, wholesale of		51.54
heating resistors, electric, manufacture of		29.71
heating, installation of		45.33
heavy haulage by road		60.24
hedge trimming, (fee or contract basis)		01.41
helical springs, manufacture of		28.74
helicopter rotors on aircraft, manufacture of		35.30
helicopters, manufacture of		35.30
herbicides, manufacture of		24.20
herbs, wholesale of		51.31
herd testing services		01.42
hides		
	originating from slaughterhouses, production of	15.11/1
	wholesale of	51.24
hides or skins, machinery for preparing, tanning, working or repairing,		
	manufacture of	29.54
high carbon ferro-manganese, production of		27.10
high tension generators, manufacture of		33.10
highways		
	construction of	45.23
	snow and ice cleaning on	90.00
hinges, manufacture of		28.63
hinnies, farming and breeding of		01.22
hire purchase and loan companies, non-UK banking sector, activities of		65.22/1
historic houses, operation of		92.52
historical museums, operation of		92.52
historical sites and buildings, preservation of		92.52
hoists, manufacture of		29.22
holding companies, management activities of		74.15
holiday camps, short-stay lodging in		55.2
holiday chalets		
	in holiday centres and holiday villages, provision of short-stay lodging in	55.23/1
	other than in holiday centres and holiday villages, provision of	
	short-stay lodging in	55.23/2
homes for the aged, activities provided by		85.31
homoeopathic preparations, manufacture of		24.42/1
homogenised food preparations, manufacture of		15.88
homogenisers, manufacture of		29.53
honey and beeswax, production of		01.25
hooks, manufacture of		28.75
hop cones, growing of		01.11
hormonal contraceptive medicaments, manufacture of		24.42/1
horns		
	motor, manufacture of	31.61
	musical, manufacture of	36.30
horse-chestnuts, gathering of		02.01
horses, farming and breeding of		01.22
hose and pipe fittings, plastic, manufacture of		25.21

with letting rooms, provision of short-stay lodging in	55.23/3
inorganic bases, manufacture of	24.13
inorganic compounds, other manufacture of	24.13
insecticides, manufacture of	24.20
instructors of sport, activities of	92.62
instruments and appliances used for medical, surgical, dental or	
veterinary purposes, manufacture of	33.10
instruments and devices for doctors and hospitals, wholesale of	51.46
insulated wire and cable, manufacture of	31.30
insulating fittings	
ceramic, manufacture of	26.23
glass, manufacture of	26.15
plastic, manufacture of	25.24
insulating work activities	45.32
insulators	
ceramic, manufacture of	26.23
glass, manufacture of	26.15
insurance agents, activities of	67.20
insurance brokers, activities of	67.20
insurance funding	66
insurance risk evaluators, activities of	67.20
inter-city coach services on scheduled routes	60.21/1
inter-dealer brokers, activities of	65.23/3
interior decorators, activities of	74.84
internal combustion piston engines and parts thereof, manufacture of	29.11
international assistance	75.21
international financial and foreign technical affairs,	
management of	75.21
International Monetary Fund, activities of	99.00
international organisations, activities of	99.00
invalid carriages with or without motor, manufacture of	35.43
investigation activities	74.60
investment funds, activities of	65.23/1
investment trusts, activities of	65.23/1
ion-exchangers based on polymers, manufacture of	24.16
iron in primary form from ore or scrap, production of	27.10
iron of exceptional purity by electrolysis or other chemical	
processes, production of	27.35
iron ore, beneficiation and agglomeration of	13.10
iron ores, mining of	13.10
iron powder, production of	27.35
iron products, finished or semi-finished, casting of	27.51
iron, manufacture of	27.10
ironing machines including fusing presses, manufacture of	29.54
ironmongery, agents involved in the sale of	51.15
irradiators, manufacture of	29.53
irrigation systems, operation of, (fee or contract basis)	01.41
isolating gases, manufacture of	24.11
isotopic separation, machinery or apparatus for, manufacture of	29.56

J

jackets	
men's, manufacture of	18.22/1
women's, manufacture of	18.22/2
jacks, manufacture of	29.22

printed, finishing of	22.23
labelling, stamping and imprinting	74.82
laboratory type sensitive balances	
electronic, manufacture of	33.20/1
non-electronic, manufacture of	33.20/2
labour organisations, activities of	91.20
labour recruitment	74.50
lac, gathering of	02.01
lacquers	
manufacture of	24.30/1
retail sale of	52.46
lactose, production of	15.51/3
ladles for handling hot metals, manufacture of	29.51
laminated glass, manufacture of	26.12
laminboard, manufacture of	20.20
lamp holders, manufacture of	31.20
lamps, manufacture of	31.50
land surveying activities	74.20
land transport equipment	
freight, renting of	71.21/2
passenger, without driver, renting of	71.21/1
land	
buying and selling of	70.12
letting of	70.20/2
landfill	45.11
landing gear on aircraft, manufacture of	35.30
landing nets, manufacture of	36.40
landscape architecture	74.20
lasers, manufacture of	33.40/2
lathes, manufacture of	29.40
launching gear, aircraft, manufacture of	35.30
laundresses, employment of by private households	95.00
laundry collection and delivery	93.01
laundry machinery, manufacture of	29.54
lavatory pans, plastic, manufacture of	25.23/2
laver, growing of	05.02
law and order activities	75.24
law courts, administration and operation of	75.23
lawn mowers however operated, retail sale of	52.46
lawn mowers, manufacture of	29.32
lawn-mowers however operated, wholesale of	51.66
lay-outs, reprographic, production of	22.25
lead	
mining and preparation of	13.20
production of	27.43
leaflets, publishing of	22.11
leaf springs, manufacture of	28.74
learned societies, activities of	91.12
leather clothes, manufacture of	18.10
leather goods	
agents involved in the sale of	51.16
retail sale of	52.43
wholesale of	51.47/2
leather or composition leather, diverse articles of,	
manufacture of	19.20

leather production machinery, manufacture of		29.54
leather		
	tanning and dressing of	19.10
	wholesale of	51.24
leaves for springs, manufacture of		28.74
lecturers, activities of		92.31/2
leeks, growing of		01.12
legal activities		74.11
leggings and similar articles, manufacture of		19.30
leisure centres, operations of		92.61
lemonade, production of		15.98
lenses, manufacture of		33.40/1
leprosaria, activities of		85.11
letterpress, printing by		22.22
lettuce, growing of		01.12
level crossing control gear, manufacture of		35.20
level gauges		
	electronic, manufacture of	33.20/1
	non-electronic, manufacture of	33.20/2
levellers, manufacture of		29.52/2
liability insurance		66.03
libraries of all kinds, activities of		92.51
lichens, gathering of		02.01
life insurance		66.01
life jackets, manufacture of		17.40/2
lifting and handling equipment, manufacture of		29.22
lifts		
	installation of	45.31
	maintenance of	29.22
	manufacture of	29.22
light metal packaging, manufacture of		28.72
light metals, casting of		27.53
lighterage activities		63.22
lighters, construction of		35.11
lighthouse activities		63.22
lighting equipment		
	manufacture of	31.50
	retail sale of	52.44
	wholesale of	51.43
lighting fittings, plastic, manufacture of		25.24
lighting sets of a kind used for christmas trees, manufacture of		31.50
lightning arresters, manufacture of		31.20
lightning conductors, installation of		45.31
lignite (brown coal), mining of		10.20
lignite tars, production of		23.10
lime, manufacture of		26.52
limestone, quarrying of		14.12
line telegraphy apparatus, manufacture of		32.20/1
line telephony apparatus, manufacture of		32.20/1
linoleum		
	laying	45.43
	manufacture of	36.63/2
linseed oil, production of		15.41
liquefied or compressed industrial gases, manufacture of		24.11
liqueurs, manufacture of		15.91

liquid fuels

    other than petroleum, wholesale of   51.51/2

    petroleum, wholesale of   51.51/1

liquid hydrocarbon fractions, draining and separation of   11.10

liquid or compressed air, manufacture of   24.11

liquids

    bottling of   74.82

    transport via pipelines of   60.30

litter boxes in public places, collection of refuse in   90.00

live animals

    agents involved in the sale of   51.11

    wholesale of   51.23

loading slings, manufacture of   17.52

lobsterlings, production of   05.02

locks

    construction of   45.24

    manufacture of   28.63

locomotives, electric and diesel rail, manufacture of   35.20

lodges, activities of   91.33

logging   02.01

logging haulage by road   60.24

logging service activities   02.02

logs, transport of, within the forest   02.02

looms, manufacture of   29.54

lorries

    manufacture of   34.10

    wholesale and retail sale of   50.10

lottery tickets, sale of   92.71

loudspeakers, manufacture of   32.30

low-energy and energy-reduced foods, manufacture of   15.88

low-sodium foods, manufacture of   15.88

low temperature carbonisation plants, production at   23.10

lubricants, wholesale of   51.51/2

lubricating oil additives, manufacture of   24.66

lubricating products for motor vehicles, retail sale of   50.50

luggage trucks, manufacture of   35.50

luggage

    manufacture of   19.20

    repair of   52.71

luminophores, manufacture of   24.12

lyes, manufacture of   24.13

M

macaroni, manufacture of   15.85

macaroni, spaghetti or similar products machinery, manufacture of   29.53

machine covers, manufacture of   17.40/2

machine tools

    interchangeable tools for, manufacture of   28.62

    manufacture of   29.40

    renting and operating leasing of   71.34

    special attachments, manufacture of   29.40

    wholesale of   51.61

machinery and industrial plant design   74.20

machinery, agents involved in the sale of   51.14

machines for transcribing data onto data media in coded form, manufacture of   30.02

machines that sort, wrap or count coins, manufacture of	30.01
machines that stuff envelopes, sort mail, manufacture of	30.01
magazines	
printing of	22.22
renting of	71.40/1
wholesale of	51.47/2
magnesite, articles containing, manufacture of	26.26
magnesium products, casting of	27.53
magnesium sulphates (kieserite), natural,mining of	14.30
magnetic or optical readers, manufacture of	30.02
magnetic tape recorders, manufacture of	32.30
magneto-dynamos, manufacture of	31.61
magnifying glasses, manufacture of	33.40/2
maids, employment of by private households	95.00
mail order goods, retail sale of	52.61
mail, distribution and delivery of	64.11
mailbox rental	64.11
maize, growing of	01.11
make-up, beauty treatment	93.02
malt, manufacture of	15.97
maltose, manufacture of	15.62
man-made fibres, manufacture of	24.70
man-made textile fibres, materials or yarns, machinery for processing of,	
manufacture of	29.54
management consultancy activities	74.14
manganese	
mining and preparation of	13.20
production of	27.45
manicure	93.02
manicure and pedicure preparations, manufacture of	24.52
manometers	
electronic, manufacture of	33.20/1
non-electronic, manufacture of	33.20/2
manure spreaders, manufacture of	29.32
maps	
lending and storage of	92.51
printing of	22.22
publishing of	22.11
marble, quarrying, rough trimming and sawing of	14.11
margarine, manufacture of	15.43
marinas	
activities of	92.62
construction of	45.24
marine and freshwater crustaceans and molluscs, taking of	05.01
marine engines and parts thereof, manufacture of	29.11
marine insurance	66.03
market research	74.13
markets, retail sale via	52.62
marmalades, manufacture of	15.33
marriage and family guidance	85.32
marriage bureaux, services of	93.05
massage apparatus, manufacture of	33.10
massage salons, activities related to	93.04
mastics, manufacture of	24.30/3
matches, manufacture of	36.63/2

mats

    cork, manufacture of 20.52

    other than of plaiting material, manufacture of 17.51/3

mattes of nickel, production of 27.45

mattings, manufacture of 20.52

mattresses and mattress supports, manufacture of 36.15

mayonnaise, manufacture of 15.87

meal of dried leguminous vegetables, production of 15.61/2

meal of oil-seeds, production of 15.41

meals on wheels, catering 55.52

measuring and controlling equipment, renting and operating leasing of ... 71.34

measuring instruments and appliances

    electronic, manufacture of 33.20/1

    non-electronic, manufacture of 33.20/2

measuring instruments and equipment, wholesale of 51.65

measuring rods and tapes, manufacture of 33.20/2

meat and meat products, retail sale of 52.22

meat and poultry meat processing, other than bacon and ham ... 15.13/2

meat dishes, prepared, production of 15.13/2

meat

    extracts, production of 15.13/2

    juices, production of 15.13/2

    machines and equipment to process, manufacture of 29.53

    pates, production of 15.13/2

    production, processing and preserving of 15.11/1

    products, production of 15.13/2

    puddings, production of 15.13/2

    rillettes, production of 15.13/2

    wholesale of 51.32

mechanical engineering, general 28.52

mechanical manipulators, manufacture of 29.22

mechano-therapy appliances, manufacture of 33.10

medallions, manufacture of 36.21

medals, manufacture of 36.21

media for sound or video recording, unrecorded, manufacture of ... 24.65

media representation 74.40

medical consultation and treatment 85.12

medical equipment, manufacture of 33.10

medical goods, retail sale of 52.32

medical laboratories, activities of 85.14

medical nursing homes, activities of 85.11

medicaments, manufacture of 24.42/1

medicated confectionery, manufacture of 15.84/2

melanges and similar spreads, manufacture of 15.43

membership organisations n.e.c., activities of 91.33

mental hospital institutions, activities of 85.11

merchandise and commodity brokers, activities of 51

merchandising displays, finishing of 22.23

metal cable, manufacture of 28.73

metal containers for compressed or liquefied gas, manufacture of ... 28.21

metal objects directly from metal powders by heat treatment, production of ... 28.40

metal ores and native metals, underground and opencast, extraction of ... 13

metal pickling substances, manufacture of 24.66

metal sand for sandblasting, production of 27.35

metal structures and parts of structures, manufacture of 28.11

metal waste and scrap, recycling of, into new raw materials	37.10
metal, forging, pressing, stamping and roll-forming of	28.40
metal-rolling mills and rolls for such mills, manufacture of	29.51
metallic closures, manufacture of	28.72
metallised yarn, manufacture of	17.54/3
metallised leathers, manufacture of	19.10
metallurgy, machinery for, manufacture of	29.51
metals	
agents involved in the sale of	51.12
treatment and coating of	28.51
wholesale of	51.52
meteorological instruments and appliances	
electronic, manufacture of	33.20/1
non-electronic, manufacture of	33.20/2
meters for water, gas, petrol, electricity	
electronic, manufacture of	33.20/1
non-electronic, manufacture of	33.20/2
methanol, wholesale of	51.55
metronomes, manufacture of	36.30
mica and articles thereof, manufacture of	26.82/2
mica, mining of	14.50
micrometers, manufacture of	33.20/2
microphones, manufacture of	32.30
microphotography equipment, manufacture of	33.40/2
microprojection equipment, manufacture of	33.40/2
microscopes other than optical microscopes, manufacture of	33.20/2
microwave ovens, manufacture of	29.71
microwave tubes, manufacture of	32.10
military aid to foreign countries, provision of	75.21
military base hospitals, activities of	85.11
military museums, operation of	92.52
military tribunals, administration and operation of	75.23
milk converting machinery, manufacture of	29.53
milk processing machinery, manufacture of	29.53
milk, production of	15.51/1
milking machines, manufacture of	29.32
milling cutters, interchangeable tools for, manufacture of	28.62
millstones, manufacture of	26.81
mine detectors, manufacture of	31.62
mineral insulating materials, manufacture of	26.82/2
mineral waters, production of	15.98
minerals and materials, mining and quarrying of	14.50
minerals, machinery for treating, manufacture of	29.52/1
minibuses, wholesale and retail sale of	50.10
mining equipment, renting and operating leasing of	71.34
mining machinery, manufacture of	29.52/1
mining, site preparation for	45.11
ministry of foreign affairs, administration and operation of	75.21
mirrors used in medicine, manufacture of	33.10
mirrors	
glass, manufacture of	26.12
installation of	45.44
mixed industrial gases, manufacture of	24.11
mobile lifting frames, manufacture of	29.22
mobile sellers, retail sale by	52.63

needles, sewing machine, manufacture of	29.54
needles, sewing, retail sale of	52.41
net and window furnishing type fabrics, manufacture of	17.60
netting made of wire, manufacture of	28.73
netting products, manufacture of	17.52
neutral spirits, production of	15.92
news agency activities	92.40
newspapers	
printing of	22.21
publishing of	22.12
retail sale of	52.47
wholesale of	51.47/2
nickel	
mining and preparation of	13.20
production of	27.45
nightclubs, activities of	55.40/1
nightdresses, women's manufacture of	18.23/2
nitric and sulphonitric acids, manufacture of	24.15
nitrites and nitrates of potassium, manufacture of	24.15
nitrogen products, manufacture of	24.15
nitrogen-function organic compounds including amine,	
manufacture of	24.14
nitrogenous, phosphatic or potassic fertilizers, manufacture of	24.15
non-defatted flour, production of	15.41
non-ferrous metal ores, mining and preparation of	13.20
non-ferrous metals, other, production of	27.45
non-ferrous metals, other, casting of	27.54
non-metal waste and scrap, recycling of	37.20
non-residential buildings, letting of	70.20/2
nonwovens and articles made from nonwovens, manufacture of	17.53
noodles, manufacture of	15.85
notaries, activities of	74.11
notary public, activities of	74.11
nozzles, refractory ceramic, manufacture of	26.26
nuclear fuel, processing of	23.30
nuclear magnetic resonance apparatus, manufacture of	33.10
nuclear plant, certification of	74.30
nuclear reactors, manufacture of	28.30
nuclear waste, treatment of	23.30
numbering stamps, manufacture of	36.63/1
nuts	
edible, production of	01.13
machines and equipment to process, manufacture of	29.53
manufacture of	28.74
preserving in sugar of	15.84/2
preserving of	15.33

O

oats, growing of	01.11
observation telescopes, manufacture of	33.40/2
oceanographic or hydrological instruments	
electronic, manufacture of	33.20/1
non-electronic, manufacture of	33.20/2
oderiferous products, manufacture of	24.63
off-road motor vehicles, wholesale and retail sale of	50.10

office box files and similar articles, manufacture of	21.21/2
office equipment, retail sale of	52.48/2
office furniture	
manufacture of	36.12
wholesale of	51.64
office machinery and equipment	
renting and operating leasing of	71.33
wholesale of	51.64
office machinery	
maintenance and repair of	72.50
manufacture of	30.01
agents involved in the sale of	51.14
office supplies	
plastic, manufacture of	25.24
retail sale of	52.47
officers' messes, activities of	55.51
oil and gas well casings, cementing	11.20
oil based lubricating oils, manufacture of	23.20/2
oil extraction service activities	11.20
oil field equipment, renting and operating leasing of	71.34
oil kernels, production of	15.41
oil nuts, production of	15.41
oil seeds, growing of	01.11
oil-rigs, transport by towing or pushing of	61.10/2
oils and fats	
chemically modified, manufacture of	24.66
edible, wholesale of	51.33
oils	
essential, wholesale of	51.55
wholesale of	51.51/2
old age and sick visiting	85.32
olive oil	
crude, production of	15.41
refined, manufacture of	15.42
onions, growing of	01.12
opacifiers and colours, manufacture of	24.30/1
open air museums, operation of	92.52
operas, production of	92.31/1
operating tables, manufacture of	33.10
ophthalmic instruments, manufacture of	33.10
optical and precision equipment, retail sale of	52.48/2
optical elements not optically worked, manufacture of	26.15
optical fibre cables for telecommunication, manufacture of	31.30
optical fibres and cables for the transmission of images or	
for lighting, manufacture of	33.40/1
optical glass, manufacture of	26.15
optical goods, wholesale	51.47/2
optical instruments, manufacture of	33.40/2
optical microscopes, manufacture of	33.40/2
optical mirrors, manufacture of	33.40/1
optical type measuring and checking appliances and instruments	
electronic, manufacture of	33.20/1
non-electronic, manufacture of	33.20/2
oral hygiene preparations, manufacture of	24.52
orangeade, production of	15.98
orbital stations, manufacture of	35.30

painters, artists, activities of	92.31/2
painting	45.44
painting of motor vehicles	50.20
paints	
manufacture of	24.30/1
retail sale of	52.46
wholesale of	51.53
pallets, box pallets and other load boards of wood,	
manufacture of	20.40
palm oil, production of	15.41
panels	
concrete, manufacture of	26.61
fibre-cement, manufacture of	26.65
plaster, manufacture of	26.62
panti-hose, manufacture of	17.71
paper and paperboard bobbins, spools, cops, manufacture of	21.25
paper and paperboard, corrugated, manufacture of	21.21/1
paper and paperboard, coating, covering and impregnation of	21.12
paper and paperboard intended for further industrial processing,	
manufacture of	21.12
paper and paperboard production machinery, manufacture of	29.55
paper in bulk, wholesale of	51.56
paper yarn, preparation and spinning of	17.17
paper, asbestos, manufacture of	26.82/1
para-medical practitioners, activities of	85.14
parachutes, manufacture of	17.40/2
parcel packing and gift wrapping	74.82
parcels, distribution and delivery of	64.11
parchment dressed leather, manufacture of	19.10
parking lot markings, painting of	45.23
parking lots	
operation of	63.21
outdoor sweeping and watering of	90.00
parking meters, manufacture of	33.50
parks	
activities of	92.72
laying out, planting and maintenance of (fee or contract basis)	01.41
paraffin, wholesale of	51.55
parquet floor blocks, manufacture of	20.30
parsley, growing of	01.12
particle accelerators, manufacture of	31.62
particle board, manufacture of	20.20
passenger coaches, railway, manufacture of	35.20
passenger land transport, scheduled, other than interurban railways	
or inter-city coach services	60.21/2
passenger transport	
by inter-city rail services	60.10/1
by interurban railways, other than inter-city services	60.10/2
by animal-drawn vehicles	60.24
passenger vessels, building of	35.11
passengers by air or via space, transport of	62
passengers by air, non-scheduled transport of	62.20/1
passengers over water, transport of	61.10/1
passengers, scheduled air transport	62.10/1
pastas, manufacture of	15.85

pastry goods, preserved, manufacture of	15.82
pastry, fresh, manufacture of	15.81
patent leathers, manufacture of	19.10
patents, preparation of	74.11
pates, meat, production of	15.13/2
paving blocks, glass, manufacture of	26.15
paving, non-refractory ceramic, manufacture of	26.30
pawnbroking, where the primary activity is in lending money	65.22/1
pea splitters, manufacture of	29.53
peaches, production of	01.13
pearls, production of	36.22
pears, production of	01.13
peat	
agglomeration	10.30
digging	10.30
manufacture of	26.82/2
pecuniary loss insurance	66.03
pedalos, hire of	92.72
pedestrian ways, construction of	45.23
pedicure	93.02
pedometers	
electronic, manufacture of	33.20/1
non-electronic, manufacture of	33.20/2
pencil leads, manufacture of	36.63/1
pencil sharpening machines, manufacture of	30.01
pennants, manufacture of	17.40/2
pens and pencils, manufacture of	36.63/1
pension funding except compulsory social security	66.02
peppers, growing of	01.12
peptones, manufacture of	24.66
percussion musical instruments, manufacture of	36.30
perfume	
manufacture of	24.52
wholesale of	51.45
periodicals, printing of	22.22
periodicals, lending and storage of	92.51
permanent way material except rails, production of	27.35
perry, manufacture of	15.94/1
personal goods, repair of	52.7
personal stationery, printing of	22.22
personnel for employment, provision of	74.50
pest control in connection with agriculture	01.41
pet animals	
breeding of	01.25
retail sale of	52.48/3
pet foods, prepared, manufacture of	15.72
petro-chemical industry, products for, manufacture of	23.20/1
petroleum jelly, manufacture of	23.20/1
petroleum products, refined, manufacture of	23.20/1
petroleum, crude, production of	11.10
pH-meters	
electronic, manufacture of	33.20/1
non-electronic, manufacture of	33.20/2
pharmaceutical goods, wholesale of	51.46
pharmaceutical preparations, manufacture of	24.42

pharmaceutical products, medicaments, manufacture of	24.42/1
phenolic resins, manufacture of	24.16
phosphates of triammonium carbonates, manufacture of	24.15
phosphates of ammonium carbonates, manufacture of	24.15
phosphates, natural, mining of	14.30
photo coin-operated machines, operation of	74.81
photo-cathode valves or tubes, manufacture of	32.10
photocopiers, printing by	22.22
photographic activities	74.81
photographic chemical material, manufacture of	24.64
photographic equipment	
manufacture of	33.40/3
retail sale of	52.48/2
photographic goods, wholesale of	51.47/2
photographic plates, manufacture of	24.64
photogravure printing	22.22
photometers	
electronic, manufacture of	33.20/1
non-electronic, manufacture of	33.20/2
photos, engravings, publishing of	22.15
photosensitive semi-conductor devices, manufacture of	32.10
physical well-being, activities related to	93.04
pianos, automatic, manufacture of	36.30
pick-ups, manufacture of	32.30
pickets, production of	02.01
piers, operation of	63.22
pies, manufacture of	15.81
pigments, prepared, manufacture of	24.30/1
pile and terry fabrics, knitted, manufacture of	17.60
pile driving	45.25
pile-drivers, manufacture of	29.52/3
pile-extractors, manufacture of	29.52/3
pillows, manufacture of	17.40/1
pilotage activities	63.22
pin-tables, manufacture of	36.50/1
pins, manufacture of	28.73
pipe organs, manufacture of	36.30
pipe tobacco, manufacture of	16.00
pipelines, long distance, construction of	45.21
pipes	
clay, manufacture of	26.40
concrete, manufacture of	26.61
fibre-cement, manufacture of	26.65
machinery for producing, manufacture of	29.56
plastic, manufacture of	25.21
refractory ceramic, manufacture of	26.26
rubber, manufacture of	25.13
pipe system construction	28.30
pitch and pitch coke, production of	24.14
pitch pipes, manufacture of	36.30
pitprops, production of	02.01
plaits and products of plaiting materials, manufacture of	20.52
planetary probes, manufacture of	35.30
plant growth regulators, manufacture of	24.20
plants bearing vegetable fibres, retting of	01.11

plants for planting or ornamental purposes, growing of	01.12
plants used chiefly in pharmacy	
or for insecticidal, fungicidal or similar purposes, growing of	01.11
plants	
parts of, preserving in sugar of	15.84/2
retail sale of	52.48/3
wholesale of	51.22
plaster articles for use in construction, manufacture of	26.62
plaster products for construction purposes, manufacture of	26.62
plaster	
manufacture of	26.53
other articles of, manufacture of	26.66
plastering	45.41
plastic	
builders' ware, manufacture of	25.23/2
materials in primary forms, wholesale of	51.55
other products, manufacture of	25.24
packing goods, manufacture of	25.22
semi-manufactures	25.21
plastic product making machines, manufacture of	29.56
plastics in primary forms, manufacture of	24.16
plate making for printing	22.24
plate warmers, non-electric domestic, manufacture of	29.72
plates	
plastic, manufacture of	25.21
rubber, manufacture of	25.13
platinum group metals rolled onto gold, silver or base	
metals, production of	27.41
platinum	
mining and preparation of	13.20
production of	27.41
playing cards, manufacture of	36.50/2
pleasure ports, construction of	45.24
pleasure-craft, renting of	71.40/1
pliers, manufacture of	28.62
ploughs, manufacture of	29.32
plugs, electrical, manufacture of	31.20
plumbing equipment and supplies, wholesale of	51.54
plumbing, installation of	45.33
plywood, manufacture of	20.20
pneumatic and wind power engines and motors, manufacture of	29.12/2
pneumatic tyre making or retreading machines, manufacture of	29.56
pneumatic tyres, manufacture of	25.11
point locks, manufacture of	35.20
polarimeters	
electronic, manufacture of	33.20/1
non-electronic, manufacture of	33.20/2
polarising elements, manufacture of	33.40/1
police forces, administration and operation of	75.24
police laboratories, operation of	75.24
polishes and creams, manufacture of	24.51/2
political organisations, activities of	91.32
pollution, measuring of	74.30
polyamides, manufacture of	24.16
polyester resins, manufacture of	24.16

precious metals	
engraving on objects of	36.22
production of	27.41
prefabricated buildings of metal, manufacture of	28.11
prefabricated buildings or elements thereof, of wood,	
manufacture of	20.30
prefabricated constructions, assembly and erection of	45.21
prefabricated structural components for building or civil	
engineering of cement, concrete or artificial stone,	
manufacture of	26.61
press photographers, activities of	92.40
press-fasteners, manufacture of	36.63/2
press-studs, manufacture of	36.63/2
presses used to make wine, cider, fruit juices, manufacture of	29.53
pressurised containers, certification of	74.30
preventoria, activities of	85.11
primary cells and primary batteries, manufacture of	31.40
printed circuits, manufacture of	32.10
printed matter, publishing of	22.15
printed paper or board, finishing of	22.23
printed sheets, finishing of	22.23
printers, for computers, manufacture of	30.02
printing not elsewhere classified	22.22
printing and writing paper ready for use, manufacture of	21.23
printing devices, hand-operated, manufacture of	36.63/1
printing ink, manufacture of	24.30/2
printing machines, manufacture of	29.56
printing machines, sheet fed office type offset, manufacture of	30.01
prisms, manufacture of	33.40/1
prison administration	75.23
prison hospitals, activities of	85.11
private investigators, activities of	74.60
private training providers, activities of	80.42/1
process oils, production of	23.20/1
process timers, manufacture of	33.50
processed meat and meat products, wholesale of	51.32
production line robots, wholesale of	51.65
professional organisations, activities of	91.12
profile shapes, rubber, manufacture of	25.13
projection screens, manufacture of	33.40/3
projectors, video, manufacture of	32.30
propagation, growth and output of animals, activities to promote	01.42
propane, production of	23.20/1
propellant powders, manufacture of	24.61
property insurance	66.03
property unit trusts, activities of	65.23/2
property, own, letting of, other than conference and	
exhibition centres	70.20/2
propylene, manufacture of	24.16
prospectuses	
finishing of	22.23
printing of	22.22
protective glasses, manufacture of	33.40/1
protein substances, manufacture of	24.66
protest movements, activities of	91.33

psychological testing apparatus, manufacture of	33.10
public houses, activities of	55.40/2
public opinion polling	74.13
public relations and communication	74.14
public service (general overall) activities	75.11
puddings, meat, production of	15.13/2
pulled wool, production of	15.11/3
pulley tackle, manufacture of	29.22
pulleys, manufacture of	29.14
pullovers, knitted or crocheted, manufacture of	17.72
pulp for paper, manufacture of	21.11
pump stations, operation of	60.30
pumps	
air or vacuum, manufacture of	29.12/1
for liquids, whether or not fitted with measuring device, manufacture of	29.12/1
punches, interchangeable tools for hand or machine tools, manufacture of	28.62
puppet shows, production of	92.34
purifying machinery, manufacture of	29.24
puzzles, manufacture of	36.50/2
pyjamas, men's, manufacture of	18.23/1
pyrites and pyrrhotite, extraction and preparation of	14.30
pyrotechnic products, manufacture of	24.61

Q

quartz, mining and quarrying of	14.50
quicklime, manufacture of	26.52
quilts, manufacture of	17.40/3
quinones, manufacture of	24.14

R

rabbit meat, preparation of	15.12
rabbits	
control of in connection with agriculture	01.41
raising of	01.25
slaughtering of	15.12
racing stables, activities of	92.62
rackets, manufacture of	36.40
radar apparatus, manufacture of	33.20/1
radiation detectors, manufacture of	33.20/2
radiators for motor vehicles, manufacture of	34.30
radio equipment, renting and operating leasing of	71.34
radio goods	
retail sale of	52.45
wholesale of	51.43
radio navigational aid apparatus, manufacture of	33.20/1
radio programmes	
production of	92.20
transmission of	64.20
radio remote control apparatus, manufacture of	33.20/1
radio transmitters, manufacture of	32.20/2
radio-telephones, manufacture of	32.20/2
radio-telephony apparatus, manufacture of	32.20/2
radioactive elements for industrial or medical use, production of	23.30
radioactive elements produced by the nuclear fuels industry, manufacture of	24.13
radioactivity, measuring of	74.30

rafters, manufacture of	20.30
railbrakes, wooden manufacture of	35.20
railings, wooden manufacture of	20.30
railroad vehicles, passenger, renting of	71.21/1
rails, production of	27.10
railway and tramway locomotives and specialised parts thereof,	
manufacture of	35.20
railway engines and parts thereof, manufacture of	29.11
railway or tramway coaches, manufacture of	35.20
railway sleepers, wooden, manufacture of	20.10
railway stations, operation of	63.21
railways	
construction of	45.23
funicular, operation of	60.21/2
preserved, operation of	92.33
underground and elevated railways, scheduled passenger transport	60.21/2
range-finders	
electronic, manufacture of	33.20/1
non-electronic, manufacture of	33.20/2
rape oil, production of	15.41
raw furskins, production of	01.25
razors and razor blades, manufacture of	28.61
reading glasses, manufacture of	33.40/2
ready-mixed concrete, manufacture of	26.63
real estate agencies	70.31
real estate projects, development of	70.11
real estate, buying and selling of	70.12
receiver or amplifier valves or tubes, manufacture of	32.10
receivers	
radio-broadcasting, manufacture of	32.30
television, manufacture of	32.30
reception apparatus for radio-telephony or radio-telegraphy,	
manufacture of	32.20/2
record cutters, manufacture of	32.30
record players, manufacture of	32.30
records	
lending and storage of	92.51
renting of	71.40/1
retail sale of	52.45
recreation programmes, public administration of	75.12
recreational activities n.e.c.	92.72
reduced-size ("scale") models, manufacture of	36.50/2
reducers, manufacture of	33.40/3
reducing and slendering salons, activities related to	93.04
reelers, manufacture of	29.54
referees (legal), activities of	74.11
refined vegetable oils, production of	15.42
refinery gases, production of	23.20/1
reflectors used in medicine, manufacture of	33.10
refractometers	
electronic, manufacture of	33.20/1
non-electronic, manufacture of	33.20/2
refrigerant gases, manufacture of	24.11
refrigerated haulage by road	60.24
refrigerating or freezing industrial equipment, manufacture of	29.23

refrigeration, installation of	45.33
refrigerators, manufacture of	29.71
refuse disposal	90.00
regional development policy, implementation of	75.13
registers, printing of	22.22
rehabilitation centres, activities of	85.11
rehabilitation services	75.23
relay transmitters, manufacture of	32.20/2
relays, manufacture of	31.20
religious articles, retail sale of	52.48/3
religious organisations, activities of	91.31
rent collecting agencies	70.32
repair materials, rubber, manufacture of	25.13
repair of motor vehicle parts	50.20
reproduction and composing	22.24
reproduction of works of art, publishing of	22.15
reprographic products, production of	22.25
reservoirs of metal, manufacture of	28.21
reservoirs	
fibre-cement, manufacture of	26.65
plastic, manufacture of	25.23/2
residential nurseries, activities provided by	85.31
resinoids, manufacture of	24.63
resins, gathering of	02.01
resistance checking instruments, manufacture of	33.20/1
resistors including rheostats and potentiometers, manufacture of	32.10
restaurant facilities operated in connection with the	
provision of lodging	55.1
restaurant meals	
with alcoholic drinks, sale of	55.30/1
without alcoholic drinks, sale of	55.30/2
retirement incomes, provision of	66.02
retirement pensions, social security, administration of	75.30
retorts, refractory ceramic, manufacture of	26.26
revolution counters	
electronic, manufacture of	33.20/1
non-electronic, manufacture of	33.20/2
rice flour, production of	15.61/2
rice hullers, manufacture of	29.53
rice, milling	15.61/2
riding academies, activities of	92.62
riding-crops, manufacture of	36.63/2
rillettes, meat, production of	15.13/2
rings, rubber, manufacture of	25.13
river works, construction of	45.24
rivers, transport of passengers or freight via	61.20
rivets, manufacture of	28.74
road coverings, manufacture of products for the manufacture of	23.20/1
road surface markings, painting of	45.23
road haulage, bulk	60.24
road wheels, manufacture of	34.30
roads	
construction of	45.23
operation of	63.21
roadside assistance of motor vehicles	50.20

sacks		
	canvas, manufacture of	17.40/2
	plastic, manufacture of	25.22
saddlery, manufacture of		19.20
safes, manufacture of		28.75
safety belts for motor vehicles, manufacture of		34.30
safety headgear, metal, manufacture of		28.75
sailboards, manufacture of		36.40
sailboats, building of		35.12
sails, manufacture of		17.40/2
salami, production of		15.13/2
salt		
	industrial, wholesale of	51.55
	production of	14.40
salted meat, other than bacon and ham, production of		15.13/2
salvage activities		63.22
sample cards, finishing of		22.23
sanatoria, activities of		85.11
sand blasting machines, manufacture of		29.24
sand		
	industrial, extraction and dredging of	14.21
	wholesale of	51.53
sandblasting		45.45
sandstone, quarrying, rough trimming and sawing of		14.11
sanitary equipment, installation of		45.33
sanitary fixtures, ceramic, manufacture of		26.22
sanitary goods, manufacture of		21.22
sanitary installation equipment, wholesale of		51.54
sanitary porcelain, wholesale of		51.53
sanitary towels of paper and cellulose adding, manufacture of		21.22
sanitary towels of textile wadding, manufacture of		17.54/3
sanitary ware, plastic, manufacture of		25.23/2
satellites		
	launching of	62.30
	manufacture of	35.30
sauce-pans, manufacture of		28.75
sauces, manufacture of		15.87
saunas, activities related to		93.04
sausages, production of		15.13/2
saveloys, production of		15.13/2
saws and sawblades		
	manufacture of	28.62
	wholesale of	51.54
scaffolds and work platform erecting and dismantling		45.25
scaffolds, renting of		71.32
scales, manufacture of		29.24
scandium products, casting of		27.53
scenery, renting of		71.40/1
scent sprays, manufacture of		36.63/2
scents, wholesale of		51.55
school buses, operation of		60.21/2
school supplies, plastic, manufacture of		25.24
science museums, operation of		92.52
scientific machinery, renting and operating leasing of		71.34
scintillation scanners, manufacture of		33.10

scissors, manufacture of	28.61
scores, musical, retail sale of	52.45
scouring pads, metal, manufacture of	28.75
scouring pastes and powders, manufacture of	24.51/2
scrap metal, recycling of	37.10
scrap	
non-metal, recycling of	37.20
wholesale of	51.57
scrapers, manufacture of	29.52/2
screen printing	22.22
screens, manufacture of	20.52
screw machine products, manufacture of	28.74
screwdrivers	
manufacture of	28.62
wholesale of	51.54
screws, manufacture of	28.74
sculptors, activities of	92.31/2
sea freight forwarders, activities of	63.40
sea mammals, catching of	01.50
sea urchins, hunting of	05.01
sea water transport	61.10
sea water, desalting of	41.00
sea-food, machines and equipment to process, manufacture of	29.53
sea-squirts, hunting of	05.01
seal, catching of	01.50
sealing stamps, manufacture of	36.63/1
seals, rubber, manufacture of	25.13
seasoning herbs, growing of	01.12
seat-sticks, manufacture of	36.63/2
seats, manufacture of	36.11
second-hand goods in stores, retail sale of	52.50
secretarial activities	74.83
secretaries, employment of by private households	95.00
securities dealers	
dealing on own account by	65.23/3
dealing on behalf of others	67.12/2
security activities	74.60
security consultancy for industrial, household and public service	74.60
security broking and fund management	67.12
security papers, printing of	22.22
seed, machines for cleaning, sorting or grading, manufacture of	29.32
seeders, manufacture of	29.32
seeds for flowers, fruit or vegetables, production of	01.12
seed potatoes, wholesale of	51.21
seeds	
retail sale of	52.48/3
wholesale of	51.21
seismometers	
electronic, manufacture of	33.20/1
non-electronic, manufacture of	33.20/2
self-service restaurant meals	
with alcoholic drinks, sale of	55.30/1
without alcoholic drinks, sale of	55.30/2
self-copy paper ready for use, manufacture of	21.23
semi-conductor devices, manufacture of	32.10

shop furniture, manufacture of		36.12
short-stay lodging facilities		55.2
shovel loaders, manufacture of		29.52/2
shovels, mechanical, manufacture of		29.52/2
shower-baths, plastic, manufacture of		25.23/2
shrimp post-larvae, production of		05.02
shutters and their frames, wooden, manufacture of		20.30
shutters		
	metal, manufacture of	28.12
	plastic, manufacture of	25.23/2
shuttle changing mechanisms, manufacture of		29.54
shuttles, space, manufacture of		35.30
sickness insurance, social security, administration of		75.30
side-cars, manufacture of		35.41
sieving belts, manufacture of		29.53
sifters, manufacture of		29.53
sight telescopes, manufacture of		33.40/2
sightseeing buses, operation of		60.23
sign plates, manufacture of		28.75
signal box equipment, manufacture of		35.20
signal generators, manufacture of		31.62
signalling apparatus, electrical, manufacture of		31.62
signalling, safety or traffic control equipment,		
	electrical, manufacture of	31.62
	mechanical and electro-mechanical for parking facilities,	
	ports, railways, roads, tramways	35.20
silencers, manufacture of		34.30
siliceous fossil meals, mining of		14.50
silicones, manufacture of		24.16
silk worm cocoons, production of		01.25
silk worms, raising of		01.25
silk, preparation of		17.15
silk-type fabrics, manufacture of		17.24
silk-type weaving		17.24
silk-type yarns, manufacture of		17.15
silver rolled onto base metals, production of		27.41
silver, mining and preparation of		13.20
single yarn, of synthetic and artificial man-made fibres,		
	continuous, including high tenacity and textured yarn,	
	manufacture of	24.70
sinking machinery, manufacture of		29.52/1
sinks		
	fibre-cement, manufacture of	26.65
	metal, manufacture of	28.75
sirens, manufacture of		31.61
sketches, reprographic, production of		22.25
skiffs, building of		35.12
skins		
	originating from slaughterhouses, production of	15.11/1
	wholesale of	51.24
skirting boards, plastic, manufacture of		25.23/2
skirts, women's, manufacture of		18.22/2
skis, manufacture of		36.40
skisuits, manufacture of		18.24/2
slag cement, manufacture of		26.51

slag wool, manufacture of	26.82/2
slaked lime, manufacture of	26.52
slacks for women and girls, manufacture of	18.22/2
slate, quarrying of	14.13
sleeping bags, manufacture of	17.40/3
slicers, bakery, manufacture of	29.53
slide fasteners, manufacture of	36.63/2
slips, women's, manufacture of	18.23/2
slurry, transport via pipelines of	60.30
smoked meat, other than bacon and ham, production of	15.13/2
smoking pipes, manufacture of	36.63/2
smoothing irons, electric, manufacture of	29.71
snack products whether sweet or salted, manufacture of	15.82
snap-fasteners, manufacture of	36.63/2
snow mobiles, manufacture of	34.10
snuff, manufacture of	16.00
soap, manufacture of	24.51/1
social sciences, research and experimental development on	73.20
social security activities, compulsory	75.30
social services programmes, public administration of	75.12
social work activities	
with accommodation	85.31
without accommodation	85.32
sockets, manufacture of	31.20
socks, manufacture of	17.71
soda, wholesale of	51.55
soft drinks, production of	15.98
software	
consultancy and supply	72.20
reproduction from master copies of	22.33
solariums, activities related to	93.04
soldering equipment, manufacture of	28.75
soldering machines, manufacture of	29.40
solid fuels	
manufacture of	10.10/3
wholesale of	51.51
sorbet, production of	15.52
sound absorbing materials, manufacture of	26.82/2
sound insulation, installation of	45.32
sound or visual signalling equipment for cycles and motor	
vehicles, manufacture of	31.61
sound recording apparatus, manufacture of	32.30
sound recording studios, activities of	92.32
sound recordings	
publishing of	22.14
reproduction of	22.31
sound, transmission of via cables, broadcasting, relay or satellite	64.20
sound-heads, manufacture of	32.30
sound-insulating materials, manufacture of	26.82/2
soups and broths, manufacture of	15.89/1
souvenirs, retail sale of	52.48/3
soya, growing of	01.11
soya-bean oil	
crude, manufacture of	15.41
refined, manufacture of	15.42

space heaters		
electric domestic, manufacture of		29.71
non-electric domestic, manufacture of		29.72
space transport		62.30
space vehicles, launching of		62.30
spacecraft, manufacture of		35.30
sparking plugs, manufacture of		31.61
spas, activities related to		93.04
speakers, activities of		92.31/2
special finance agencies, activities of		65.22/4
special purpose machinery n.e.c., manufacture of		29.56
spectacle frames, manufacture of		33.40/1
spectacle lenses, manufacture of		33.40/1
spectrometers		
electronic, manufacture of		33.20/1
non-electronic, manufacture of		33.20/2
spectrum analysers, manufacture of		33.20/1
speed changers, manufacture of		29.14
sperm banks, activities of		85.14
spice crops, growing of		01.13
spices		
manufacture of		15.87
wholesale of		51.37
spiegeleisen, production of		27.10
spindles and spindle flyers, manufacture of		29.54
spinning machines, manufacture of		29.54
spiritualists' activities		93.05
splints, manufacture of		33.10
split poles, production of		02.01
sponges, gathering of		05.01
spools		
paper and paperboard, manufacture of		21.25
wooden, manufacture of		20.51
spoons, metal, manufacture of		28.61
sport and game schools, activities of		92.62
sport facilities, construction of		45.23
sport fishing, requisites for, manufacture of		36.40
sport programmes, public administration of		75.12
sporting activities		92.62
sports arenas, operation of		92.61
sports equipment, renting of		71.40/1
sports goods		
manufacture of		36.40
retail sale of		52.48/3
wholesale of		51.47/2
sportsmen, activities of		92.62
spray guns, manufacture of		29.24
spraying of motor vehicles		50.20
spraying machinery for agricultural use, manufacture of		29.32
springs, manufacture of		28.74
sprinkler systems, installation of		45.33
squeegees, manufacture of		36.62
stable-lads, employment of by private households		95.00
stadiums		
construction of		45.23

operation of	92.61
stage productions, production of	92.31/1
stage set designers and builders, activities of	92.31/1
staircases, wooden, installation of	45.42
stairs, manufacture of	20.30
stalls, retail sale via	52.62
stamps, retail sale of	52.48/3
staple fibres, not carded, combed, or otherwise processed	
for spinning, manufacture of	24.70
stapling machines	
machine tools, manufacture of	29.40
office, manufacture of	30.01
starch derivates, wholesale of	51.55
starches, manufacture of	15.62
starter motors, manufacture of	31.61
stationery	
paper, manufacture of	21.23
retail sale of	52.47
wholesale of	51.47/2
stations for the handling of goods, operation of	63.21
statuary, concrete, plaster, cement or artificial stone, manufacture of	26.66
statuettes	
ceramic, manufacture of	26.21
plastic, manufacture of	25.24
wooden, manufacture of	20.51
steam baths, activities related to	93.04
steam cleaning	45.45
steam cleaning machines, manufacture of	29.24
steam collectors, manufacture of	28.30
steam generators, manufacture of	28.30
steam turbines and other vapour turbines, manufacture of	29.11
steam, production, collection and distribution of	40.30
steatite (talc), mining and quarrying of	14.50
steel bending	45.25
steel centrifugally cast tubes, manufacture of	27.21
steel elements, not self-manufactured, erection of	45.25
steel in primary form from ore or scrap, production of	27.10
steel products	
finished or semi-finished, casting of	27.52
flat rolled, in coils or in straight lengths, manufacture of	27.32
steel open sections by forming on a roll mill, manufacture of	27.33
steel solid bars or sections by cold drawing, manufacture of	27.31
steel tube fittings, manufacture of	27.22
steel, manufacture of	27.10
steering boxes, manufacture of	34.30
steering columns, manufacture of	34.30
steering wheels, manufacture of	34.30
stencil duplicating machines, manufacture of	30.01
sterilisers, manufacture of	33.10
stevedoring	63.11
stiffened textile fabrics, manufacture of	17.54/3
Stock Exchange money brokers, activities of	65.23/3
stock exchanges, activities of	67.11
stock haulage by road	60.24
stokers, mechanical, manufacture of	29.21

telex and teleprinter apparatus, manufacture of	32.20/1
telex communication	64.20
tenders, manufacture of	35.20
tennis courts, construction of	45.23
tents, manufacture of	17.40/2
terminal facilities, operation of	63.21
terminals for issuing of tickets and reservations, manufacture of	30.01
terminals, computer, manufacture of	30.02
terry towelling, manufacture of	17.21
test benches	
electronic, manufacture of	33.20/1
non-electronic, manufacture of	33.20/2
test boring	
for construction	45.12
incidental to oil and gas extraction	11.20
test drilling	
for construction	45.12
incidental to oil and gas extraction	11.20
testing instruments and appliances	
electronic, manufacture of	33.20/1
non-electronic, manufacture of	33.20/2
testing of calculations for building elements	74.30
textile fibres	
other, preparation and spinning of	17.17
wholesale of	51.56
textile industry machinery, wholesale of	51.63
textile part of electric blankets, manufacture of	17.40/3
textile plants, growing of	01.11
textile production machinery, manufacture of	29.54
textile products, washing and dry cleaning of	93.01
textile raw materials, agents involved in the sale of	51.11
textile softeners, manufacture of	24.51/1
textile wadding and articles of wadding, manufacture of	17.54/3
textile wall coverings, manufacture of	21.24
textile weaving, other	17.25
textile wicks, manufacture of	17.54/2
textile yarn	
impregnated, coated or sheathed with rubber or plastic,	
manufacture of	17.54/3
machinery for processing of, manufacture of	29.54
textiles and leather finishing materials, manufacture of	24.66
textiles	
agents involved in the sale of	51.16
finishing of	17.30
renting of	71.40/2
retail sale of	52.41
rubberised, manufacture of	25.13
wholesale of	51.41
theatre halls, operation of	92.32
theatrical presentations, live, production of	92.31/1
theme parks, operation of	92.33
thermal insulation, installation of	45.32
thermionic valves or tubes, manufacture of	32.10
thermocopiers, printing by	22.22
thermometers	

tomatoes, growing of	01.12
tone arms, manufacture of	32.30
tonic waters, production of	15.98
toolholders, manufacture of	29.40
tools	
manufacture of	28.62
wholesale of	51.54
tooth brushes, electric, manufacture of	29.71
toothpaste, manufacture of	24.52
torsion bar springs, manufacture of	28.74
toughened glass, manufacture of	26.12
tour operators, activities of	63.30/2
touring clubs, activities of	91.33
tourist guides, activities of	63.30/3
towels	
paper, manufacture of	21.22
retail sale of	52.41
towing of motor vehicles	50.20
town and city planning	74.20
toxic waste, treatment and destruction of	90.00
toys	
professional and arcade, manufacture of	36.50/1
wholesale of	51.47/2
tracing cloth, manufacture of	17.54/3
tracksuits, manufacture of	18.24/2
tractors	
agricultural, wholesale of	51.66
for semi-trailers, manufacture of	34.10
used in agriculture and forestry, manufacture of	29.31
renting of	71.31
walking (pedestrian controlled), manufacture of	29.31
trade unions, activities of	91.20
trading stamp activities	74.84
traffic regulation, administration and operation of	75.24
trailers and semi-trailers	
agricultural, manufacture of	29.32
manufacture of	34.20/2
renting of	71.21/2
trailers, wholesale and retail sale of	50.10
training of dogs for security reasons	74.60
training of pet animals	92.72
trains	
disinfecting and exterminating activities for	74.70
electrical toy, manufacture of	36.50/2
tramway, scheduled passenger transport	60.21/2
transformers	
electric, manufacture of	31.10
wholesale of	51.65
transistors, manufacture of	32.10
translation activities	74.83
transmission apparatus for radio-broadcasting, manufacture of	32.20/2
transmission belts	
plastic, manufacture of	25.24
rubber, manufacture of	25.13
transmission or conveyor belts or belting, manufacture of	17.54/2

transmission shafts, manufacture of	29.14
transmitter-receivers, manufacture of	32.20/2
transplant organ banks, activities of	85.14
transponders, manufacture of	32.20/2
transport documents, issue and procurement of	63.40
transport equipment, except motor vehicles, motorcycles and bicycles,	
wholesale of	51.65
transport insurance	66.03
transport operations by road, sea or air, arranging or	
carrying out of	63.40
trash, collection of	90.00
travel accessories of leather and leather substitutes,	
retail sale of	52.43
travel accessories, wholesale of	51.47/2
travel agency activities	63.30/1
travelling libraries, banks etc, manufacture of	34.10
trays, paper, manufacture of	21.22
tree pruning, (fee or contract basis)	01.41
trench digging	45.11
tricycles, delivery, manufacture of	35.42
tricycles for children, manufacture of	36.50/2
trolley bus, scheduled passenger transport	60.21/2
trolley-buses, manufacture of	34.10
troughs, fibre-cement, manufacture of	26.65
trousers, men's, manufacture of	18.22/1
trucks with driver, renting of	60.24
trucks	
manufacture of	35.50
without drivers, renting of	71.21/2
trusses, manufacture of	33.10
trusts, preparation of	74.11
tubes	
collapsible, manufacture of	28.72
fibre-cement, manufacture of	26.65
glass, manufacture of	26.15
plastic, manufacture of	25.21
refractory ceramic, manufacture of	26.26
rubber, manufacture of	25.13
seamless steel, manufacture of	27.22
tubes (valves) or bulbs , machinery for producing, manufacture of	29.56
tubs, wooden, manufacture of	20.40
tulip bulbs, wholesale of	51.21
tulles and other net fabrics, manufacture of	17.54/1
tunicates, hunting of	05.01
tuning forks, manufacture of	36.30
tunnelling machinery, manufacture of	29.52/1
tunnels	
construction of	45.21
operation of	63.21
turbines and parts thereof, manufacture of	29.11
turbines, renting and operating leasing of	71.34
turbo-jets on aircraft, parts of, manufacture of	35.30
turbo-propellers on aircraft, parts of, manufacture of	35.30
turf for transplanting, growing of	01.12
Turkish baths, activities related to	93.04

turn-tables (record decks), manufacture of	32.30
tutors, employment of by private households	95.00
twine, manufacture of	17.52
typewriter ribbons, manufacture of	36.63/1
typewriters	
manufacture of	30.01
renting and operating leasing of	71.33
wholesale of	51.64
typing	74.83
tyre and tube repair, fitting or replacement	50.20
tyre cord fabric of high-tenacity man-made yarn, manufacture of	17.54/3
tyre flaps, manufacture of	25.11
tyre rebuilding and retreading	25.12

U

ultra-violet lamps, manufacture of	31.50
ultrasonic diagnostic equipment, manufacture of	33.10
ultrasonic sounding instruments	
electronic, manufacture of	33.20/1
non-electronic, manufacture of	33.20/2
umbrellas	
manufacture of	36.63/2
wholesale of	51.47/2
underlay, needlefelt, manufacture of	17.51/3
undertaking	93.03
underwear	
men's, manufacture of	18.23/1
women's, manufacture of	18.23/2
unemployment insurance, social security, administration of	75.30
unexposed materials, manufacture of	24.64
uniforms, work, renting of	93.01
unit trusts, activities of	65.23/2
United Nations, activities of	99.00
universal AC/DC motors, manufacture of	31.10
unloading cushions, manufacture of	17.52
upholstered chairs and seats, manufacture of	36.11
upholstering	36.14
uranium ores, mining of	12.00
uranium, enriched, production of	23.30
urban communication and powerlines, construction of	45.21
urban pipelines, construction of	45.21
urea, manufacture of	24.15

V

vaccines, manufacture of	24.42/1
vacuum cleaners, manufacture of	29.71
vacuum flasks, manufacture of	36.63/2
valances, manufacture of	17.40/3
valet car parkers, services of	93.05
valets, employment of by private households	95.00
valves, manufacture of	29.13
vanadium, mining and preparation of	13.20
vans, manufacture of	34.10
vans up to 3.5 tonnes, renting of	71.10
vapour generators, manufacture of	28.30

varnish removers, manufacture of	24.30/1
varnishes	
manufacture of	24.30/1
retail sale of	52.46
wholesale of	51.53
vases, concrete, plaster, cement or artificial stone,	
manufacture of	26.66
vats, wooden, manufacture of	20.40
vegetable fats or oils, machinery for the extraction or	
preparation of, manufacture of	29.53
vegetable hair, gathering of	02.01
vegetable juice, manufacture of	15.32
vegetable materials used for plaiting, growing of	02.01
vegetable milling	15.61/2
vegetable oils, processing of	15.42
vegetables	
growing of	01.12
machines and equipment to process, manufacture of	29.53
preserving of	15.33
retail sale of	52.21
unprocessed, wholesale of	51.31
vehicle motors, testing and regulating apparatus, manufacture of	33.20/2
vehicles drawn by animals, manufacture of	35.50
vehicles, motor, manufacture of	34.10
vending machines, retail sale by	52.63
veneer sheets, manufacture of	20.20
ventilating or recycling hoods, manufacture of	29.71
ventilation ducts, cleaning of	74.70
ventilation equipment, non-domestic, manufacture of	29.23
ventilation, installation of	45.33
venture and development capital companies and funds, activities of	65.23/5
vermouth, manufacture of	15.95
vessels only engaged in processing and preserving fish	
by freezing, activities of	15.20/1
vessels only engaged in processing and preserving fish	
other than by freezing, activities of	15.20/2
vessels, commercial, building of	35.11
veterinary activities	85.20
viaducts, construction of	45.21
vibration insulation, installation of	45.32
vices, manufacture of	28.62
video games, manufacture of	36.50/2
video production	92.11
video recording or reproducing apparatus, including camcorders, manufacture of	32.30
video recording, reproduction of	22.32
video tape projection	92.13
video tapes	
distribution of to other industries	92.12
renting of	71.40/1
videos, wholesale of	51.43
vinegar, manufacture of	15.87
vinyl acetate, manufacture of	24.16
vinyl chloride, manufacture of	24.16
viscometers	
electronic, manufacture of	33.20/1

non-electronic, manufacture of	33.20/2
vitrifiable enamels, manufacture of	24.30/1
vocational rehabilitation	85.32
voltage checking instruments, manufacture of	33.20/1
voltage limiters, manufacture of	31.20
voltage regulators, manufacture of	31.61

W

wadding, medical impregnated, manufacture of	24.42/2
wagon and locomotive frames, manufacture of	35.20
wagons, manufacture of	35.20
waistcoats and similar articles, knitted, manufacture of	17.72
waiters, employment of by private households	95.00
walking-sticks, manufacture of	36.63/2
wall covering	45.43
wall coverings	
plastic, manufacture of	25.23/2
wooden, installation of	45.42
wallpaper	
hanging	45.43
manufacture of	21.24
retail sale of	52.48/3
wholesale of	51.44
walrus, catching of	01.50
war ammunition, manufacture of	29.60
war veterans' associations, activities of	91.33
warehouses, operation of	63.12
warpers, manufacture of	29.54
warships, building of	35.11
wash basins	
metal, manufacture of	28.75
plastic, manufacture of	25.23/2
washers and similar non-threaded products, manufacture of	28.74
washing and drying machines, manufacture of	29.71
washing machines, laundry-type, manufacture of	29.54
washing powders in solid or liquid form, manufacture of	24.51/1
waste disposal	90.00
waste disposers, manufacture of	29.71
waste	
collection of	90.00
wholesale of	51.57
watch glasses, manufacture of	26.15
watch straps, non-metallic, manufacture of	19.20
watches	
manufacture of	33.50
repair of	52.73
retail sale of	52.48/3
wholesale of	51.47/2
watchman activities	74.60
water heaters	
electric domestic, manufacture of	29.71
non-electric domestic, manufacture of	29.72
water projects, construction of	45.24
water taxis, operation of	61.10/1
water transport, activities related to	63.22

installation of in any material	45.42
metal, manufacture of	28.12
plastic, manufacture of	25.23/2
wooden, manufacture of	20.30
windscreen wipers, manufacture of	31.61
wine	
based on concentrated grape must, manufacture of	15.93/2
from self produced grapes, production of	01.13
of fresh grapes and grape juice, manufacture of	15.93/1
wings on aircraft, manufacture of	35.30
winnowers, manufacture of	29.53
winter sport arenas and stadiums, operation of	92.61
winter sport clubs, organisation and operation of	92.62
wire products, manufacture of	28.73
wire, steel, by cold drawing or stretching, manufacture of	27.34
wired glass, manufacture of	26.11
wires	
for domestic use, wholesale of	51.43
for industrial use, wholesale of	51.65
wiring sets, manufacture of	31.61
wood chips, manufacture of	20.10
wood flour, manufacture of	20.10
wood goods, retail sale of	52.44
wood in the rough, production of	02.01
wood marquetry, manufacture of	20.51
wood wool, manufacture of	20.10
wood	
drying of	20.10
other articles of, manufacture of	20.51
products of primary processing, wholesale of	51.53
retail sale of	52.48/3
sawmilling, planing and impregnation of	20.10
wholesale of	51.53
wooden beadings and mouldings, manufacture of	20.30
wooden caskets and cases, manufacture of	20.51
wooden containers, manufacture of	20.40
wooden flooring, unassembled, manufacture of	20.10
wooden goods intended to be used primarily in the construction industry, manufacture of	20.30
wooden ware, wholesale of	51.47/2
wool carbonisers, manufacture of	29.54
wool scourers, manufacture of	29.54
wool, raw, production of	01.22
woollen-type fabrics, manufacture of	17.22
woollen-type fibres, preparation and spinning of	17.12
woollen-type weaving	17.22
woollen-type yarns, manufacture of	17.12
word processing machines	
renting and operating leasing of	71.33
manufacture of	30.01
work-accident insurance, social security, administration of	75.30
workholders, manufacture of	29.40
works trucks, manufacture of	29.22
workwear, manufacture of	18.21
World Bank, activities of	99.00

worsted-type fabrics, manufacture of   17.23
worsted-type fibres, preparation and spinning of   17.13
worsted-type weaving   17.23
worsted-type yarns, manufacture of   17.13
woven fabrics of glass fibres, manufacture of   17.25
woven pile fabrics, cotton-type, manufacture of   17.21
wrapping machinery, manufacture of   29.24
wrestling clubs, organisation and operation of   92.62
writing compendiums, manufacture of   21.23

X

X-ray tubes, manufacture of   33.10
X-ray or alpha, beta or gamma radiation apparatus, manufacture of   33.10

Y

yarn
    asbestos, manufacture of   26.82/1
    rubberised, manufacture of   25.13
    wholesale of   51.41
yeast, manufacture of   15.89/2
yellowcake, manufacture of   12.00
yellowcake to uranium tetrafluoride and hexafluoride, conversion of   23.30
yogurt, production of   15.51/3
young persons associations, activities of   91.33
youth hostels   55.21
yttrium products, casting of   27.53

Z

zinc
    mining and preparation of   13.20
    production of   27.43
zoological gardens, operation of   92.53

Printed in the United Kingdom for The Stationery Office
Dd 300722 2/97 C70 59226 559/1